Talented Teachers

The Essential Force for Improving Student Achievement

A volume in
The Milken Family Foundation Series on Education Policy

MILKEN FAMILY FOUNDATION

Two Decades of Advances in Education and Medical Research

The Milken Family Foundation (MFF) was established by brothers Lowell and Michael Milken in 1982 with the mission to discover and advance inventive and effective ways of helping people help themselves and those around them lead productive and satisfying lives. MFF advances this mission principally through the various programs it initiates and carries out in the areas of education and medical research.

Guided by a belief that "the future belongs to the educated," Lowell Milken created one of MFF's signature initiatives—the Milken National Educator Awards—in 1985 as a means to attract, retain, develop, and motivate high caliber individuals to teaching. The program has evolved from spotlighting a dozen California educators into the nation's largest and most visible teacher recognition program now in 47 states and the District of Columbia, annually honoring 100 outstanding teachers, principals and specialists with individual, unrestricted $25,000 prizes. They join a national network of nearly 2,000 Milken Educators committed to excellence in the teaching profession, and in demand as an expert resource base for local, state and national education policy makers.

The nation's students benefit from the commitment of many capable teachers. Yet experiences with Milken Educators and thousands more teachers in classrooms across America made it increasingly apparent that if every child is to have access to quality teachers K–12, far greater numbers of talented people are needed to teach. Thus in 1999, Lowell Milken introduced the Teacher Advancement Program (TAP) as a complementary initiative to the Milken Educator Awards. TAP is a research-based school improvement model to restructure and revitalize the teaching profession by offering sustained opportunities for career advancement, competitive compensation, performance-based accountability, and professional growth—all crucial to attracting the quantity of talented professionals required for America's classrooms. In just a few short years, the Teacher Advancement Program has been implemented in over 70 TAP schools across the nation with more in the planning stages, and preliminary research findings confirm the value to students and teachers alike of this comprehensive education reform strategy.

The Milken Educator Awards and Teacher Advancement Program are but two of the Milken Family Foundation's education-driven initiatives. Others include the Milken Scholars Program, the Milken Archive of American Jewish Music, and the Milken Festival for Youth. In the realm of medical research, Foundation efforts include the American Epilepsy Society/Milken Family Foundation Epilepsy Research Award, Grant & Fellowship Program as well as the Prostate Cancer Foundation, created by Michael Milken in 1993 and today the world's largest philanthropic organization dedicated to better treatments and a cure for prostate cancer.

For additional information concerning Milken Family Foundation initiatives in education and medical research, visit *www.mff.org.*

Talented Teachers

The Essential Force for Improving Student Achievement

Edited by

Lewis C. Solmon
Tamara W. Schiff
The Milken Family Foundation

MILKEN
FAMILY
FOUNDATION

INFORMATION AGE
PUBLISHING

80 Mason Street • Greenwich, Connecticut 06830 • www.infoagepub.com

Library of Congress Cataloging-in-Publication Data

Milken National Education Conference (2003 : Los Angeles, Calif.)
  Talented teachers : the essential force for improving student
achievement / edited by Lewis C. Solmon.
      p. cm. – (The Milken Family Foundation series on education
policy)
  The major portion of the book is from the proceedings of the 2003
Milken National Education Conference which was held in Los Angeles in
May 2003.
  Includes bibliographical references and index.
  ISBN 1-59311-116-9 (pbk.) – ISBN 1-59311-117-7 (hardcover)
  1. Teachers–Rating of–United States–Congresses. 2. Academic
achievement–United States–Congresses. I. Solmon, Lewis C. II. Title.
III. Series.
  LB2838.M493 2004
  371.14'4–dc22

                                                              2004002894

CONTENTS

Part VI
Leadership

FOREWORD

The Milken Family Foundation has assembled a splendid set of papers on the exceedingly important topic of teacher quality. Teacher quality is a major determinant of the future success of students as well as of our nation's future.

Along with students themselves, teachers are central figures in the learning process, and their quality is of great concern not only to parents but also to citizens and their government representatives. In the extraordinary No Child Left Behind federal legislation, the central place of teacher quality illustrates its importance in the views of President George W. Bush and Democrats and Republicans in Congress. The recent passage of accountability legislation to measure teaching effects in all 50 states suggests the urgency of improving teacher quality.

Parents, citizens, educational leaders, and policy makers know that something must be done to improve teacher quality and to recognize and better compensate excellent teachers. The distinguished contributors in this volume provide many stimulating insights on how these things might best be accomplished. A thoughtful reading should provide an excellent basis for rethinking and reforming education policies and practices to improve teacher quality and student achievement.

—Herbert J. Walberg
Distinguished Visiting Fellow
Hoover Institution, Stanford University

Talented Teachers: The Essential Force for Improving Student Achievement, pages vii–xiii
Copyright © 2004 by Information Age Publishing

ACKNOWLEDGMENTS

In preparing this book we had the pleasure of working with many talented people who made this project significantly easier and of high quality. First and foremost, we appreciate the efforts of Kimberly Firetag who guided the production of these proceedings, contributed to the organization of the volume, and oversaw the editorial process. Our appreciation goes out to Debbie White, Daren Reifsneider and Felice Meyers who meticulously edited the initial conference transcripts to turn the document into a readable form. Much appreciation to Larry Lesser and the Milken Family Foundation Production Department for their technical talents in videoing the conference sessions and then providing us with transcripts of each session. Thank you also to the Milken Family Foundation Communications Department under the leadership of Bonnie Somers for providing input and editorial guidance.

Thank you to all of the contributors to this publication who participated in the Milken Family Foundation's 2003 National Education Conference, and a special acknowledgement to Dr. Herb Walberg for connecting us with George Johnson, President and Publisher of Information Age Publishing Inc. IAP has graciously agreed to publish these proceedings in a timely manner so we can share the conference information with a broad audience. Mr. Johnson has been encouraging, supportive and helpful throughout the publication process. Finally, special gratitude goes to Lowell Milken, chairman and co-founder of the Milken Family Foundation for his ongoing support and contributions to the goal of improving the educational experience for all children.

PREFACE

Lewis C. Solmon and Tamara W. Schiff

Thirty years ago, *A Nation At Risk* alerted Americans to the low achievement levels of students in our public K–12 system. Despite ongoing educational research, increased K–12 spending, and endless "school reforms" since then, not much progress has been made. This lack of progress is evident when we look at the latest results on the National Assessment of Educational Progress (NAEP) Nation's Report Card or when we compare achievement of U.S. students to that of their counterparts in other developed nations from the Third International Mathematics and Science Study (TIMSS).

The education community has spent years trying to determine what the problems and solutions are to the low achievement levels of all too many of our students. We have said that low achievement is a social and family problem beyond the reach of the schools; we have spent more money on education; we have reduced class size in some grades and added learning technology; we have de-tracked and identified learning disabilities; we have removed walls and put schools within schools. There were some more harmful things as well, like eliminating phonics and mandating whole language, or giving up the learning of multiplication tables in favor of "new" math. Regardless of the practicality or logic behind any of these efforts, we have seen little widespread success in raising student achievement significantly.

Clearly, some reforms have shown promise, particularly the setting of high curricular standards, assessing students to see the extent to which they are achieving those standards, and having consequences for students, teachers, and schools, both positive and negative, for meeting or failing to

Talented Teachers: The Essential Force for Improving Student Achievement, pages vii–xiii
Copyright © 2004 by Information Age Publishing

meet the standards. However, what the research tells us, and what we know intuitively, is that for these processes to increase student learning, high-quality teachers are required.

No longer can schools blame low student achievement on factors beyond their control. Recent research has shown that about half of student achievement can be attributed to such factors, but also *about half is dependent upon the schools themselves.* Moreover, we now have data that shows that the most important school-related factor influencing student achievement is *the quality of the classroom teacher.*

This book explains to policymakers, parents, business leaders, and teachers themselves the importance of talented teachers in increasing student achievement. It is based on the proceedings from the 2003 Milken National Education Conference (NEC), which was held in Los Angeles in May 2003. In the early 1980s, Lowell Milken, chairman and co-founder of the Milken Family Foundation, created an awards program to acknowledge educators' crucial contributions to our national well-being. His belief was—and is—that one way to attract, retain, and motivate talented people to the teaching profession is to recognize and reward outstanding educators' achievements, enhance their resources and expand their professional influence and growth. For almost two decades the program, which is the largest teacher recognition program in the nation, has rewarded thousands of exemplary K–12 teachers, principals, counselors, librarians, and other specialists—each with an unrestricted financial prize of $25,000.

Award recipients are also invited to attend the Milken Family Foundation's annual National Education Conference where they have the opportunity to learn and participate in forums concerning critical educational issues, policies, and programs. The 2003 NEC, "Teacher Quality: Opportunities for Future Success," generated discussions on many of the critical issues relating to teacher quality. The resulting proceedings comprise the major portion of this book. In addition to the conference proceedings, we invited panelists to submit supplemental articles, adding greater depth to their examination of these teacher quality issues. Each chapter begins with the discussions from the conference and concludes with the companion articles.

PART I

The first chapter sets the stage by discussing the general issue of the achievement gap. The proceedings provide supporting data and reasons for differences in achievement, then propose ways to solve this very serious problem. The five panelists and moderator come from a wide variety of political and educational perspectives, and so present a diversity of views:

Lowell Milken, the chair of this session, brings to this discussion both a business perspective and two decades of work at the Foundation in the K–12 education field; Nina Rees, U.S. Deputy Under Secretary of Education for Innovation and Improvement, provides a perspective from the federal government's point of view; and David Driscoll, Massachusetts Commissioner of Education, addresses the issues from the experience of a state that has faced problems, yet has had success; Jeanne Allen is president of the Center for Education Reform, a national, independent, nonprofit advocacy organization providing support and guidance to individuals, community and civic groups, policymakers, and others who are working to bring fundamental reforms to their schools; Tavis Smiley, hosts a nationally syndicated radio show on NPR and is particularly concerned with issues of equality; and Jerry Brown, the current mayor of Oakland, CA, is a former governor of California, a lawyer, and the founder of two leading charter schools.

The panel discusses various reasons for the achievement gap, from lack of student motivation, low parental involvement and expectations, lack of will to fix the problems, low socioeconomic status of communities and families, poor facilities, inadequate amounts of books and supplies, money not flowing to the classrooms, lack of classroom discipline, and the unpredictable nature of many of the sources of money going into education. They also suggest solutions to help narrow the achievement gap in schools. These include directed spending on programs that have been proven effective, various types of school choice such as charter schools, more money coupled with stronger accountability systems, investment in early childhood education as well as adult education and after-school programs, implementing high-stakes exams with accountability, and paying talented teachers more money. Yet, the panel agrees, none of these solutions will work without a high-quality, talented teacher in the classroom.

PART II

Once we have established the importance of high-quality teachers, we must be able to identify which teachers should be so classified. To risk oversimplification, the studies demonstrating the importance of high-quality teachers identify such teachers as those whose students have demonstrated exceptional learning gains. Then they show that such teachers continue to get higher achievement gains from their students compared to other teachers of equally able students. However, the studies beg the question of what it is about high-quality teachers that makes them able to get greater learning gains from students.

Thus, Part II focuses on how to determine who is a quality teacher. Most observers cannot define a "quality teacher," but as Justice Potter Stewart said in trying to explain pornography, "[they] know it when they see it." Lewis C. Solmon begins the discussion by suggesting three dimensions of teacher quality: teacher inputs, teacher behaviors, and student outcomes. The panelists each tackle one of these dimensions: Eric A. Hanushek, senior fellow at Stanford University's Hoover Institution, talks about the importance of looking at how much a teacher's students learn; Lee S. Shulman, president, Carnegie Foundation for the Advancement of Teaching, discusses the importance of preparation; and Herbert J. Walberg, professor emeritus of education and psychology at the University of Illinois at Chicago, talks about teacher behaviors. Philip Bigler, Professor, James Madison University and a past recipient of the Milken Educator Award, then presents the teacher's perspective, addressing the importance to teachers of having the ability to change, to take advantage of learning technology, to be aware of the contributions they make, and to have inspiration and compassion. All panelists stress subject matter competency.

PART III

An often-debated requirement of high-quality teachers is the requirement of a teaching credential and state certification (license) in order to be in a classroom. Such licenses generally require attending a program in a college of education, without which, some argue, one is not prepared to teach. Others point to the fact that many successful teachers in private, religious, or independent schools have nothing more than rigorous subject-matter preparation in the form of an undergraduate major in an academic discipline from a strong undergraduate program. They argue further that the paucity of the scientifically based knowledge of pedagogy makes education school courses problematic at best.

The federal K–12 education reform, No Child Left Behind (NCLB), underlined the importance of this debate. NCLB mandates that every new teacher hired must meet the requirements of a "highly qualified" teacher, and that by 2005–06, all teachers in core academic subjects must be highly qualified. NCLB defines "highly qualified" as fully licensed or certified, no waivers or emergency credentials, at least a bachelor's degree, demonstrated subject matter knowledge through a state test, and teaching skills also demonstrated through a state test (elementary).

The federal law has answered the certification question with a resounding "yes." But the debate is not over. In the discussion we present, Arthur Wise, president of the National Council for Accreditation of Teacher Education (NCATE), argues for the value of certification, and Michael Podgursky, Middlebush Professor of Economics and Chairman of the Department of Economics at the University of Missouri–Columbia, counters with the need for greater flexibility regarding who can teach.

PART IV

The need for certification is only one of the controversial aspects of NCLB. In order to address more of these issues, we invited Chester E. Finn, Jr., president of the Thomas B. Fordham Foundation and former Assistant Secretary of Education, to present his analysis of the law. Finn, as it turns out, is quite ambivalent about the wisdom of NCLB, so he decided that the best way to express that was to *debate himself!* He covers the most important parts of NCLB, including issues about the federal role in education as embodied in the legislation, the notion of state standards set to a national timetable, and whether it is realistic to expect these standards of *every* child. He also questions whether testing should take place every year, whether it should be at so many grade levels, and whether it should be limited to just three subjects. Furthermore, he asks whether NCLB leads to draconian school interventions and he asks whether NCLB is a precursor to vouchers or something else. Finally, he debates what it means to be a qualified teacher, and he raises the question of whether NCLB is an excess of behaviorism or indeed a roadmap to a needed overhaul of the education system.

PART V

With research underlining the importance of high-quality teachers for student achievement, and the mandate of NCLB for highly qualified ones, the next question has to be how we can attract, motivate, develop, and retain high-quality teachers in our nation's public schools, particularly those schools in our most challenged inner cities and rural areas. Part V describes one approach, the Teacher Advancement Program (TAP).

In 1999, Lowell Milken introduced a comprehensive whole school reform model called the Teacher Advancement Program to improve teacher quality in the United States and, in turn, enhance student achievement. Within six months of its formal introduction, the Milken Family Foundation began implementation of the TAP program in public schools. Lewis C. Solmon discusses the need for a program like TAP and its underlying principles. TAP provides teachers with a career path and advancement opportunities; compensates expert teachers for their skills and responsibilities; restructures the school schedule to accommodate teacher-led, site-based professional development; introduces competitive hiring practices;

and pays teachers based on how well they instruct and how much their students learn. TAP has developed an extensive research-based teacher evaluation system that uses master teachers and the principal as evaluators after they are trained and certified as being qualified to do so, and teachers are evaluated five or more times each year. These design components change each school's structure, making the teaching profession more attractive, the job conditions more manageable, and the pay for high-quality teachers much better.

John Schacter presents the preliminary evaluation results from six TAP elementary schools in Arizona. The findings show that all TAP schools increased student achievement in math and language arts each year. The highest-performing TAP school gained 56% while the lowest-performing gained 11%. TAP schools outperformed control schools by 13% over two years. Forty-eight percent of TAP classrooms realized achievement gains compared to 38% of classrooms in control schools. Finally, schools that rigorously implemented TAP produced gains that were 51% greater than control schools. These results occurred in high- and low-performing schools, as well as in large and small urban communities.

As the Milken Family Foundation began to implement TAP around the country, it became clear that leadership at the state, district, and especially the school level is crucial to TAP's success. Accordingly, we invited Warren Bennis, Distinguished Professor of Business Administration at the University of Southern California, to address the state education chiefs and other policy leaders who attended our conference. Bennis has been called "the Dean of Leadership Gurus." He suggests five things for every education leader to consider. First, leaders should use the bully pulpit to engage others in the ideals of what education can do. They need to be out there every day talking about the value of education. Next, they need to maintain a positive outlook. They also have to be change agents who honor and cherish symbols of history, tradition, and stability while emphasizing symbols of change and revision. Further, education leaders must make others proud of themselves. They need to keep reminding themselves of the important job they are doing, and remember the contributions they are making. Finally, they must be passionate about their work. A committed, enthusiastic, and fervent leader breeds similar emotions in those around them.

Some of Dr. Bennis's other ideas are presented in this chapter.

IN SUM

Quality teachers are absolutely central to assuring excellence in the educational experience of every young person in America. Indeed, good teachers are to education what education is to all other professions. They are the indispensable element—the sunlight and oxygen—the foundation on which everything else is built. That is why we, as a nation, must make it a national goal to place a talented teacher in every classroom in America. (Lowell Milken in *The Growth of the Teacher Advancement Program: Teaching as the Opportunity 2002*)

In order to create and develop the human capital of teachers in America's classrooms and in turn increase academic achievement of students, individuals considering a career in teaching must be provided a set of skills, the support for developing those skills, a path for advancement, and the reward for achieving at high levels and making an impact in their work. Although many approaches to improve teacher quality have been suggested, the Teacher Advancement Program embodies the elements with the greatest hope to make improvements in the teaching force that will have a direct, positive impact on the achievement of students.

This book provides readers with the opportunity to hear what experts in the educational community think about the myriad issues involved in improving the quality of all teachers in our nation's classrooms. One final note—this book reflects the proceedings of our National Education Conference that was held in May, 2003. Since that time, the Teacher Advancement Program has grown from roughly 30 schools to over 70 schools nationwide, and that growth is continuing. Similarly, additional student achievement results have been reported from Arizona and South Carolina. For the most updated information on the Teacher Advancement Program, please visit the Milken Family Foundation website at http://www.mff.org.

INTRODUCTION

William J. Bennett

We talk a great deal in Washington about how to promote excellence in education. The Milken Family Foundation's Educator Awards and the Teacher Advancement Program are doing just that. These programs are examples of the kind of performance-based compensation we should be using to reward teachers and to achieve the end of excellent education. A Roman poet says, "Here, too, the honorable finds its due and there are tears for passing things; here, too, things mortal touch the mind." I salute the Milken Foundation for saying that excellence should be recognized, rewarded, applauded, and honored.

We often use the word "excellence" without explaining why it is important. I do not consider "excellence in education" to be a pat refrain or a self-evident goal unworthy of mention for American teachers. My favorite novelist, George Eliot, says that excellence is good because it encourages us about life generally. Excellence in education encourages children and their friends and families about life generally; the benefits of a good education extend well beyond the classroom and well beyond the present day. A good education is the foundation for a happy and successful life, and its benefits extend to all those who spend time with its primary recipient.

The question then arises: how do we define excellent education? I am chairman of an online education company that offers a virtual curriculum to children across the country, and we have had to face the same challenges in designing excellent educational materials that the nation's public schools faced when I was Secretary of Education and face still today. It is

Talented Teachers: The Essential Force for Improving Student Achievement, pages xv–xviii
Copyright © 2004 by Information Age Publishing

difficult to decide exactly what to teach and how to teach it because of the ever-changing state of science and the humanities and educational theory. But I do believe that there is a body of knowledge that our children ought to know when they leave school. We want educated children to graduate from our high schools—children versed in the great works of literature and the great ideas, not in the minutiae of process and the maneuverings of bureaucracy.

Once we have decided what we want our children to learn, we must confront the real problem of ensuring that they learn it. Any child's education starts in the family. The decline and, in many cases, collapse of the American family has had the single most consequential impact on American education. A teacher cannot assume that every child has parents who are prepared to do their work and meet their responsibilities, and that places a heavier burden on schools. But it remains the case that while not every teacher is a parent, every parent is a teacher—a child's all-but-indispensable teacher. I have seen children saved by education even when a parent was not present, but it remains the rule in nearly all cases that parents' presence and involvement is critical to children's success in education and in life. I asked a psychiatrist whom I visited early in my tenure what children need to succeed. He said, "A child needs at least one adult with a deep, irrational attachment to that child that overrides almost everything else." In other words, for a child to succeed, he needs at least one adult who is absolutely crazy about him. That is the work that we have to attend to.

Outside of the family, people from across the gamut of America's educational system should be actively involved in a child's education—rules cannot simply be mandated by policymakers in Washington. I got the single most important piece of professional advice I have ever received in my life from my wife, Elayne Glover Bennett, who is a former elementary school and special education teacher and who still works in the public schools of the District of Columbia. "Don't just stand there and make pronouncements from on high," she said to me when I was Secretary. "Find out what you're talking about first." I asked her why I should have been any different from the other Cabinet members. "Because you're a teacher," she replied. So off I went to about 125 schools where I normally taught a class or two. I met with teachers, talked to people, and listened a lot. I taught third grade and seventh grade and eleventh grade. At some places the door was shut in my face before I got in because I was not certified. But in most places, I was welcome for at least one or two classes. And in attending I saw wonderful teaching and I saw horrible teaching. When I saw the horrible teaching, I wanted to scream and shout and report people. When I saw the great teaching, I wanted to stand and applaud, to give people recognition and awards. It was great to be able to attend those classes; I developed friendships around the country with teachers and some principals, administrators, and parents—people with whom I am still in touch and whose advice I solicit in developing virtual curriculum materials. I had a wonderful time teaching in their classrooms and I learned a lot about American education, and I think that the teachers who saw that I was teaching had more regard for my opinion because of it. When we take policymakers out of their offices in Washington and put them in the places affected by their decisions, we are rewarded more than once. Not only do the administrators take back a more intimate knowledge of American education, but the educators feel more connected to their supervisors, and so the policies the supervisors create are more successful.

Despite all the great teaching I saw, it was clear to me from my time in the classrooms that there were too many unenthusiastic and incompetent teachers. If I were running a school system today, I would focus on only one thing for the first six weeks of the job: gathering together the best talent I could find—the best teachers, people in love with their subjects. George Eliot wrote of a character who loved his work so much that "one could not tell where the subject matter left off and the man began." American schools need teachers who are equally entwined with what they do. Our schools need to find those people, whether they be licensed or not, who are deeply competent in their subject, who can communicate with young people, and who are of exemplary character. We should hire them and let them do what it is they want to do—within a curricular framework, of course. But the great teacher is irreducible, and we should not try to force all teachers to teach in the same manner. If we staff our schools with passionate and intelligent teachers, we will dramatically improve American education without having to micromanage: after all, so much of education is that magic that goes on between teacher and child, the passing of fire from one to another. The teachers I saw as I went around the country who inspired me and with whom I have stayed in touch were teachers who passed on that fire.

Once the schools hire great teachers and give them their curriculum, they must not become complacent. That fire a teacher passes to a student will die if it is not kindled. When I was a graduate student in philosophy, there was a professor from Germany, an expert on Kant and Hegel, who fascinated me because he seemed to know everything. I asked him, "Professor Hartman, just how do you work?" And he said, "Mr. Bennett, I'm sure just like you, I get up in the morning. I start to read, I have a cup of tea. Then sometimes I look and it's 7:00 P.M., and I've just been reading all day." I said, "Well, sometimes I get up in the morning, I start eating and watching television, and I look at my watch and it's 7:00 P.M. I've not done a thing!" I love the idea of enthusiasm for learning, but students must be pressed, or—as I did some—they drift. There is much temptation in the human heart, in life, in television, in the street. Raising children and teaching are both about consistency. That early thirst for learning is lost unless children are guided. Students must be constantly, consistently challenged, from the very earliest ages all the way through high school, or the race between education and catastrophe will be lost.

Just as we must continue to push our students, so must we push our schools and teachers. Even after we hire teachers who love their subjects, we must promote growth by reviewing for excellence; nor can we afford to let our schools go unevaluated. We have to make distinctions between good and bad teaching, good and bad curricula and schools. We should honor the great people—administrators and teachers who are doing a great job. We should not honor the people who are not. We should not be afraid to make hard distinctions, and if we're serious about it, we need to reward and honor excellence.

People say American education is underfunded. Some American education—the excellent education—is underfunded, but some American education is getting too much money. We should identify the high quality and the low quality and fund them commensurately, and we should get our priorities straight. Instead of purchasing new computers that become obsolete in a matter of months, we should increase the salaries of great teachers. We need to tell the truth about American education. Nobody in the system who is doing a high-quality job has anything to fear from any honest assessment or criticism.

"Sunlight is the best disinfectant," Justice Brandeis said. The more sunlight we shine on the system, the better chance we have to improve it and the better chance we have to do more broadly what we are doing with the Milken Awards—which is bringing honor and praise to those who deserve it.

This volume is helping to spread that sunlight. It is a compilation of thoughts from experts who have reflected on the hard work of achieving excellence. It is my hope that readers will profit from these ideas as they pursue excellence in education across this country.

Part I

EQUITY AND EXCELLENCE

CHAPTER 1

EQUITY AND EXCELLENCE

Ensuring a High-Quality
Educational Experience for Every Child

Lowell Milken, Jeanne Allen, Mayor Jerry Brown, David Driscoll, Nina Rees, and Tavis Smiley

Introduction by Jane Foley

I am here to introduce a man who needs no introduction to this audience, but it's worth a moment to reflect on why Lowell Milken, an extraordinary, successful businessman and chairman of this Foundation since its inception in 1982, is also uniquely qualified to help our distinguished panel focus on and articulate the challenges and solutions for ensuring that no child is left behind.

We have often heard Lowell speak about how his life has been shaped and strengthened through strong family bonds and outstanding teachers. While a freshman in high school, he wrote an autobiographical essay in which he concluded, "The future is very bright for a person with a fine education and I look forward to it." Lowell's vision for American education for all students is the same start in life that he had, and so at the age of 33, Lowell co-founded the Milken Family Foundation.

Talented Teachers: The Essential Force for Improving Student Achievement, pages 3–46
Copyright © 2004 by Information Age Publishing
All rights of reproduction in any form reserved.

For over 20 years, under Lowell's vision and direction, the Foundation has been advancing its mission by implementing national programs in education and medical research that identify talented people and provide them with resources, all to enable individuals to achieve even higher levels of success and performance, and connect them within powerful networks. Lowell is relentless in his quest to create and develop comprehensive solutions grounded in research to improve American education, and as such, has been a leader in groundbreaking education reform.

Over the years, Lowell has expanded our thinking and propelled us to action. Many examples come to mind. In 1985, Lowell publicly recognized the important contributions of outstanding educators with the creation of the Milken Educator Awards program, and since then has been celebrating the achievements of the nation's best educators, and activating them in state and national networks that help elevate the entire teaching system.

In the later part of the 1980s, Lowell saw that meaningful use of education technology would require sound research, focused professional development, and effective and instructional applications if it was going to be a tool to improve student achievement. The Milken Exchange on Education Technology was subsequently launched to promote and accelerate program and policy initiatives that would ensure meaningful outcomes for students.

In the early 1990s, Lowell challenged us at these annual education conferences to restore high quality to American education by addressing our most basic beliefs—equity and excellence. He set forth a program of high standards, linked to assessment and accountability, that would strengthen the system and develop the potential in all students. In 1997, he proposed a comprehensive program of early childhood education. Many of its provisions are now enacted into law.

In 1999, Lowell unveiled a comprehensive school reform model, the Teacher Advancement Program, to address both the teacher quantity and quality crises. Today, TAP is active in dozens of schools across the country and the early results are most promising in realizing student achievement gains, retaining and motivating talented teachers to stay in the profession, and in attracting talented young people to the teaching profession.

I have had the good fortune over the years to see Lowell's insight, analysis, and ideas on reform in action from both the school and national perspectives, which leads me to one conclusion: When Lowell Milken talks about the future of American K–12 education, it is a good idea to listen. Let's now hear from Lowell and our panelists as to their ideas for how we can develop an education system with equity and excellence for every child.

Lowell Milken

Our panel topic of this morning is "Equity and Excellence: Ensuring a High-Quality Educational Experience for Every Child." This subject has been of great interest to me and to our work at the Foundation for two decades. Believing as I do that education is the means most conducive to building human capital, it is essential that the nation, states, school districts, and schools do everything in their power to ensure that every child in America is afforded a rigorous educational experience.

For over three decades, our nation's K–12 system has tried with little success to significantly improve the academic achievement of low-performing children. And while some progress has been made in closing resource gaps, the fact is that the academic achievement gap between students rich and poor, majority and minority, urban and suburban, remains at unacceptable levels.

In a nation of more than 50 million children in K–12 public education, as many as nine million students, the majority of whom are poor, are not receiving a quality educational experience. And while geographically the system is consistently failing poor minority and non-minority students across the United States, the vast majority of these low-achieving students live in highly populated inner-city areas or poor rural areas.

It may be hard to imagine, but it was 20 years ago that one of the most important education reform documents of the 20th century, *A Nation at Risk*, was issued. And while in the wake of *A Nation at Risk*, educators and policymakers said they would focus their attention and efforts on student achievement, two decades later, little progress has been made. Today, once again, this problem has taken on a new sense of urgency, driven in large part as a result of legislative action and court cases on a range of issues, increases in student and school achievement information, as well as widespread calls for holding the K–12 system of education accountable. At the federal level, and in every state and district, policymakers are struggling to address low academic achievement among many K–12 students and the gaps in achievement among income and racial ethnic groups.

Starting from the belief that all children can learn, what are the steps that need to be taken in order to remedy the current state of affairs? What are the strategies and solutions that will reduce the academic achievement gap? Is it a matter of resources? Is it dependent on introducing new and innovative approaches? Is competition within the K–12 system required to change a system that historically has been slow to change? Is the remedy finding ways to attract, retain, and motivate talented educators to teach in our low-performing schools? Are solutions dependent on federal action, initiatives like No Child Left Behind where states are mandated to have all children make adequate yearly gains in achievement levels?

These are some of the issues we will explore, and to do so, I am especially pleased to have five opinionated and talented panel members to advise us.

Tavis Smiley is a nationally syndicated radio host who has spent his life mastering the art of being heard. The third oldest of 10 children, he earned a degree in law and public policy from Indiana University and began his career as a top aide to former Los Angeles Mayor Tom Bradley. Tavis now reaches millions of Americans daily over the radio waves on NPR's *The Tavis Smiley Show* and on ABC Radio Network with *The Smiley Report;* on television as a reporter and analyst for everyone from CNN to C-SPAN; in print as an author of six books; and as a philanthropist, dedicated to educating and empowering young leaders in the black community.

Next, Nina Rees is Deputy Under Secretary for Innovation and Improvement of the U.S. Department of Education. Nina oversees a $2 billion budget for 25 competitive grant programs and implementation of the public school choice and supplemental services provision of the No Child Left Behind Act. An integral part of the team that drafted the original blueprint for NCLB, Nina served as an education policy advisor to Vice President Richard Cheney and the Bush 2000 Campaign. From 1997 to 2001, she was chief education analyst for the Heritage Foundation where she honed her commentary skills on such programs as *CNN Inside Politics* and the *CBS Evening News.* During that time, Nina worked closely with federal and state legislators on reforms targeting disadvantaged students including school choice initiatives for low-income students.

Jerry Brown is currently the Mayor of Oakland and formerly a two-term governor of the State of California. During his terms in the 1970s, Governor Brown presided over a state where 25% of the nation's new jobs were created. As governor, he broke new ground by appointing an extraordinary number of women and minorities to prominent government positions. Governor Brown's bid for the 1992 Democratic Presidential Nomination, during which he refused any contributions over $100, garnered enough voter support to continue until the Democratic National Convention where he lost the nomination to Bill Clinton. Today, he is serving his second term as Mayor of Oakland, with urban revitalization as his focus. Believing in the power of education to lift young people out of poverty and to enable them to lead productive lives, the Mayor has made education reform the key component of his work. For example, he has opened two charter schools in the Oakland Unified School District, the Oakland School for the Arts, and the Oakland Military Institute.

Dr. David Driscoll is Commissioner of Education for the Commonwealth of Massachusetts. David also happens to be from a family of 10 children, and the youngest no less. David has been in public education for 39 years with broad experience at the classroom level as a middle and high school math teacher, at the district level as superintendent, and currently at the state level as commissioner. As commissioner, David has launched and implemented a number of important initiatives ranging from strengthening the state's future teaching force to improving the state's school and district accountability systems. And under David's leadership, Massachusetts was one of the first five states in the nation to have its No Child Left Behind accountability plan approved.

Jeanne Allen is a national voice for school choice and accountability in K–12 education. Jeanne founded the nonprofit Center for Education Reform in 1993 to deliver practical K–12 research and assistance to parents and neighborhood leaders throughout the country. Having authored the school reform handbook, *How to Improve Your Schools,* Jeanne is a strong advocate of bringing the power of ordinary people to bear on policy decisions that affect their local communities. Lawmakers, reform leaders, and journalists alike often seek Jeanne's expertise, and her commentaries have appeared in more than 200 publications, ranging all the way from *Good Housekeeping* to the *Wall Street Journal.* She earned her bachelor's degree in political science from Dickinson College and has worked at the U.S. Department of Education in a senior post.

Before we pose questions to the panel members, let's take a brief look at the academic achievement gap from a few different perspectives.

To begin, let's look at the results of the recently released UNICEF report on the achievement gap from an international view. This report provides an analysis of the educational performance in 24 of the world's industrialized nations (Chart 1.1). This study ranks countries by the size of the gap

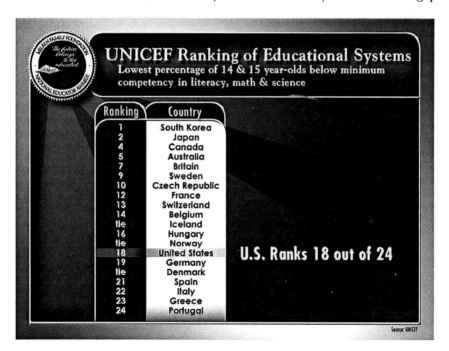

Chart 1.1.   UNICEF ranking of educational systems.

between low achievers and average students by using various test results in reading, math, and science and literacy. South Korea and Japan have the lowest percentage of 14- and 15-year-olds below minimum competency. The United States by comparison does not fare well with a ranking of 18th out of 24 countries.

Nationwide, we see the achievement gap between black and white and Hispanic and white children in the NAEP reading long-term assessments. As shown in Chart 1.2, while some progress was made during the period from 1971 to 1988, since that time period, the gap is widening again.

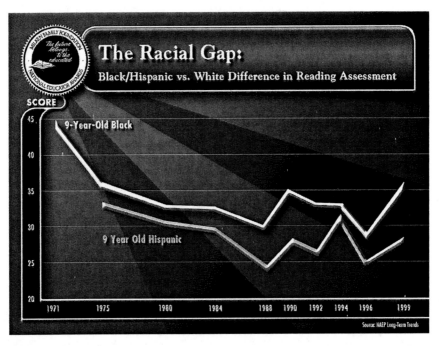

Chart 1.2.   The racial gap.

Looking at student achievement nationwide based on income level, Chart 1.3 shows NAEP fourth-grade reading and math scores during the period 1996 through 2000. Students on free or reduced-price lunch have made little progress in recent years, while substantial gains have been made in math among students not eligible for free and reduced-price lunch.

As you can see, the measurement level used is that of a "proficient" achievement level on NAEP and other standardized exams (Chart 1.3). There is a good reason for using this measure, for it is our belief that a level of "proficient" is the achievement level children must attain if they're going to be prepared for gainful employment in the 21st-century. It's also

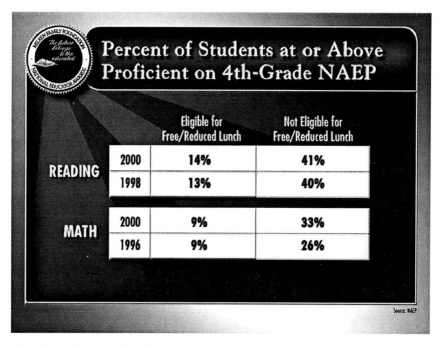

Chart 1.3.   Percent of students at or above proficient on 4th-grade NAEP

the level that NCLB speaks to, though states are free to determine their own "cutoff" scores for state-mandated exams.

The next three charts highlight the achievement gap among ethnic groups by state. In looking at fourth-grade 2000 NAEP math results by certain participating states, Chart 1.4 shows the percentage of African American students who are at an achievement level of proficient. As you can see, among the 32 states that participated in NAEP, 21 had only 1–5% of black students scoring at a proficient level in fourth-grade math; in eight states, only between 6 and 10% of children score at the proficient level; and in three states only 11–16% score at a level of proficient. Chart 1.5, which includes the respective scores for Hispanic children, shows results only marginally better. Of a total of 38 states reporting data for Hispanic children, not one state has more than 17% of Hispanic students achieving a level of proficient on the NAEP exam. By comparison, the scores for white students, included in Chart 1.6, show significantly higher results.

Looking more carefully at the data, we find that the real determinant is one of poverty. And tragically, since the vast majority of black and Hispanic children happen to be poor, their achievement results are correspondingly markedly below those for children in high income levels. This disparity is seen, for example, in academic achievement results in California. Chart 1.7

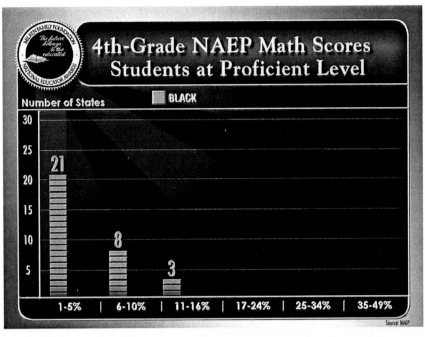

Chart 1.4.   4th-grade NAEP math scores: Students at proficient level.

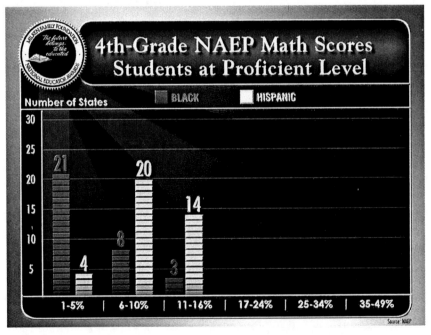

Chart 1.5.   4th-grade NAEP math scores: Students at proficient level.

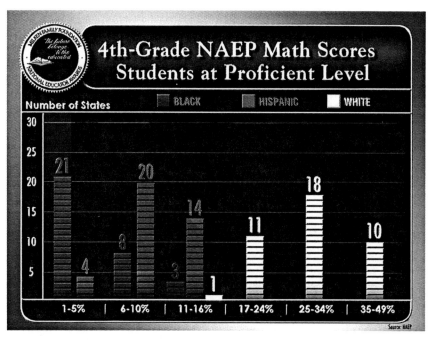

Chart 1.6.   4th-grade NAEP math scores: Students at proficient level.

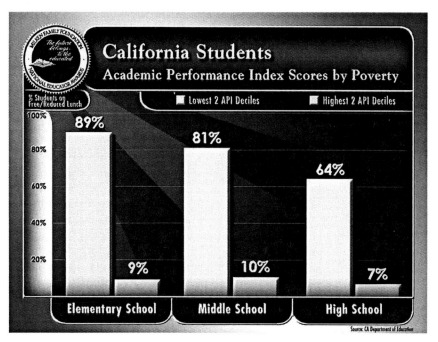

Chart 1.7.   California students: Academic performance index scores by poverty.

shows the highest two deciles and the lowest two deciles in student performance on California's Academic Performance Index. Among those students in the highest two deciles, only nine percent are on free and reduced-price lunch. In contrast, 89% of elementary students who score in the lowest two deciles are on free and reduced-price lunch.

While we could go on and on presenting examples showing a vast disparity among students at different income levels, among students from different racial/ethnic groups, and between urban and suburban students, respectively, there is little point in doing so. What we need to address now is *what are the solutions and strategies to address and remedy these disparities?*

Let's begin our discussion with the issue of money. Does the achievement gap exist in large measure because we have not adequately funded low-performing schools? What role does money play in the process of improving student performance for low-performing students and schools?

Dr. David Driscoll

It's a lot more important than people think it is. You know the old saying about you don't solve the problem of education by throwing money at it. Those of us in education say, why don't we try it just once? I'll just give you a few statistics to demonstrate my point. Special education costs are going through the roof across the country. Full funding is supposed to be 40%. It's at about 18% at the federal level. That would be $250 million to my state, which has arguably among the highest percentage. Only 3.2% of the federal government budget is spent on education in comparison to 26% on defense.

I'm not against defense, but I think there must be a balance. So I won't accept the fact that people say, well we spend billions of dollars, we're not getting any results; therefore, money is not the answer. While money is part of the answer, it's certainly not the whole answer. Number one, it's very important that money be predictable, so you don't run into the situation that I didn't think I was going to be in again. After 10 years of steady money, with more money going to the poorer districts, we now have a $3 billion deficit and the extra funds are gone. The $70 million endowment for teacher quality, gone. Forty million dollars for MCAS remediation, gone. And then when we talk about money, predictability is key. Second, it's going to cost billions of dollars to run education, because that's what it costs when you open the doors everyday. I don't think it's a huge amount of money, but I think more money is needed. For example, salaries for teachers in hard-to-staff schools. I think we need to invest a lot more in early childhood education. So there are areas that are going to cost a lot more money.

Tavis Smiley

I agree with David that we ought to try this once. I've said many times that the answer to solving the education crisis in this country, certainly with regard to public education, might not be throwing more money at the problem, but I can assure you, it's not taking money out of the public school system. And we keep debating and arguing about whether or not that is a legitimate thing to do, certainly around the issue of school choice.

It's not just a problem of money, but I think more so it is problem of will. Because if we had the will, the courage, the conviction, and the commitment in this country to solve this education achievement gap, we would do something about it. I suspect that all of us in this room, while we could debate whether or not the war with Iraq has been a good thing or a bad thing, I think all of us obviously support our troops fighting for our security abroad. But I have been baffled by the speed, the deliberate speed with which we found money that we did not have to finance a war halfway around the world. It just seems to me, then, that if we had the will to really solve this problem, we would find the money to solve the problem.

It is clearly, as Lowell mentioned earlier, a problem that has existed in this country for decades. So not even trying to point fingers at Republicans or Democrats or anybody in between or on either end, the point is that over a period of time, every president, every single president says he wants to be the education president. We have not had the will, the courage, the conviction, and the commitment to put our money where our mouth is, and deal with this issue.

So the question becomes why do we not have the will? Why? There may be a thousand reasons, but we must find the political will to deal with this problem.

Lowell Milken

David and Tavis, you say that we need to increase funding for education, but have we been getting results for the money we do spend?

I am constantly asked by businesspeople just why are student NAEP scores so disappointing when, as a nation, we seem to be spending ever-increasing amounts to fund K–12 education? We see, for example, in Chart 1.8, that while spending has increased overall by about 100% during the past two decades, NAEP reading scores among 9-year-olds have been flat. Moreover, since 1965 we have spent over $150 billion on Title I programs. Yet, despite substantial expenditures to support high poverty schools, we find that 60% of all poor children scored below basic on the 2000 NAEP reading exam (Chart 1.9).

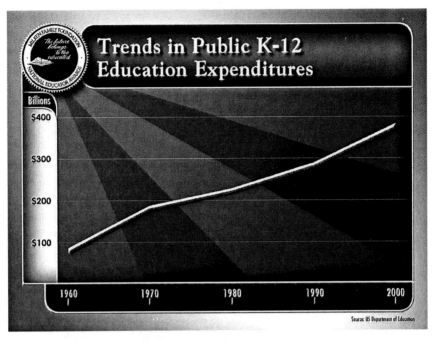

Chart 1.8.   Trends in public K–12: Education expenditures.

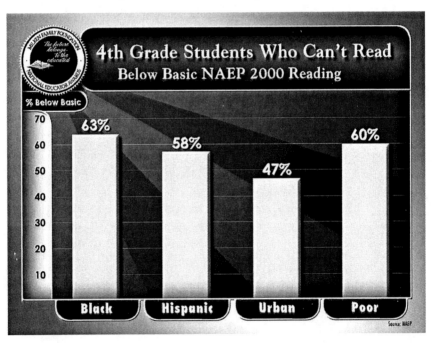

Chart 1.9.   4th-grade students who can't read: Below basic NAEP 2000 reading.

And yes, while much of the increased expenditures have not been directed to the classroom but rather to special education and other related programs, what do you say to citizens about these dismal reading results? What do you tell them when they say that the system is not doing its job with the monies that it is already spending?

Mayor Jerry Brown

I want to make two points. One, money in government is spent most of the time based on the competition of the claimants who operate at the government level. So in other words, health care gets a certain percentage as does education, prisons, military, infrastructure, and so on. If you look at the overall picture, people are willing to support a certain amount in taxes, and that amount doesn't change all that much. It actually rises slowly. And this increase is divided among those various claimants.

Now if you think about how underfunded social security is; if you think about the tremendous escalation in health care costs; if you think about the new international role we're going to play; then you have to ask, with all those very powerful demands, will education be able to squeeze them out and get a bigger share? The answer, I believe, is no. Or will the taxpayer be willing to assume a much greater percentage of burdens relative to the overall gross domestic product? The answer to that is also probably no. So whether right or wrong, it's not going to happen. That's my first point.

Second, you started to mention that the money goes to pay a teacher, or to buy a classroom, or to pay janitors, or to buy pencils. But if you look at where the problem is, it's in these mostly low-income areas, where you have the shadow of segregation and race that still haunts society. People are marked by this history. And then you add it to the disproportionate allocation of funds and income success. And then that's just reproduced in the classroom. When you're poor, you have stresses, you have uncertainty, somebody gets sick, they can then lose their job, and that has serious repercussions.

There are major crises, fears, threats, crime, tension, and dysfunctionality, which are a part of the daily experience. These aren't corrected by paying teachers more money or building schools. So in one sense, the measure is not how much the teachers get paid, or how much we pay for this budget item we call education, but how much money the parents make. And if every parent had a living family wage, and went to work everyday, and was above poverty, you'd find those statistics changing. But the chances of that happening are not high.

Lowell Milken

Mayor, you may be correct, but we still have a responsibility to provide every one of these children with a quality education. These children still, for the most part, show up to school every day, and they are in school for five to eight hours. We cannot "fail" our responsibility because of the complexity of the situation or the competing interests involved.

Nina Rees

I want to address a couple points that have been raised before I get to your last question. The first is that we are not spending enough at the federal level. The U.S. Department of Education received a larger increase than any other agency at the federal level this year. But the fact of the matter is, at the federal level, we only invest 8% of total funds spent on education. So primarily, funds for education come from state and local property taxes. Therefore, I don't buy this notion that we're not funding education enough at the federal level.

Now, having said that, let us go back to the special education question, the fact that we're not committing up to the 40% that we promised. The notion that the federal government was supposed to pay up to 40% of special ed funds was based on a faulty notion that it takes twice as much money to educate a special education child. And since then we have found that many of the children who get labeled as children with disabilities are children who would not be labeled as such if they were provided good reading instruction at an early age.

The approach that the President and the Secretary have taken, and rightfully so, is one of increasing funding, but also increasing the level of accountability associated with these funds. The goal is to measure student progress on an annual basis, and by student subgroups, so that no child falls through the cracks. This means that looking at student achievement in the aggregate, which is what we're doing right now, is no longer sufficient.

One of the problems is the fact that we are pouring money into states and localities, but we don't have a lot of data as to what they're doing. So again, the No Child Left Behind Act has increased the amount of information that states and localities have to provide so we can see where the money is going, how it's being spent. At the end of the day, we're pouring more funds into programs that work and eliminating wastes that are currently happening within the system. It's wrong to spend more money on a program that we know is not proven to be an effective way of raising student achievement. It's a waste of taxpayer dollars. No business would be able to survive under that model. I think that we need to take a look at how we're spending our funds for education right now.

Tavis Smiley

Nina made the point that she didn't buy the argument that we were not spending enough money on education, so let me respond to that right quickly if I can. First of all these increases are relative. That's why I said earlier, it's not about taking shots at Republicans or Democrats; it is that as a country we have not had the will. So these increases are relative to what we have been spending, or not spending, in the past.

These increases, I suspect, or these charts reflect what we were spending before we found this $80 billion that we didn't have for this war in Iraq that I raised earlier. And the third thing is simply this. And we have these conferences, with all due respect to Lowell, and I am so grateful for the Milken Foundation for having the courage to have this conversation, and so appreciative that all of you are here to be a part of this conversation. But at a certain point this becomes conjecture. 'Cause if you go to inner-city schools in Oakland, if you go to inner-city schools right here in Los Angeles, somebody who's brighter than I am asks me, where is the money being spent? They still don't have computers, the schools are still dilapidated. They still don't have books. I mean, when you walk in these schools, and see these conditions, I keep hearing and seeing that we're spending money. But when you walk in these schools, the money is not getting to where it needs to be. That's the bottom line.

Nina Rees

All we're trying to say is that it's not managed well. So unless you find a way to get principals, teachers, and local superintendents the means to see where their money is going and how it's being spent, we're going to be faced with the same thing you're seeing in Oakland and Jersey City. They spend more per pupil than any other city in the nation, yet their test scores are worse than any other state in the nation.

Jeanne Allen

The issue of money is really not as complicated as we're all making it sound. It's a wonderful thing to be able to say we need more money. In our personal lives, we all want money. But each of us has to make decisions everyday about how to spend it. But in education we have to get very, very clear about what's happening. When a dollar is allocated, whether it's the federal or state government, it doesn't just go into education. If it just went to education, and money was "sitting" in classrooms going to teachers, going to programs that work, being governed by people closest to our children, we wouldn't be having this debate.

But once the money starts to move, it's pulled apart and the California Department of Education, or the Arkansas Department, and so on, give it first to this contract, to that person, to that grown-up. And by the time it reaches the classroom, there's no control, no accountability. And if you have a program that actually works, you can't buy it anyway, because you would have to go all the way back to the loop where it started. Tavis or David say that we don't have the will. We have the will. But there is a huge blob sitting between our money and our kids that's preventing us from doing what's right. And until we have the will to actually say break this down and start giving it to people who need it, and who can make the most difference with it, you can talk about money all day long; but that doesn't change how it's spent.

Mayor Jerry Brown

Here's the problem with government spending. When you see a problem, you throw some money at it. Suppose there are 10 people with that problem. When you throw money at it, pretty soon there are 20 people who find out they have that problem too. Then you throw more money at it, and now you have 40 people with that problem. So special ed is a guarantee. Now, forgetting how much the federal government is supposed to give us, if you can come within those boundaries—and by the way there are aggressive parents who want that, and they all have lawyers, and they have a right to a lawyer—then you get it. So you can divert money into that out of the desire or the frustration with the school you have. So there are perverse incentives that work in the system that Jeanne described, and I think you're implying as well. It's very hard to take them out of the system.

Dr. David Driscoll

The deal that was made in Massachusetts in 1993 was we're going to give you money. And in fact it's been billions of dollars over 10 years. But you're going to get results. And, I think we've done that. And I want to brag a little bit about it. Let's look at Chart 1.10 for a moment. Here are the results of the MCAS. It shows in this particular case all of the various ethnic groups. Now I don't want to oversell this, but you can see that the gap is closing. However, it's a gap to pass so it's meeting the minimum at the 10th-grade level. Nevertheless, that's remarkable progress. And if we look at Chart 1.11, it's even more so when you look at the various groups like LEP kids.

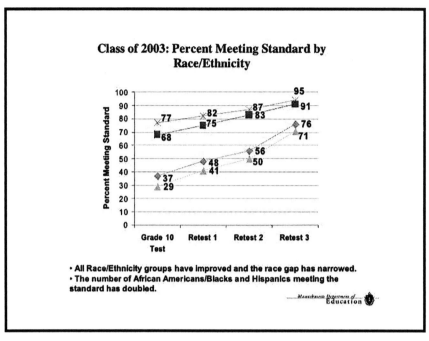

Chart 1.10.   Class of 2003: Percent meeting standard by race/ethnicity.

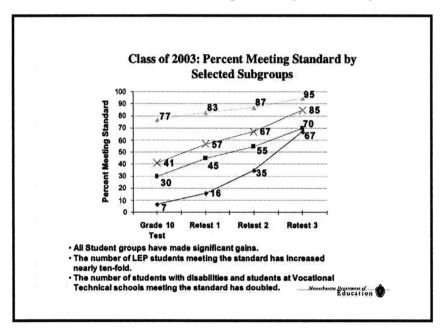

Chart 1.11.   Class of 2003: Percent meeting standard by selected subgroups.

Only 7% of our LEP kids were passing just a few short years ago and look what's happened. So I would argue that we have in fact met the requirements of the people of Massachusetts and they have funded us because we do have results. And for your purposes, Lowell, only 10% of Hispanic kids were proficient and above in 2000, and it went to 26% in 2002. At the sixth-grade level in math, we went from 9% to 12% for Hispanics, and 9% to 14% for blacks. Also 36–41% for whites so all boats are rising. So the gap remains, and yet black and Hispanic kids are doing that much better. I would argue that in Massachusetts, with billions of dollars being spent, but having it tied to accountability and in our case a high-stakes exam, we can in fact get results and we can get support from the business community and the general public. When you take money and you spend it wisely, and it's focused on proven, sound research-based programs that drive student learning, you can get support. And it's early childhood education. It's adult education, it's after-school programs, it's the whole gamut of programs.

Lowell Milken

Let's move on to the critical role that teacher quality plays. Many of you in this audience are familiar with an ever-growing body of research that shows that teacher quality is the single most important school-related factor that drives student performance. Research studies show that effective teachers can significantly boost the student achievement of low-achieving students, students performing at or near grade level, and gifted students as well. And certainly all of our own personal experiences would confirm that good teachers really do make a difference.

But despite all the evidence that good teachers can make a significant difference in student performance, in all too many low-performing schools today, we find that the students who need help the most have the least trained and least experienced teachers to help them succeed.

Let's take a brief look at the results of a comprehensive New York study on teacher quality (Chart 1.12). Researchers found that over a 15-year period:

- Poor non-white and low-performing students attend schools with less-qualified teachers.
- In urban areas, teachers with greater skills were more likely to leave.
- Salaries for the New York City School District teachers with master's degrees were 15–25% lower than their suburban counterparts.
- Schools in which more than 20% of students were scoring at the lowest level have consistently less-qualified teachers than the other schools.

- In poor performing schools, 35% of the teachers had failed their general knowledge or liberal arts and science exam compared to 9% in schools in which none of the students scored at the lowest level.
- Transfer and quit behaviors among teachers are consistent with the findings that the more qualified teachers seize the opportunities to leave the more difficult working conditions and move to more appealing environments.
- Teachers are more likely to leave poorer urban schools, and those who leave are likely to have greater skills than those who stay.

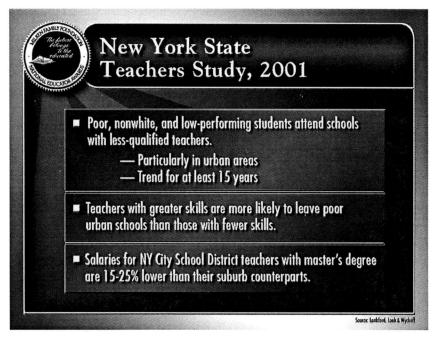

Chart 1.12.   New York state teachers study, 2001.

New York is hardly the only state experiencing these problems. In California, schools with the highest percentage of minority students have more than one in five teachers who are not certified. Furthermore, in the vast majority of the state's low-performing schools, at least one-third of the teachers are in their first or second year.

In most large urban districts, turnover in high-poverty schools is extraordinarily high in the first three years. In Philadelphia, for example, public school teacher turnover is around 40%. And in the 1999–2000 school year, 50% of teachers had come to their schools within the previous two years. Many have commented that this kind of turnover leaves children in a system where there is a revolving door of teachers every year. And we've all seen the statistics on out-of-field teaching, where simply too many teachers do not have sufficient training and knowledge of the courses they are being asked to teach.

We could go on and on, but the facts are clear that regardless of the measure of teacher qualification—whether it's experience, certification, academic preparation, knowledge of academic content, or performance on licensure tests—we assign students who need the most help to teachers with the weakest academic foundations. This is unacceptable. But just how do we get talented educators to teach in our low-performing schools?

Tavis Smiley

I think these numbers speak for themselves. I'm sitting here staring at this screen, taking in all these statistics, but I keep coming back to the same point. You can save a lot of money that is spent to do these studies if you just went to the schools and spoke to the kids. They will tell you everything that these charts bear out. I believe that teachers are the most undervalued resource in our society. No question about that. I would hasten to add that as these numbers point out, it's not that some of these kids can't learn, it's that some of these teachers can't teach. And that's the problem that we have in schools.

We have to pay teachers more money. We have to reward those teachers who will do the yeoman's work of going into the district, going into the schools, where the kids most need their help. And I don't believe you have to be a veteran teacher to be a good teacher. It's about passion, it's about experience, it's about drive, it's about a lot of things. So, you don't have to be a veteran teacher to be a good teacher, but you have to be a teacher that cares about those students.

However, it doesn't matter to me how we get those teachers to care about those students. If it's money, then I'm all for it. If it means paying them to make them care, then so be it. But as you mentioned earlier, Lowell, the fact is that every one of us in this room has a story about a teacher who cared about his or her students. I will be 39-years-old at the end of this year and to this day I still keep in constant touch with my second-grade teacher. She happened to be a white woman and I was the only African American student in that classroom. I would not be doing what I am doing today were it not for this woman who told me that I was as gifted, as talented as anybody else in that classroom. It's about getting teachers who care about the students they teach. We have to get the teachers who are most qualified, as these charts indicate, to the students who most need their help and not to do that, I believe on our part, is child neglect.

Lowell Milken

A governor said that a poor education is a high form of child abuse, yet we have permitted this state of affairs to go on for 30 years. While we cannot mandate that effective teachers must teach in low-performing schools, I believe that there are innovative ways to attract talented teachers to teach in hard-to-staff schools.

Dr. David Driscoll

I think the first thing is to shine a light on the problem. I mean as obvious as it is, no one ever talks about it. It's like the number of kids we lose, black and Hispanic, from the 9th grade to the 12th grade. No one ever talks about it, yet it is a huge national problem. There have been a number of attempts, including Teach for America which has had some success. In addition, KIPP Academy and other charter schools located in inner cities. We have them in Boston.

We have our bonus program where we took mid-career people including doctors, lawyers, black and Hispanic adults, and the attrition rate was about 30%, which is less than the norm. Naturally, once they went into the schools with this idealism, they found all those terrible conditions. This is a huge problem. And it's not going to be solved overnight. But the first thing we have to do is recognize it's a huge problem. Moreover, what business would start out saying, well, here's our problem, because obviously student achievement and this gap are our problems, what business would say, well, there's our problem, but we're not going to deal with it?

Lowell Milken

Our research at the Foundation tells us that we will not be able to make the gains in student performance in our lower performing schools unless we are able to attract and retain talented teachers to those schools. We know in business, for example, that when a critical problem is identified respecting a product or service, the enterprise will ask its most talented people to address the issue. They do not assign the least experienced or least competent staff members to remedy the crises. Why in K–12 education have we permitted the opposite approach to be taken?

Jeanne Allen

The system discourages talent. Those new teachers are the least pre-pared for bureaucracy, though they are often "fired up" with idealism. They tend to walk into a school, and they meet the teacher who was put there because they were the least effective, and they have a principal who is the least effective, and the entire environment says if you came here to do a good job you're in the wrong place.

So you go back to this notion that you're giving prospective teachers, people you want to attract to the profession, a chance to do something good, but we give them absolutely no control; no tools whatsoever.

The new teachers are introduced into a system where everyone at that school has already decided that they've given up. They blame everything from the poverty to tests, and by doing so, they convey to the new teacher that they won't make a difference. It is discouraging.

There's a wonderful article written by a Teach for America graduate detailing his experience in a D.C. public school. Basically run out by his colleagues for trying to move, he ends up in a D.C. charter school and is doing exactly what he wanted to do but was not allowed to do, in a class-room with the identical kids who now listen to him and are learning. If we do not change the conditions and the climate of that school with external pressure and force out mediocrity, nothing we do will change.

Lowell Milken

When we look at the efforts of state and large school districts to recruit and retain qualified teachers, we find that both states and school districts generally do not target their efforts to the hard-to-staff or high poverty schools. I would submit that the states and districts are not doing enough to provide the kinds of incentives to get teachers to teach in hard-to-staff schools.

Earlier this month, we conducted a number of focus groups with highly qualified educators. Some of the participants once taught in hard-to-staff schools and left while others still teach in hard-to-staff schools. These focus groups spoke volumes about the challenges that high-quality teachers face when they are in "hard-to-staff" schools—challenges that directly conflict with their desire and ability to teach children. We heard about the poor state of facilities, how teachers were often asked to hold class in play yards amidst helicopter and traffic noise, or in classrooms with inadequate heat and air conditioning. Others saw themselves as glorified babysitters because of the absence of discipline and instructional vision.

The teachers we spoke to worked in schools where both teachers and students came and went from semester to semester and from year to year. They all were concerned with their safety and the level of security at the school site. Some told stories of being stalked, or feeling uncomfortable with the high fences and bars on every window, while others worked on campuses where the school police often outnumbered teachers' aides. However, despite the seriousness of these problems, they were not the main reasons high-quality teachers gave for leaving these hard-to-staff schools. Rather, the key reason focused on a lack of support and leadership from principals and colleagues, and the standard salaries they were receiving for enduring such work conditions.

Teachers are very willing to tackle many of these challenges, but in order for them to remain motivated and stay in hard-to-staff schools, or more importantly, in order to attract new teachers to these environments, they told us that certain key elements needed to exist. First, there needed to be financial incentives—teachers who taught in hard-to-staff schools need to earn more money than those teachers in less difficult settings. And importantly, teachers said they would not only need a strong instructional leader in the school, but also they would need to have other talented teachers, perhaps five or six in an elementary school of 600 students, join them. I believe it is unrealistic to assume that we are going to attract a highly qualified teacher for every classroom in short order. However, with a core group of talented educators in place, they can mentor inexperienced teachers and lead the way to improve the skills and behaviors of all of the teachers in these schools. Do you think this type of approach would make a difference?

Tavis Smiley

I also think it is unrealistic to attract a highly qualified teacher in every classroom. Maybe we're just dead wrong to continue to assume as we have and to believe this notion that folks who go into teaching go into it for purely altruistic reasons. We don't assume that about anybody else in our society. Yes we want to be supported, we want to have the resources to do our job, but if in the world that we live, particularly in the economy that we're dealing with now, people have to make a living.

I was looking at a study the other day that suggested that even among African Americans, I mean back in the day when black folk couldn't do anything else but teach, there was a greater percentage of African Americans who went into the teaching profession. Thankfully, now we live in a society where there are other options for African Americans and people of color to pursue, so the number of African Americans now who are going into the teaching profession has gone down.

I submit that in part, what that survey that I was reading suggests, is that even African Americans understand that we live in a world where you have to make a living. I think maybe we are making a huge mistake, assuming that in this particular society, in this world, and let me add then, particularly given that we have a whole new generation, this hip-hop generation, who we're going to be relying on down the road to choose teaching as a profession. They want compensation, they want to be remunerated. So the fact of the matter is that, when you look at this long term, the problem does not get any better. We want to get this generation to go into teaching, but we're not going to reward them? I think we're setting ourselves up.

Mayor Jerry Brown

As you outlined from the focus group videos, some of those teachers said that discipline is a big problem—the ability to have the teacher in charge of the classroom; enough time for teacher training, collaboration, team building; to allow the principal to be in charge and build the school that he or she wants. And ironically, all the new rights, the new reforms, the proliferation of more rules and laws—all well intentioned—are removing and reducing the discretionary authority at the school site.

There's less scope of maneuver and therefore less authority and less control, because it's all micro-managed by the federal government, the state, and it's just freezing progress. It's not working. So, it's pretty clear, even if you don't have the money, which we've said we're not going to get for a while, if ever, that you have to have a structure and discipline. And if some student has to go out of the classroom, you have to be able to do that without fear of a lawyer, without fear on the part of the principal, and that doesn't exist today.

The teachers are prisoners in a system that every year grows more complicated, with more rights and rules, but the end result is exactly what those statistics say: a lack of significant improvement. So you have to return power to the principal, the principal picks the teachers, and they create the program. And then you'll get something better and that sounds very much like a charter school, or a small school, or one of those other kind of experiments that other people here are going to talk about.

David Driscoll

I think the City of Boston has had some great success over the last 10 years as well. Terrific superintendent and a lot of things happening, including early retirement programs, which allowed us to bring in a lot of younger teachers. They hired a lot of teachers, class size went down. Your idea of bringing five mentor teachers is a great concept, as are the principles in TAP. But it also can be those 19 teachers, who with the stick of MCAS and with the requirements of studying data, we're seeing in our schools, particularly in Boston, really tremendous progress forward. We've had nine years, and not a strike in Massachusetts, a heavy union state because there's been this critical mass, there's been collective bargaining, there's been policy changes, there's been lower class size, there's been a sense of accomplishment. We are seeing it at Dorchester High School and at Charleston High School, they're winning awards and kids are doing much better.

However, as of today, the superintendent has had to close five schools and lay off 400 teachers, which gets back to this. We build them up and then we break them down again. But it's a huge problem, as you suggested. We're not going to come up with simple answers. But I think the idea of having mentor teachers is a good one, we also have charter schools and we have some competition there as well. The proof is in the kids getting better, but we have a long way to go. And you pointed out a problem that everybody just wants to ignore and it's an outrageous thing that we ignore this problem.

Nina Rees

One of the requirements of No Child Left Behind is the option for the states to define what a highly qualified teacher is. States have a great opportunity to go back and revamp the certification system. Part of being highly qualified will entail making sure that your teachers pass a test of some kind, they have a bachelor's degree and that they are state certified. I would submit that a lot of these conditions that states have put in place for a teacher to become certified actually act as barriers to individuals going into the profession of teaching.

When you talk to individuals who are trying to attract folks into teaching, they would also agree with everyone on this panel in that there are just so many structural barriers to attracting good teachers into inner-city districts. Even though there is a good, strong pool of individuals who are ready to go into inner-city districts, the process is so long that by the time they fill out the paperwork and wait for the different forms to go through, the suburbs usually go in and attract these teachers before they are able to go into the inner-city setting.

I'm talking mainly about teachers who are coming through alternative certification, including the New Teachers Project and Teach for America. One of the chronic things that they tell us is that they attract these individuals, but the process it takes between the time they fill out their paperwork and they go through their background check is so complicated. Most individuals don't have three months or more to wait and see if they got the job. So the suburbs tend to attract them. That's one problem that I think they ought to really pay attention to if they want to attract good individuals into the profession of teaching.

Aside from that, I think we haven't been able to figure it out very well. At the federal level we're going to launch a few studies to look at what really makes a quality teacher. We have the different characteristics of teachers who are qualified, but we don't know enough about what we need to do in order to attract qualified people into the profession and keep them in the profession.

One of the attractive points about what you are doing through the TAP program is targeting different individuals who are interested in teaching and then really offering them the support and the training that they need, along with research for us to see how well they're doing. I commend your organization for taking the lead on this issue because a lot of other organizations need to be focused on this area if we want to make a difference in education.

Lowell Milken

Let's turn our attention to the issue of instituting new approaches to improving student learning among low-performing students. If a school consistently fails to improve student performance, should alternative options in the form of public and private choice be available? Some argue that if we cannot fix low-performing schools, we should liberate the children from these schools by allowing families other choices.

Some see charter schools as an answer since they have greater freedom from state and district regulations and increased opportunities to innovate. Can charter schools play a more significant role in reducing the achievement gap? Or, as some argue, should we attach school funding to the "child's back" and let parents use the funding to attend any school of their choice, private or public?

Jeanne Allen

Now you're on to something. You can see in Chart 1.13 the growth of charter schools. What is important is that charters unite all the reforms we're talking about. It brings together the issue of money, which in most cases, in most states is going directly into classrooms. Teachers and principals, and oftentimes parents, have an opportunity to actually look at what it

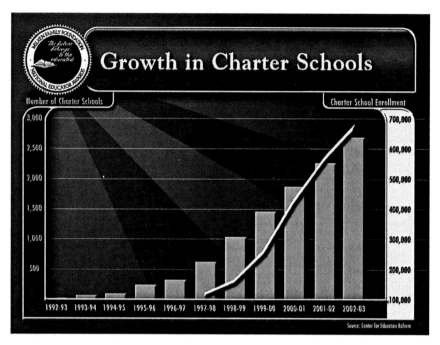

Chart 1.13.   Growth in charter schools.

is they want to do with kids from scratch. And they decide on schools that succeed because a charter school has to perform to stay in business or it loses its contract.

And everywhere we have charter schools that open up in hard-to-educate areas, parents run to these schools, in droves. It is compelling when you look at Philadelphia and L.A., St. Paul and Chicago, that when you open up an option and say anybody can come (and they're open by lottery, and they still have to abide by the same standards), people flock to them. Parents have an option to be empowered, and they run to charter schools in such numbers that their waiting lists often surpass the enrollment. Chart 1.14 shows data on waiting lists. Look at the last bullet, 73% of charter schools have waiting lists as large as 50% of their current student enrollment. And these schools are small on average, which is attractive. But the fact is that there are more people who want to go there than available seats.

We have data that confirms charters are taking the lower end of low-performing students overall and making progress in finite time periods. In fact, there are a disproportionate numbers of low SES, minority, and disadvantaged children clustered in charter schools. Why? Because the need is greatest in those areas and parents, no matter what their income, no matter what their color, understand that which other people have, that is, rich

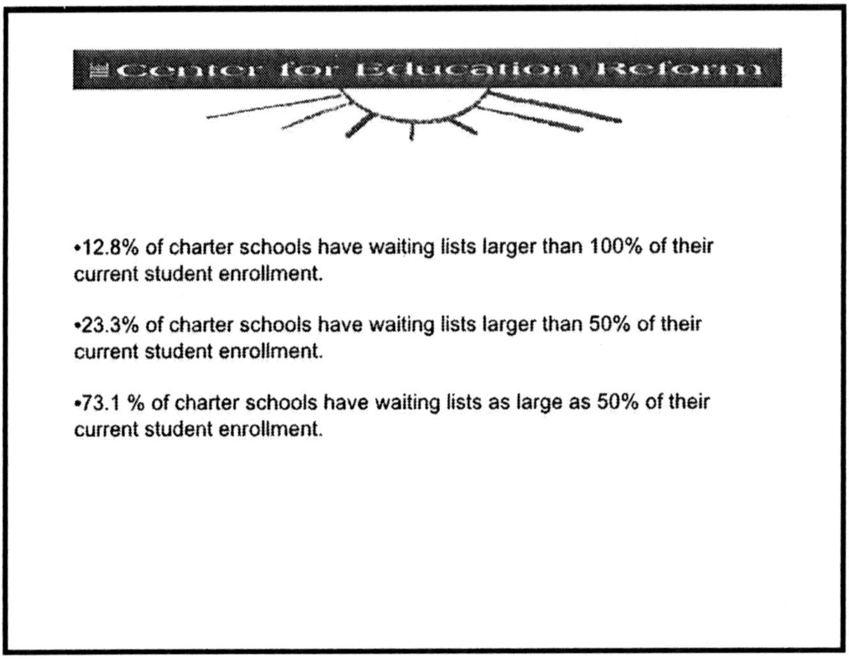

≡Center for Education Reform

•12.8% of charter schools have waiting lists larger than 100% of their current student enrollment.

•23.3% of charter schools have waiting lists larger than 50% of their current student enrollment.

•73.1 % of charter schools have waiting lists as large as 50% of their current student enrollment.

Chart 1.14.   Charter school waiting lists.

people and affluent people who can move to nice suburbs and pick other schools, is probably not a bad thing.

And given the opportunity, they run to these schools. And this is one of these reforms that benefits educators in particular; when they have an opportunity, they are starting these schools. Young recruits out of education colleges or through alternative routes are choosing to teach in charters over traditional public schools. This fact doesn't get nearly enough attention.

Mayor Jerry Brown

I started two charter schools in Oakland: the Oakland School for the Arts and the Oakland Military Institute with the California National Guard. The Oakland Military Institute features uniforms, a sergeant in every classroom, a lot of marching, a lot of discipline. We get about 98% attendance rate, a lot of participation from parents. The Oakland School for the Arts is an audition-based school—again even more participation from the parents. I think the problem is the overregulation of these schools.

Every year in the state capital, the school industry wants to reimpose all the regulations, so a charter school becomes identical to the very institution that it was carved out from and from which it should be distinct. But I can tell you this, the student gains haven't been as dramatic as I'd like, but we're able to make change. We're able to modify based on what is. So I think that the notions here are really freedom, diversity, and flexibility. And the enemy of that is re-regulation inside this monopoly system.

And I think the key word came out in the Supreme Court opinion in 1926, *Pierce v. The Society Sisters*, wherein the Supreme Court said children are not the creatures of State. Instead, they are members of a family who have the absolute right to choose the kind of educational environment for their children. I think the charter school exemplifies that in terms of the interest it generates, the participation, and the flexibility. You can make mistakes, but then you can correct those mistakes because you can get new principals, you can get new teachers, and you can change the way things are run. You're not encumbered by many of the things that are considered basic to the regular public school system.

Lowell Milken

David, why do you think in many states there are interest groups trying to restrict the number of charter schools?

David Driscoll

Well, I do think that there's no question the people within school systems are resistant to change. There's no question about that. And as much as I would defend public education, I think it has to change as well. And I think there has to be this sense of urgency to recognize these kids only have these years and we have to make a difference. And I would agree with Jeanne. In Boston we have waiting lists where we have charter schools. They've had trouble getting principals. They've hired some Boston principals to become principals of the charter schools, but it's hard work. And they get tripped up with the mechanical things like lunches and buses and other things.

However, I think it's definitely part of the landscape and I think it's been a positive thing in many ways. I think it's provided some competition, which has been healthy for Boston. But there's no question about resistance. In fact, our former governor had to cut the budget. We have a reimbursement that goes to the school to kind of blunt the loss of funds to charter schools. And the governor, faced with this deficit a year ago, cut out the reimbursement. And it resurrected the war again between public schools and charter schools. Such that I mean it got ugly. We had public hearings to expand charter schools, which we did. Crowds don't bother me, but they came and they were angry. I think there is a lot of resistance. And, for example, the last time we finally got the cap lifted, the heavily Democratic legislature influenced by the unions saw to it that they have things like being able to form a union, teachers had to be certified, things like that. So it definitely exists. There's a competition there and it can get ugly politically, which is too bad because I think they're a proper part of the mix. I think the results are still mixed in our state. The results aren't quite what they should be in many charter schools. But clearly, they are offering an alternative to parents and families.

Jeanne Allen

You actually have great charter schools, David, which is wonderful. Charters in your state are outperforming traditional public schools in comparable neighborhoods. They are taking lower-SES students and making faster gains with them overall. This is what we see nationwide; that in a value-added way, year by year charter students are making gains. The problem is, despite David's leadership, Massachusetts fixes the enrollment of charter schools at 2% of the overall population of the state.

Now if we really have a sense of urgency (and I'll come there and stand with you in front of the news cameras), you need to recommend that 25% of kids should be allowed in charter schools and go up against those who oppose growth because there's no question about the success that Massachusetts has made on the state tests. Changes are occurring across your state due to the competition introduced through charters. The people in Boston and elsewhere in the state started saying, we had better do something or we're going to be out of it. Don't you agree? I mean, it's a huge ripple effect?

David Driscoll

I agree. We've hit the cap in Boston, in fact. So there cannot be an additional charter school now in Boston. We can talk about the results and I think there are certainly some pockets of terrific results. I think there are some areas that we have concerns as well. So I guess that's life.

Lowell Milken

Chart 1.15 shows how many students were eligible for transfers from failing schools and how many actually transferred. Nina, why do you think that

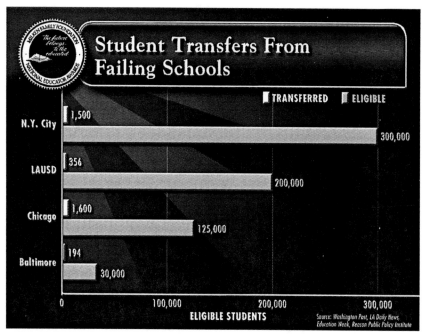

Chart 1.15.   Student transfers from failing schools.

so few parents of children in low-performing schools are taking advantage of NCLB's requirement that school districts allow students in failing schools to transfer to higher performing schools within their school district and provide transportation for the students who transfer?

Nina Rees

I think that with any reform you need to give it a few years before you make any conclusive statements. Let me just point out, as an example, New York City, because I spent a few days there recently to look at how they were implementing this provision of the law. It's very clear that once you notify districts that they may not be communicating with parents in an effective way about the availability of choices, they do put in an effort to go back and make their letters clearer and give parents more time to pick and choose schools.

The other thing that you need to pay attention to is that most parents tend to want to keep their kids within the vicinity of where they reside. So they're not likely to want to bus the child a half hour across town to go to another school, regardless of how well that other school is performing.

One of the incentives that this provision of the law has created in districts like Philadelphia where superintendents have more autonomy over how they spend their budget is to create charter schools. This provision should be adopted in such a way as to attract educational entrepreneurs into the business of creating new schools, and to creating good after-school programs. More importantly, they should make the public schools responsive so that more parents believe in the system enough to keep their kids in that school.

In places like Portland, Oregon, many parents ended up keeping their children in the schools that their children were currently attending even though the school was in need of improvement. Primarily this was because when they looked at the test scores, they noticed that only a small percentage of kids in that school were not doing well. And since the subgroup was different from the subgroup that the rest of the kids belonged to, they decided not to make the transfer. I think it's important to study this very carefully.

It's important for us at the federal level to enforce this provision of the law, that is, to put pressure on the states to hold the districts accountable. Also, it is important to provide information to districts on how you create schools within schools, how you create capacity in your districts. More importantly, I think the burden is really on creative-minded superintendents to seize this opportunity to bring in individuals to build charter schools in states where charter school laws exist. States also should revamp their charter school laws so they're increasing the cap on the number of charter schools that can be built. Otherwise, you are going to be left with a system where a lot of schools identified are in need of improvement and not a lot of good alternatives will be available to parents.

Tavis Smiley

While I support public schools, and I went to public schools all of my life, I think there is something wrong with the public school system to some extent when it does not encourage parental involvement. I've learned one thing as I've traveled this country into schools in the suburbs and to schools in the inner city. And that is the schools that do best in this country, without regard to public or private, charter or public, the schools that do best in this country are the schools where parents are involved. Those are the schools I think that do best. And to an extent, there's something wrong with the public school system that does not encourage and does not empower parents to be involved in that system. That's number one.

Every chance I get, as I do all the time to speak to audiences, predominantly of African Americans, I say to them, that we as black parents, we as parents of color, have to have the will to make this thing work. I believe that. The schools that do best are the schools where parents are involved. And so, this year we celebrate the 35th anniversary of the wonderful publication of the book, *The Fire Next Time* by James Baldwin, one of the greatest essayists this country's ever known. Baldwin said that race is not a personal reality, race is not a human reality, race is a political reality. The governor was right. When you happen to be a person of color, it's a more difficult field you have to navigate just for being a person of color.

But that notwithstanding, I say to black audiences all the time that we have to understand that Malcolm X was right, that education is our passport to the future. That tomorrow belongs to those who are prepared for it today, and I'm not going to let black parents off the hook when they don't step up and involve themselves in the educational excellence of their children. Parents have to do that, there's no substitute. But now that we close on this third point, something completely radical that may change this whole conversation here. I believe that people of color, as all these studies and surveys and graphs point out, for whatever reasons, are having a more difficult time navigating this thing called education.

As Mayor Brown remarked earlier, we are not going to solve the money problem any time soon, and because all these problems are connected, particularly when you're a person of color, what do we do? I think that the way to get away from this debate about charter schools or vouchers is to do something radical.

What would happen in this country if we had a constitutional amendment that guaranteed every child in this country equal assess to a high-quality education? What would happen if we made it one of the precepts of this country that every child ought to be guaranteed not just life, liberty, and pursuit of happiness, not just a right to free speech, not just a right to carry a weapon or the right to vote? But what if we, through our constitution, guaranteed every child in this country, no matter race, no matter color, no matter gender, no matter religion, a right to an equal high-quality education? If we ever did that as a country, it would end all of this conversation and we wouldn't have to be back here 20 years from now discussing this. And that's radical...

But, if we decide as a people that we want equal high quality, then we decide that.

Mayor Jerry Brown

Now you're not a lawyer, right?

Tavis Smiley

No, I'm not.

Mayor Jerry Brown

Okay, I'm a lawyer. I can tell you every time you make a new right, you create a new lawsuit. Now here's the problem: there already is a federal right to an equal, fair education. And what that means is that you cannot discriminate against the student for acting up, disrupting the class, or simply doing nothing. They have a right to this thing called an education that you just have to give somebody. But the fact is, it's not just about education, it's about learning. And you can't control the schools, I would argue, by the proliferation of a lot of rights that get misinterpreted. If you want to say, hey Johnny, you're not doing anything, shape up or I'm going to have to send you over here, or we're going to do something different with you, then you violate their right to get this thing called an education, which is just sitting there and not necessarily learning. And that destroys the power of the principal and the teacher. So I think we've gone a long way down that rights kind of road. The fact is that you can't solve education with litigation. We saw significant improvement with teachers in charge, with principals who can replace teachers, and with parents who can make known what they want to do.

Tavis Smiley

Respectfully, I disagree. I cannot think of a more fundamental right that these children in our society have, than the right to an equal, high-quality education.

That's why we're here today. We are in this room debating today because there are too many segments of our society that do not have that guaranteed right to an equal, high-quality education. What you spoke of are the things they have the right to not be subjected to. It's the difference between having the right to vote, and the right to not have your vote infringed upon. To not be harassed, and have to pay a poll tax. It's the Voting Rights Act that protects your right to vote, that's different from having the right to vote if we gave every child in this country, again, a guarantee to an equal, high-quality education. In a matter of weeks, we start tracking our way to the 50th anniversary of *Brown v. Board of Education*. We are still having this debate 50 years later, which is the essence of what *Brown v. Board* was about, because every child in this country is not guaranteed an equal, high-quality education, and if we did that, we wouldn't be here today.

Mayor Jerry Brown

Yes, we have a right. We have a right in California, because I signed the law, to a bilingual education. And then pretty soon the people who got out of the Spanish immersion were only 1% a year, and you had people seven years later still not knowing English. So you go in with a right, but then the interest group kind of takes over, and you get a bureaucracy, you get a whole movement, and it turns out to be something other than what you want. So I agree with you that, from a macro perspective, there's great deprivation. Many perverse incentives enter in.

David Driscoll

There are two things I do as commissioner in Massachusetts everyday. One is I get that sense of urgency to help every child. And the second thing I do is prepare affidavits to go to court. We're being sued left and right, as the federal government left it to states to decide the rights of education. And we were fortunate in Massachusetts to have a gentleman by the name of John Adams that wrote our constitution. So we have what you're talking about.

And in fact, our Education Reform Act came as a result of the very words of John Adams. We had kids and parents that sued, saying that the Commonwealth of Massachusetts was not living up to its constitutional obligation to all children. And fortunately the legislature passed the Education Reform Act as the case was being decided. But the court, the Supreme Court of Massachusetts decided that in fact, the funding system and the entire system was unconstitutional. And therefore John Adams, back in the 18th century said the people of Massachusetts, the Commonwealth of Massachusetts, shall cherish their children. Cherish did not have an effective meaning. It meant a sense of duty. And so we're in court and we're going to be back in court, because we've had 10 years of a foundation formula, by which monies went to the urban areas. By which we are making progress. And the court is watching it very carefully. But now with the money cut back, we're back in court. Ironically, the Supreme Court of Massachusetts used KERA, the Kentucky Education Reform Act, as its definition of a high-quality education for students.

Sort of a copout in my opinion. Although the words are wonderful. And so we have what you're talking about. And by the way, every state is different, unfortunately, with respect to the constitution. Fortunately for us, we had John Adams. So that will play out. And it's interesting how it will play out. Because if we keep this gap, we are closing it, we only have 6% of our kids fail on a third-grade reading test. We are making great progress now across the board. But I'm not sure we're going to face up to the constitutionality. We certainly aren't as we lay off teachers and close schools and cut back on early childhood programs and early literacy programs. So that constitutional requirement is right here in River City in Massachusetts.

Jeanne Allen

The real issue is one of equality of opportunity—the opportunity to actually select and participate directly in the education of your child. So that rather than the state, or the constitution, or somebody who again has absolutely nothing to do with education fixing this notion that is in most constitutions anyway, you as a parent, Tavis, me, David, the people out in South Central Los Angeles say, "I'm going to make that decision if you are going to pay for that high-quality education that I define."

Audience Question

Great conversation, but what about the importance of curriculum? Maybe the reason we're spending a lot of money and not producing student results is because we're not teaching the right things at the right time and in the right manner to our students. How important is this issue of our curriculum development across math and science? What should be the focus of states on making sure that when we put that teacher in front of those kids, they've got a quality curriculum that they're teaching?

Nina Rees

Well I think the state folks should address that issue, but one of the things we've done at the federal level is to really go in and conduct rigorous evaluations and research of what works in classrooms. Right now the only thing that passes the high bar that we've set is in the area of reading. I encourage you all to contact us if you want to know of research-based methods of teaching reading. Unfortunately, in the other fields, we do not have the evidence we need to promote anything at the national level. But we do encourage states to take on this challenge of actually researching what they're putting into classrooms, to tease out what exactly it is about the effective practices of teachers and effective schools that make a difference. Until you have that evidence, it's very difficult to go about replicating things at the state and national level.

David Driscoll

I think it's the meat of the sandwich. Our reform is about curriculum frameworks, about the standards, and then about the testing, the assessment, and high-stakes testing that goes with that. That's the engine. And I think states have made great progress in establishing the right standards, what kids ought to know and be able to do by grade level. Another thing in education, it's not necessarily a science, sometimes it's an art. If you don't like high-stakes testing, you can go to Arizona State and read their study.

If you do like high-stakes testing, then you can go to Stanford and read that study. That's education. But I think high-stakes testing has obviously made a tremendous difference. Look at Chart 1.16. Guess what subject is high stakes, and what year it kicked in. I'll give you a hint, its mathematics and its 2001, and it's now over 90% of our kids have passed the test. So I think the curriculum, the standards, and the assessment are crucial.

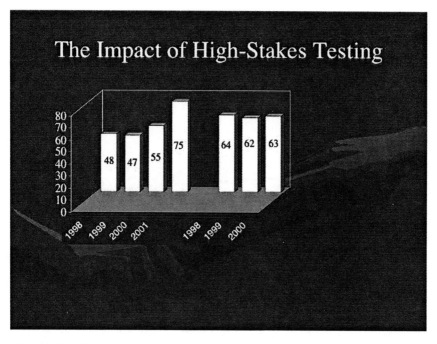

Chart 1.16.   The impact of high-stakes testing.

Audience Question

I am a principal of an at-risk inner-city elementary school by choice. We have 100% free lunch students at our school and we're making progress. But I would argue that an achievement gap exists in large measure because we haven't focused enough on prevention. Have you found any studies that have prevented the achievement gap due to providing early education to enhance cognitive ability?

Lowell Milken

Yes, there is no question that a key element is early childhood education. According to a recent study by University of Chicago economist James Heckman, the most economically efficient investment that society can make is in the very young. You can see the results on Chart 1.17. For every dollar spent on early childhood education, he found a return of $5.70. Heckman argues that investing in preschool education is more cost effective than similar investments in K–12, college, post-graduate education, or even job training. Young children have a longer period to recover the returns on their investments; and since knowledge begets knowledge, preschool begets continued education and early success yields later success.

Heckman's research confirms in clear economic terms what was found in academic, societal, and socioeconomic terms from the Perry Preschool longitudinal study. The Perry Preschool Project followed African American students from their preschool experience through adulthood and found that the children who participated in the program when compared to a control group of students had significant differences in life experiences. Perry children achieved at higher academic levels than the other children,

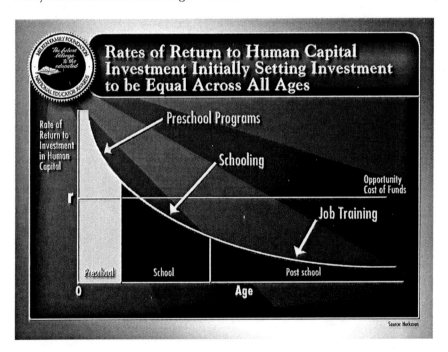

Chart 1.17.   Rates of return to human capital investment initially setting investment to be equal across all ages.

as measured by higher graduation rates, better grades, higher standardized test scores, and fewer placements in special education classes. These children also had fewer arrests, and more were employed and self-supporting than those who had not been in preschool. While this is only one study, it appears that investing in "quality" early childhood programs can consequently decrease the number of students who need remedial education or drop out of society later in life.

Yet the benefits and returns of a strong early education program cannot be maximized without a solid K–12 education. One can only imagine how much greater an impact the Perry program could have had if all the students then had access to a high-quality elementary and secondary educational experience. Yes, we need to ensure that all children are afforded a high-quality early education, but we must have a K–12 system that supports and even extends these initial impacts.

Jeanne Allen

I just want to add that there's no question that really strong educationally based preschool programs work. However, we also know that any gains made in preschool are short-lived if that child is not also in an elementary program that challenges them and demands high expectations. The kind of standards in Massachusetts, those in Colorado, that hold kids to high standards make for good schools. Some in those states are trying to deflate the levels at which kids have to succeed.

We know that the higher you raise expectations, even if it's tough, the higher children achieve. That's the key, no matter what, and particularly with disadvantaged kids.

Audience Question

What can be done to help federal and state governments understand that we cannot mandate excellence? We have to inspire excellence in our schools and in our teachers.

Mayor Jerry Brown

There's the paradox—the federal government mandating excellence. But it's an order coming from on high from 3,000 miles away. It ultimately depends on the teacher and we live and die by that. The only other enforcers are the parents. I don't see this. Either mandate it from on top or you let the parents choose what they want.

Nina Rees

As the Department of Education representative up here, I want to convey that we're not mandating. We're simply saying if you're going to accept this money, you need to make sure you're showing us results. That's it. You don't need to accept the money if you don't want to. How else would you go about reforming the system? How else can you argue that you should continuously spend money? Over $150 billion over a period of 25 years has been spent on Title I alone and you saw that chart earlier.

I don't want to upset the crowd with this, if you look at what we've done so far in talking to state officials, the undersecretary and the secretary have met with almost every single state official to work on their state plans. If you talk to the Council of Chief State School Officers and the Educational Leaders Council and all the different representatives in Washington who represent these chief state school officers, they will admit that we have put a real good-faith effort in making them understand the little things they need to do in their state plans in order to make some changes to comply with the federal law.

Most states, in fact 38 states, already have an accountability system in place. So they are not starting from scratch. We're not telling them to do things that they haven't been doing before. All we're saying is if you're going to do this, you need to show us how you're measuring student progress. Yes, it's going to be on an annual basis, as opposed to what you were doing before. But most localities are already testing on an annual basis. The difference is that we have set standards that every child needs to make adequate yearly gains. It's not on the school-wide basis or district basis, it's every child.

And that is to go back to the point earlier, which is that we want to close the achievement gap. We want to create a sense of urgency so that creative superintendents at the local level can take on the banner and go argue for the changes they need to make change possible. That is what Superintendent Vallis of Philadelphia tells us whenever we meet with him about the power he now has at his disposal to go ask for the reforms that he wasn't able to get last year when these things were not in place.

Lowell Milken

I would now like to ask each panelist if there is a final thought you would like to leave with this audience.

David Driscoll

Well, I thank you for permitting me to participate on the panel. It is a great opportunity to address many of the challenges in education. The system is complex, but we are on to something. We're moving forward. Teachers are using data like they've never used it before. We're looking at a lot more writing by kids. We're looking at support across America for public education that we've never seen before.

We've seen this focus on teacher quality. Lowell Milken and his brother deserve such tremendous credit for doing something that is just extraordinary. That is, celebrating the dignity and the nobility of teaching. So we do get discouraged. We look at some of these results and for every yin, there's a yang. It's a tough society and there's a lot of ways to make excuses. But we're on to something. We're moving forward, but we can't oversell it either. It's a question of carrots and sticks.

For the teacher before that talked about mandates, we have to have some mandates but we have to implement them with some common sense, and allow goals that can be reached. While I might have some complaints about No Child Left Behind, I'll live with them as long as we can. Along with my teachers and administrators, we'll figure out ways to implement adequate yearly progress over a reasonable amount of time.

Tavis Smiley

I think we need to answer the question that the superintendent raised. I think the answer is we need to take this spotlight and ask America the central question as I see it. The central question is when are we going to have the courage, the conviction, and the commitment to find a way to guarantee every child in this country an equal, high-quality education? That's what we have to do. It may be revolutionary to some people, but nobody in this room has given me a good answer for why it is that we cannot guarantee every child in this country equal, high-quality access with the resources for a quality education.

Nina Rees

There's one chart that you failed to show and I wanted to just point that out. Chart 1.18 from Caroline Hoxby. I just wanted to put that out there for you all to take a look at because that's one of the areas that people haven't really delved into too much. She basically looked at different areas that had a lot of competition between the public and private schools. She found in

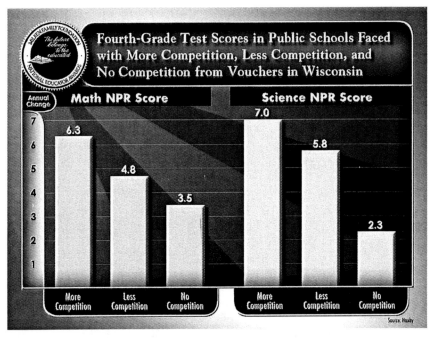

Chart 1.18. Fourth-grade test scores in public schools faced with more competition, less competition, and no competition from vouchers in Wisconsin.

areas that have more competition, test scores tend to go up. We need to do more research in this area, but I think it's important to put that out there because as we're trying to come up with different interventions, it's important to understand the value that choice offers in increasing the number of good schools in particular districts.

But going back to the No Child Left Behind Act, I was involved in drafting this law. Let me just tell you one thing that people often forget. This was a law that the President crafted with the help of the great senator from the state of Massachusetts Senator Ted Kennedy and the congressman from the great state of California, Congressman George Miller. One of the debates we had for months was over this question of is it fair to demand that all of our children ought to be proficient within a certain period of time.

The members who were the most adamant in making sure this happened were members like Mary Landrieu from Louisiana, again a Democrat. So, this is not a partisan issue for us. To the president certainly it's not a partisan issue. He wants to approach this the same way he approached the issue in Texas, which is to look at it from a bipartisan perspective and make sure that we are working with states to ensure that they're raising student achievement.

Many times, you look at barriers that have been placed before you; and they are not necessarily Federal or state barriers. But they are things that could easily be waived. Not all of them, of course but some of them are things that we can help you with. The Office of Innovation and Improvement is a grant-making office. We have a number of grants up for competition. I want to encourage you all to please come see me so I can tell you a little bit more about this office.

The No Child Left Behind Act is based on four pillars including high standards, accountability, and choice. Our belief is that if you create momentum and pressure from the top, and free up individuals at the bottom with information and choices, you will be able to speed the pace of change. This cannot happen if superintendents and folks at the local level are not seizing this opportunity to go after the reforms that they want to bring about in their school system.

I think it's important for those of you who have a little bit more autonomy in shaping the way things are done in your districts to seize this opportunity to make the arguments for change, such as merit pay for teachers who are doing a good job, or raising the cap on charter schools. Really bringing the unions to the table and negotiating better ways to bring quality individuals to the classroom. Because if you don't seize this opportunity, you've basically missed a great opportunity to bring about change and help thousands of low-income students.

Mayor Jerry Brown

Since we are all learners and questions often stimulate more thought than answers, my question is, given the way society is organized, and given where it's likely to go following the same organization, will the proliferation of more standardized tests reduce the gap or will it actually provide a quantitative measurement and rationalization for an increasing gap?

David Driscoll

I just think we have to stay the course. Those people outside of education have to recognize how difficult it is. But we need to keep demanding, those inside of education have to recognize that things have to change. We just have to keep working together. I think we're making progress. If we start fragmenting and pointing fingers, we're going to get into trouble. I think we've got to work together. We are making progress but we have to stay with it for the sake of the kids.

Jeanne Allen

I just want to address the teachers who are struggling to build those effective schools and who sense that there are always mandates and things that are keeping you back from doing what you do best. Effective laws influence effective schools and there aren't a lot of people out there (despite the groups' interest and their money) fighting, to get you the kind of autonomy and control you need; to be left alone to do your job and be held accountable for what you're doing in the classroom. To be rewarded for it. You have to be vigilant, we can't afford to just sit back and hold hands and work together. There's an awful lot of people that are working against you having local control, and you have to be vigilant and make sure that doesn't happen.

Lowell Milken

While there may be no single strategy to solve the problem of the achievement gap among students in our nation, my experience in more than two decades of work in K–12 education and in operating and owning businesses tells me that the single most important factor that must be addressed is the human capital in low-performing schools. We need to reverse the trend where talented teachers leave inner-city schools to teach in the suburbs, and we need to encourage talented teachers who teach in the suburbs to move to urban schools. If we're going to be successful in achieving comprehensive education reform, we need to find ways to incentivize talented young people to go into teaching and to develop, motivate, and retain them to stay in the teaching field. This issue has and continues to be a major focus of our work at the Foundation and at this conference. No doubt, it is an enormous challenge, but finding the answer to this challenge will not only help close the achievement gap, but also will help to ensure that every child in our country receives a high-quality educational experience.

Part II

HOW TO DETERMINE WHO IS A
QUALITY TEACHER

CHAPTER 2

HOW TO DETERMINE WHO IS A QUALITY TEACHER

Lewis C. Solmon, Philip Bigler, Eric A. Hanushek, Lee S. Shulman, and Herbert J. Walberg

Welcome to the panel that will answer this question once and for all: What is a quality teacher? Now actually Bill Bennett just alluded to the same quote that I had planned to start with. But I'll start with it anyway. The quality teacher is like Potter Stewart's explanation of pornography. In 1964, just as Stewart tried to explain hard-core pornography by saying in part, "I shall not attempt to further define the kinds of material I understand to be embraced within that shorthand description. And perhaps I could never succeed in intelligently doing so. But I know it when I see it." Everyone, teachers and the principal at a particular school, parents and even the kids themselves, know who the quality teachers are when they see them even if they cannot be specific about what makes excellent teachers.

There's quite a bit of debate about the characteristics and behaviors that make a teacher truly exemplary. What I want to do is to go through the list of how No Child Left Behind defines a "qualified teacher." When it talks about "qualified," it means fully licensed or certified, demonstrated subject matter knowledge, teaching skills, and at least a bachelor's degree. We hear different people saying different things. Everything from liking children, to being up to date, to constantly learning, to sharing ideas, to strong verbal ability, to being a hard worker. All of those really are supposed to contribute to a teacher's ability to help students learn. In some sense, that's

Talented Teachers: The Essential Force for Improving Student Achievement, pages 49–85
Copyright © 2004 by Information Age Publishing
All rights of reproduction in any form reserved.

what a quality teacher is: one who enables kids to learn. But how do we know who they are before the fact?

In my reading of the literature, it seems that there are three dimensions of teacher quality. One is teacher inputs or what she brings to the table or into the classroom. One is a teacher's behaviors or what he or she does in the classroom. The third is student outcomes or how she changes students for the better. When we talk about changing students for the better, we can divide those student outcomes into cognitive, behavioral, or affective. There are a lot of issues about if a kid does well on a test but does not have civic responsibility, and is that okay? Or if a kid doesn't do well on a test but has better health habits and prosocial behaviors, does that mean that the teacher is doing a good job?

Whether we like it or not, public policy today is focusing us and directing all education policy toward the student achievement test. Basically, you propose a policy, and the first question that state legislators and the people in Washington ask is will this increase student achievement? And so, that's one thing that I'm sure we've got to look at. How difficult it is to measure student achievement and what are the appropriate measures of student achievement?

But that's all to come in the next two hours. And we have a very prestigious group of experts on our panel today. First, Eric Hanushek is the Paul and Jean Hanna Senior Fellow at Stanford University's Hoover Institution and Research Associate at the National Bureau of Economic Research. A leading expert on education policy, specializing in economics and the finance of schools, Rick has published numerous articles in professional journals and written several books including *Improving America's Schools* and *Making Schools Work*. He's previously held appointments at the University of Rochester, Yale, and the U.S. Air Force Academy. His government service includes positions as Deputy Director of the Congressional Budget Office, Senior Staff Economist for the Council of Economic Advisors, and Senior Economist for the Cost of Living Council. Dr. Hanushek is a distinguished graduate of the United States Air Force Academy and served in the U.S. Air Force from 1965 to 1974. His Ph.D. in economics was from MIT.

Rick will be followed in the discussion by Lee Shulman, who is the eighth president of the Carnegie Foundation for the Advancement of Teaching. He is also the Charles E. Ducommun Professor of Education and Professor of Psychology at Stanford University. His research group laid the conceptual foundations for reconsideration of the nature of teaching, the nature of teaching knowledge, emphasizing the role of content understanding, and pedagogical process. Between 1985 and 1990, Lee and his colleagues conducted the technical studies and field tests that supported the creation of the National Board for Professional Teaching Standards. He was previously Professor of Educational Psychology and Medical Education at Michigan State University. He is a past president of both the American Educational Research Association and the National Academy of Education. Dr. Shulman has been honored with the American Psychological Association's E.L. Thorndike Award for distinguished psychological contributions to education. And in 2002, he was elected a fellow of the American Academy of Arts and Sciences.

Third is Herbert J. Walberg, Professor Emeritus of Education and Psychology at the University of Illinois at Chicago, and a Distinguished Visiting Fellow of Stanford University's Hoover Institution. A recipient of a Ph.D. from the University of Chicago, Herb has written and edited more than 55 books and 350 articles—I think he has the record of everybody I've introduced this week—on such topics as educational effectiveness and exceptional human accomplishments. Among his latest books are the *International Encyclopedia of Educational Evaluation* and *Psychology and Educational Practice.*

Herb is a founding fellow and vice president of the International Academy of Education, headquartered in Brussels, and has presented lectures to educators and policymakers throughout the world. He served on the National Assessment Governing Board and is a fellow of several academic institutions. He's currently the chair of the board of Chicago's Heartland Institute, a think tank providing policy analysis for the U.S. Congress, state legislatures, the media, and the public.

Finally, we have Philip Bigler, an actual career teacher. Somebody in my office had this unique idea that if we want to talk about what a quality teacher is, maybe we should ask one. He has recently moved to higher education, though. He is a 1999 Virginia Milken Educator and 1998 National Teacher of the Year. Philip is director of the James Madison Center at James Madison University in Harrisonburg, Virginia, where he teaches history, American studies, and political science. A 25-year veteran of the teaching profession, he helps his students realize that civilization rests upon the foundations of the past and that they are the inheritors of a rich, intellectual legacy. Under his tutelage, students have debated current issues, as a member of the Greek polls argued constitutional law before a mock supreme court and collected oral histories from residents of the Soldiers and Airmen's Home. For two years he was historian of the Arlington National Cemetery, after which he returned to the classroom. Mr. Bigler is associate director of the Stratford Monticello Teacher's Seminar and has authored four books.

Eric A. Hanushek

I want to say at the beginning how thrilled I am to be here. I think this is an amazing gathering of people here of the talent that I think is so important. And I want to thank the Milken Foundation for putting on this affair.

I think it's superb. What I wanted to do today was to quickly talk about the research on teacher quality and how it relates to a set of policy issues. And then from that actually get back a little bit to TAP and talk about how this all relates. As an overview, let me say at the beginning that I think teacher quality is the largest issue facing the U.S. and our public schools today. In that regard, there are two leading policy proposals of how to ensure that there are high-quality teachers in the schools. The first is to tighten up on who can be eligible and who can be in the classroom teaching. The second is essentially to loosen up on that. I'm going to try to talk through what we know from the research literature today, and then the final point I want to talk a little bit about is the overall issue of the teacher labor market: salaries, entering the teaching force, and so forth. The market constrains what we can do in terms of teacher quality. Part of this is almost preaching to the choir here.

Let me give you a couple indications of why I say teacher quality is most important. These also relate to a couple of studies that I have done. Let me say at the beginning that I take Lew's third definition of teacher quality as the essential definition. That is, that teacher quality is the ability to get more learning out of a group of students and to increase the amount of their achievement. We know that families are extraordinarily important in determining one's education. There is no denying that families are very important. But at the same time, people over a long period have misinterpreted what that means. People have said that the *Coleman Report*, the monumental study of American schools in the mid-1960s said that we should not pay attention to schools because the only thing that matters is the families. In my estimation, that report and that finding is dead wrong.

Let me first tell you what the studies that we've been doing in terms of achievement in Texas say. They say that quality teaching is much more important than the things that we've been arguing about like class size reduction. But importantly, it said that, if you had an above-average teacher for five years in a row, you could wipe out the average deficit faced by low-income kids. The simple fact is that we don't guarantee that any student gets a good teacher for five years in a row. And that I think is the issue.

A second indication of the quality of teachers comes from a study I did some time ago in Gary, Indiana: an all-black school with essentially all poverty kids. The difference between a good teacher, one at the top of the distribution, and a bad teacher was one year of learning. So, that a bad teacher got half of a year gain in student achievement, a good teacher got a year and a half of gain in one academic year. Now again, you simply have to multiply that by a few years of having a good teacher and you can see that teachers can have enormous leverage. But we don't have a system in place now to ensure that everybody gets those good teachers.

So, what have we done? What we normally try to do is to measure characteristics of teachers and assume that has something to do with quality. We measure whether they have a master's degree or not. We measure the level of experience. We sometimes give them tests of a variety of sorts. As a general rule, none of these are very highly correlated with the performance of teachers in the classroom. That is the underlying problem that we face if we pursue this idea of instituting requirements before somebody can teach, because it's not very related to what we see in the classroom. The simple fact is that there's a lot of heterogeneity of teachers. Teachers that look the same on paper and on these requirements are very different in the classroom and they produce very different amounts of learning. There are substantial differences within individual schools. It is not all about getting a good principal to ensure that there are good teachers. But in fact there are a lot of differences that we see.

The most popular current policy is to tighten up on the requirements for entry into teaching. And then we need to compensate teachers to try to make sure that that doesn't completely choke off the supply of entering teachers. The most elaborate versions of these call for combined actions by education schools, by students, and by the schools themselves. But in large part these are ideas about substituting decision making through regulations and rules of who can enter for decision making at the schools.

Now the potential gains of such policies are pretty obvious. We can conceive of getting smarter teachers because they're required to pass higher tests and more difficult exams. We can get better preparation from the education schools, if it's more closely linked to the performance of their students when they go out to teach. We can generally raise the minimum quality. And parts of the other aspects of further training and salaries may in fact improve career development. The potential drawbacks though, on the other hand, are also something to pay attention to. The first and obvious point is, if you add more requirements to get into teaching, it makes it more costly for any individual to prepare to go into teaching. Simple economics would suggest that, if it's more costly to get into teaching, you're going to restrict the potential number of people who would be willing to go into teaching.

First, you might eliminate a number of well-motivated and potentially good people. These are people who would go into teaching for a short period of time because they think it's important, but don't necessarily want to commit completely to a career at the beginning. Second, you will also obviously, in a general sense, retain all of the current shortages we have of special education teachers, language teachers, math and science teachers. If you make it more costly to get in, you're not going to do anything about the specific shortages that we have. Further, by making it more costly and making people work harder, even if you raise the rewards for it, you're going to lock in people who aren't necessarily well suited for the job, once they find out. Not everybody knows when they're 20 years old if they're going to be a good teacher or want to do it forever. But you will tend to lock them in if you in fact follow the tightening version.

So, the tradeoffs here are clear. You potentially get better teachers, but it depends crucially on whether the things that you require, the new things you require, are closely related to the quality in the classroom. And that's something that I don't think that we know at the current time. Second, whether it works at all depends upon what is the supply response, whether you get a lot more people interested in teaching or a lot fewer people interested in teaching.

One of the versions of this is the proposal to grade teachers by giving them tests beforehand. All of the current evidence we have suggests that the testing of teachers, giving somebody a paper-and-pencil test or cognitive test, is a very imprecise measure of quality of the teacher. We also know that it has a very adverse effect on trying to attract more minority teachers into schools, implying you'll particularly hit that part of the market. Then, finally, one of the problems is that you always have to set cutoff levels on these tests. And we frankly don't know anything about where to set those. These are somewhat arbitrary decisions. But they have the effect of cutting back on who enters teaching.

Let me talk about the other side of this question, that is loosening up. The first was all about the potential advantages and disadvantages of tightening up on teachers getting into the profession. Now, I'll talk about the opposite. My basic starting point, and my interest in this, is a fundamental fact that I believe is true: If we're interested in student performance, there is no substitute for focusing on student performance. And that's how we have to think about teaching. If we're interested in the performance of our students, that's where we should put our attention. This is a very different issue than focusing on the prior characteristics of teachers coming into the profession.

And it implies strengthening the role of the teachers and the principals in the local schools and local school districts. One of the aspects of the prior decision rules of tightening up on teaching is that it's eliminating the role of the local schools and the local districts in making decisions. The alternative that is very important is to try to make the role of the people in the schools much more important. That's how you will get judgments about the quality. I don't want to go into all the details of the incentives that can do that at this point. Ideas of merit pay, ideas of more competition in schools, and so forth are ways that you can try to change the incentives at the school level.

Rather, let me follow on to talk a little bit about how this relates also to teacher labor markets, because those are issues that always come up. One of the things that we know is that women, in particular, have had a lot more opportunities over the last 30 or 40 years. Instead of just being teachers and nurses, they can go into being doctors and managers and lawyers. One of the things this has done is put a lot on schools because the alternative wages to women teachers have risen very rapidly. It also holds for males that the wages of college graduates have soared in the last 20 years. Teacher salaries have simply not kept up with the wages in the labor market. This has led to very specific shortages of people who have specialized skills. Math and science teachers is always the example used. But other people, with very specific skills that have alternatives elsewhere, find that teaching is not particularly attractive.

What do we say about that? Well, the obvious thing is, if salaries aren't keeping up and if we aren't getting the people we want, maybe we should raise teachers' salaries. And I think that is the answer, except for one thing. Overall salary increases aren't very strong incentives and don't provide the right solutions. Chart 2.1 shows the percentage of college workers who earn less than the average teacher. The higher that graph, the better teachers are doing relative to other college workers. The top two lines are for females and what has happened to women teachers relative to salaries in

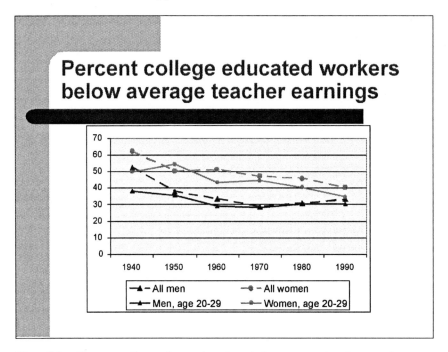

Chart 2.1.   Percent college educated workers below average teacher earnings.

the market for other female college graduates. What you see is that that has steadily declined over the last 40 years. It only goes out to 1990, but it the trend has continued. For men, you see that it declined through the 1960s, and often 1970 has remained rather flat.

There are a lot of other people in other occupations earning more than teachers. So, what do we do in the face of a situation like that? Well, if we thought of trying to restore the right-hand side to the pictures on the left-hand side, restore teachers to their position in the overall distribution of salaries around the country, we might like that as a normative policy idea. But it would be very, very expensive.

Even with the expense of it, there are a lot of people that would support it with a caveat. There are a lot of people that would support the idea of much higher salaries for good teachers. The problem is that there is absolutely no public support for the idea of much higher salaries for poor teachers. And that's where you run into the policy dilemma. Just saying that we have to pay teachers more will never restore teachers to their position in the past if we do not add a dimension of looking at the quality of the teachers. There's an economic theorem: Bad teachers like money as much as good teachers! So, in reality, if we raise teachers' salaries in an across-the-board way, not only would it be expensive but it would have detrimental effects on the schools, at least in the short run for some period of time. What you would see that everybody wanted to stay and teach in schools longer, that is both good and bad teachers. Without some mechanism that in fact selects who we want to stay in the schools and who we want to get the higher salaries, I think that it's just a pipe dream to call for significantly higher salaries.

That's why I come back to this idea that I had at the very beginning and I'm going to end with this. We have two fundamental options facing us to deal with teacher quality, where teacher quality is in fact the issue. We can tighten up on who gets into the profession and then try to reward everybody who gets in with higher salaries. Or we can loosen up. By loosening up, I mean allow more people into the profession but make stronger decisions, clearer decisions about who is performing well in the classroom. We would work to retain the really good teachers, but not necessarily all teachers who enter the profession. I think that that's the only hope that we have on this important issue.

Lee S. Shulman

I begin by offering greetings from the grave, from Andrew Carnegie to the Milken family. I feel that I carry Mr. Carnegie's responsibilities seriously these days. When I became president of the Carnegie Foundation, I had a written letter that Andrew Carnegie wrote in 1905 establishing the Carnegie Foundation for the Advancement of Teaching. In that letter, he states the mission of our foundation, and it is one that I think we share with the Milken Family Foundation. It is, and I quote, "to do and perform all things necessary to encourage, uphold, and dignify the profession of the teacher." My sense is that in a very real way, the Milkens are carrying out, both as philanthropists and as supporters of the teaching profession, the mission that Andrew Carnegie stated so eloquently nearly 100 years ago. And for that, I want to thank the Milken family on behalf of all of us. Andrew Carnegie invested probably more than anything in the establishment of libraries all over the world. The Milkens are investing in teachers, but libraries and teachers are very similar: They get better and better over time, becoming more and more generative, and their impact is utterly limitless, unpredictable, and ineffable over time.

Since there were references to Ronald Reagan earlier at lunch, I too can't help remembering something about Reagan. One of the people whom I succeeded was Clark Kerr, whom many of you may remember as having been the architect of the California higher education system and the president of the University of California System, until Ronald Reagan, in his first act as governor fired Clark Kerr. A few days later, Clark was speaking to an assemblage much like this one where he was introduced as the president of the University of California. He was quick to correct the master of ceremonies and to say that no, he was no longer the president of the university. Thanks to Mr. Reagan, he had ended his term as president exactly as he had begun, "fired with enthusiasm." Fortunately for the Carnegie Foundation and for American higher education, Kerr subsequently devoted his time and energy to directing the Carnegie Commission for Higher Education Policy, which led to many important innovations, including what we now know as Pell Grants. And that's my Reagan story.

I have spent the last 40 years obsessed with teaching. I have taught and I have engaged almost endlessly in studying what I see as one of the great miracles of our species—the act of teaching. If you really think about it, teaching is so demanding that it should be both physically and intellectually impossible. It is simply the most difficult task that human beings try to accomplish.

I spent 10 years of my career doing research on medical practice and medical education. I have studied surgeons, oncologists, pediatricians, and psychiatrists. Let me tell you something: Teaching on an average day in an elementary school classroom is more difficult than any act engaged in by any physician in any specialty, with the possible exception of managing an emergency room during a natural disaster. Think about it: what would our lives as teachers be like (I'm speaking to my colleagues in teaching now) if before you even had to teach a kid, we could send all the other kids out of the room to a "waiting area" and deal with just one student at a time?

There just is no question that the incredible burden of endless flow of responding and initiating to a group of enormously diverse kids with no breaks to speak of is a cruel and unusual calling. And yet that's what we're here to talk about: What are the qualities of a good teacher? And what I'm going to be drawing on in my remarks will be a variety of sources, because I think this question is only partially answerable by carefully conducted, statistically controlled social science research; though, as a social scientist and psychologist, I value that kind of work enormously.

I want to suggest that there are seven attributes to teaching quality. I won't have time to make the full argument for each, but I feel that I want to make them as clearly as possible. These attributes begin by my saying something to the teachers here—the awardees—that I know you wish I wouldn't say. If you occasionally watch old movies on cable, one that particularly gets recycled is this teenage horror flick called *I Know What You Did Last Summer*, parts 1, 2, and 3 (I don't know how many summers they're into right now). My version of that is *I Know What Each of the Awardees is Secretly Thinking*. What you are thinking is, "I didn't really deserve this award. If they only knew…." You're waiting for somebody to come in, tap you on the shoulder, and say, "I'm terribly sorry, but there's been a mistake…"

I spent five years of my life designing the structure of what has become the National Board for Professional Teaching Standards, with its very heavy emphasis on sampling from an entire year of a teacher's work by means of a portfolio process, rather than depending on a two- or three-hour examination. Those of us who know about teaching know that the classroom is where you see teaching. And every National Board Certified teacher I know has said, "Why me? There are better teachers in the school. I wish *they* had been candidates."

This is attitude related to the first attribute of teacher quality: High-quality teachers are much more self-critical than average or mediocre performers. We've got evidence about this, and there's a lot of interesting research to support the claim. In fact, one of these studies, done by a couple of social psychologists from Cornell and Illinois, hit the front pages of newspapers about three years ago, showing that across a variety of fields, the more competent people were, the more likely they were to underestimate their competence. Indeed, this phenomenon is, in fact, part of the explanation for competence. Because if you're constantly underestimating how good you are, you're constantly working to get better. You always think you can get better, and believe me, those of you who get those $25,000 checks are not going to return home and sit on your laurels; you're going to push that bar higher. You're going to push it higher because you don't think you deserve it, because you think now you've got to live up to that level. It is an attitude built into one of the quality indicators of competent and outstanding teachers; they are highly self-critical. I find it in medicine, engineering, and other fields as well.

This self-criticism is related to the second characteristic, which is that high-quality teachers are characterized by unimaginable levels of energy, of passion, of zeal, and of motivation. What is fascinating about the energy and motivation of high-quality teachers is that it isn't entirely explainable in the language of either behavioral psychology or economics, because energy and motivation are not increased just because the teachers get positive results. Teachers are like men and women of faith; they're like Don Quixotes; they've internalized a set of values, a set of beliefs, and those beliefs drive them. It's not that they ignore the results, but they also have come to understand that very often the results are not immediately attainable the next day, the next week, the next month, even that very year. And so there is a kind of persistent passion or zeal that characterizes outstanding teachers.

The third characteristic is that quality teachers are highly skilled practitioners—no surprise. But they are so highly skilled that much of what they do has become automatic, has become routinized in the same sense that the work of a surgeon or pilot becomes routinized. You sit in a classroom and marvel at the way a skilled elementary school teacher manages the seven transitions that she has to manage within a 40-minute period, the way she works with one child who's having difficulty reading and somehow is monitoring 33 other kids in six groups, none of whom can get away with anything. That's not in any of your methods courses—these incredibly sophisticated routinized skills characterize good teaching, and let me tell you something, somebody with a bachelor's degree in English and lots of motivation doesn't walk into a classroom knowing how to do that. You've got to learn to do that.

Fourth, quality teachers are deeply knowledgeable and intellectual about the subjects they teach, and that's as true in second grade as it is in twelfth grade calculus. We have a growing body of evidence that in those countries that have been doing better on the Third International Mathematics and Science Study (TIMSS) than we have, one of the things that's happening is that their teachers are always asking students more conceptual questions, questions about why two ideas link together. Well, you can only ask those questions if you deeply understand those ideas yourself. If you don't, you avoid them like the plague. Deep, flexible, sophisticated knowledge of the content is absolutely an attribute of teachers who also recognize that they can't possibly know everything, which is why high-quality teachers teach some things better than others and recognize it.

A fifth attribute is that teachers of quality are moral agents who are motivated, even driven, by a moral vision. They care about the learning and achievement of their students, but that's not where their concern ends. They have a vision of the kind of society, the kind of democracy, the kind of civic community that they want to create and be part of. Those images, those dreams, are absolutely central to the work of high-quality teachers. Often, that's a role that standards try to play. When we began our work with the National Board, I was very skeptical about how valuable it would be to have groups of teachers come together and establish standards of practice, standards of teaching, and standards of learning. I just didn't think it was going to be important. I was wrong.

My wife Judy Shulman works with National Support Groups. She was talking to a teacher in Oakland who described studying the standards as preparation for becoming a year-long candidate for the National Board and who said she realized that many of the standards described aspects of excellence that she had never previously considered. She began developing a vision of what she could be, a vision that was in part stimulated by these standards. It was like reading a biblical text; it really set a bar for her. She began to feel that she was committed to higher standards of teaching performance even during her candidacy period. She then described the extraordinary joy she felt when she learned that she had become national Board Certified. This meant that there was evidence that other teachers examining the artifacts of her work—the evidence of her teaching, the evidence of her students' learning, the evidence of what she knew—had deemed her an accomplished teacher. She described saving the note that said she was certified in her pocket, and as she walked into the classroom, she thought, "I'll never be the same again; I will always set a higher standard for myself." And then she described bad days, days where she thought, "I should give it back." You'll have that feeling as Milken Educators as well. But she described a day in her Oakland fourth grade where everything came together, where the hours and hours of planning and design at the kitchen table paid off. But the point here is that at the end of that day, she just shouted out, as this was a *National Board Banner Day*, that everything really goes well. She was meeting her own higher standards. Rather than becoming complacent and proud when they receive recognitions like Board Certification or Milken selection, quality teachers develop even more demanding visions. So a sense of vision is important in creating and sustaining high-quality teachers.

High-quality teachers are not flying solo. Well, sometimes they are—we have the heroic image of a Jaime Escalante, and we write newspaper articles and books about the ones who fly solo. But all of us know that most of the time a high-quality teacher is somebody who draws from and contributes to a community of teachers, a group of other people who don't get the Most Valuable Player award. But part of your feeling is that they deserve to share the award. And in the presence of a teaching community, of a professional community, extraordinary things are possible. In its absence, it's so very, very hard.

That's part of the genius, I must say, if I may compliment my hosts, of the Teacher Advancement Program (TAP). It doesn't take a single indicator, valorize it, and say, *that's* quality. If you look at TAP, the largest percentage of the weight is on what the teacher knows and does, how he acts, how she performs as a teacher in a school. A much smaller percentage is the amount of learning that their kids did that year. An even larger percentage is how well the kids in the whole school did. What a lovely recognition that it takes a village to teach well, that we are not flying solo. And it's captured in the Milken model.

Finally, quality teachers have an impact. Yes, they are effective. All those things come together to make an impact on kids, on their measurable learning, on their own zeal and love for what they're studying. But teachers also understand, as I said before, that you will not always see the impact immediately, that teaching is like both an iceberg and an embryo. You only see the tip when you watch, but there's so much more going on beneath the surface. And the impact is not on the little creature as you see that little creature at the moment; the little creature cumulates and grows over time. And for that reason, we have to care a lot about the kind of human being a teacher is. That is, we must be concerned with how much the teacher knows, and what they can do, but with the formation of the character, values, virtues, and vision.

There you have my model of the seven features of teacher quality: (1) self-critical reflectiveness, (2) passion and zeal, (3) skilled practice, (4) deep knowledge of subject matter, (5) moral agency, (6) membership in a learning community, and (7) impact on students.

Let me offer, in conclusion, four challenges. The first challenge is related to the strategies we have available to improve the quality of a teacher. My colleague Rick Hanushek has proposed two strategies: loosen up the standards for entry or tighten them. But there's a third alternative to loosening up entry and tightening up entry into the profession of teaching, and that is do not depend on entry to do all the work of qualifying teachers. Do what every other profession does seriously—educate the professionals. *The education of teachers must be done better and better and better.* If many people are dissatisfied with the quality of contemporary teacher education, the solution is not to stop doing it. Instead, the answer is to take it more seriously. We need more and better teacher preparation, not less of it. We must invest in the education of teachers with the kind of seriousness that we now invest in the education of physicians, engineers, and even members of clergy.

You know, if you want to become an Episcopal minister, you can't get an emergency credential, even if you've got a Ph.D. in counseling psychology or in theology; you spend three years studying for the ministry, five years for the rabbinate. There are no viable alternative routes. In the same vein, teaching is serious work. It's enormously difficult. People have to learn to do it and they're never done learning it, and one had better remember that. Even though it may be cheaper to hire people off the street, it's not the way we ought to go.

The second challenge is all of you who won the award are mysteries. The essence of your genius remains hidden and veiled. We will give you an award, and you will go back to your schools, and we will not know what you are actually doing when you teach. One of our projects at the Carnegie Foundation is to design a systematic project to "out" great teachers, to document, make public, display, what is it that good teachers do, how they think, how they are self-critical, how they grow, and make this knowledge available in both protected and public websites, so that other teachers and members of the public can learn from the wisdom of your practice. You have an obligation to make your work public.

And thus my third challenge is for Lew and the Milkens to stop keeping the Milken Educators a secret. Let's see if we can do something, not statistically and in general, but something to make this work public. It is not enough to celebrate these teachers one day a year, culminating in a magnificent award ceremony. When you have discovered great art, you have an obligation to use your resources to make it public, accessible, and in a form that other educators can build upon.

Finally, my fourth challenge is to keep standards for teaching high, even though Rick Hanushek is absolutely right—as a consequence we could create more teacher shortages. But the answer is not to celebrate great teachers on the one hand, and then to hand out emergency credentials irresponsibly on the other hand. When I think about emergency credentials, I'm reminded that for many years the most popular TV program we Americans would watch was called *ER*. Never forget that in that TV program, the "emergency" in the title referred to the patients, the physicians were well prepared and deeply committed professionals who had met the highest standards of the medical profession. In our schools we are now in danger of doing just the opposite. Parents continue to send the best and smartest kids they have to schools, and too often they encounter teachers who are the emergency cases! Teachers like the Milken Educators must become the models for our teaching standards. We must continue to seek the best, the brightest, the most committed and accomplished, and the most carefully prepared teachers into our classrooms. We know the kids are coming. Our schools cannot be emergency rooms for teachers.

And so, from Mr. Carnegie's Foundation to the Milken Family Foundation, I bring warm congratulations and encouragement. You enrich our mission "to do and perform all things necessary to encourage, uphold, and dignify the profession of teacher." And to the teachers who have achieved this remarkable recognition, I can only say, "Relax. You really do deserve these awards. You have earned them."

Herbert J. Walberg

I'd like to add my sense of gratitude to the Milken family, to Lew Solomon and the other staff members at the Foundation not only for the wonderful programs that they've had, but this conference itself. I've learned so much here. I've been much stimulated by what I've heard already. I'd also like to add to the others, congratulations to the award winners, not only from this past year but in previous years.

I think I have some familial insight into teaching. My mother had 10 sisters and one brother, and six of them were Hoosier schoolteachers. And, I myself began teaching in the Chicago public schools in 1958, so I go back a long way in the field of teaching. I'd also like to make a confession. Two of the people that you've already heard from very much stimulated me to do the work that I'm going to be reporting on today. When Bill Bennett was Secretary of Education and Checker Finn was Assistant Secretary for the Office of Educational Research and Improvement, they said something is known about effective teaching. And, I had known both of them somewhat, and I had given some efforts to that over some years. And they said how about helping us put something together. Well, some of you may have been around for a quarter century or so may remember *What Works*.

It was a little pamphlet and it had about 40 ideas in it or principles that were based upon research but we made a great deal of effort to express it in user-friendly language. Some 600,000 copies were printed. We have odd priority. There was a huge amount of interest in that booklet and since it was about the time of *A Nation at Risk*. This came after Sputnik in 1958 as well, when there was a great sense of concern about improving American education. The experience helping to put that booklet together and to select principles for the book stimulated me to do work of a similar kind in the subsequent years. And so I helped the U.S. Navy put principles together, and I'm now for the fourth year editing a series for UNESCO, the United Nations Educational Scientific and Cultural Organization, on effective educational practices.

There is a huge hunger among educators and practitioners for what works in teaching. These booklets are distributed to 150 countries throughout the world but they're also available on the Internet. And they are not copyrighted, so they can be downloaded and they can be republished as they are, so different countries around the world can reprint those booklets because other countries are just as interested in, as we are, in improving our student achievement levels.

And the point has already been made that this is not a matter of Democrats and Republicans; the nation has spoken. The Congress and 49 states have all been very supportive of accountability tests, standards, and things of that nature. I would like to acknowledge the American Board for the Certification of Teacher Excellence that enabled me to synthesize some of the work that I had done over many years. This conference paper enabled me to bring together a lot of the work that I had done for many years across these different areas. The paper regrettably has 91 footnotes, and, I'm not going to be able to go into that kind of detail in the 12 or so minutes that I may have left here. But, if there are some points that I don't explain sufficiently well or don't touch on at all, I would encourage you to take a look at the paper. And there are many references in it, so you can look at the original material if you wish.

The American Board is, I think, doing a wonderful job at developing tests. Their main point is that if you don't know the subject you're going to have a lot of difficulty in teaching it. So the tests rely very heavily on subject-matter knowledge. However, there is a professional knowledge test on it as well, because there is the expectation that teachers need to know scientific findings about what works in education. My premise is that teaching and learning are fundamentally psychological processes, and that we need to think about the actual acts of teaching and how the specific behaviors and proclivities of teachers and conditions of teaching have the greatest impact on student achievement.

Psychologists, at least my breed of psychologists, like randomized field trials, just as in medicine and other fields, where you randomly assign, let's say, students to several different instructional procedures. You measure them before and after. And you compare the two. We can't, moreover, give too much credibility to a single study.

Maybe it was done with sixth-grade girls in Gary, Indiana. Does it have any implication for 12th-grade boys in San Diego, California? Obviously not. So we like to have many studies done in a wide variety of circumstances, and then we use statistical procedures to bring those studies together. We can use the technique of meta-analysis to actually measure the effects, and a great number of policymakers, of course, are interested in the relative effectiveness of various teaching strategies and procedures.

I want to say, partly in response to some of the other things that have already been said at this conference, that teaching is enormously important. Obviously that's why we're here, but there are eight other factors that are also important. I've tried to synthesize hundreds of studies in the field of educational psychology that have attempted to statistically link or do randomized studies to link conditions the children are in, both in school and outside of school, to how much they learn. Chart 2.2 shows nine educational productivity factors.

Nine Educational Productivity Factors

Factor	Proportional Learning Influence
A. Student Aptitude	
1. Ability or preferably prior achievement as measured by the standardized tests	.92
2. Development as indexed by chronological age or stage of maturation	.51
3. Motivation or self-concept as indicated by personality tests or the student's willingness to persevere intensively on learning tasks	.18
B. Instruction	
4. Amount of time students engage in learning	.47
5. Quality of the instructional experience, including method (psychological) and curricular (content) aspects	.18
C. Psychological Environments	
6. Morale or student perception of classroom social group	.47
7. Home environment or "curriculum of the home"	.36
8. Peer group outside school	.20
9. Minimal leisure-time mass media exposure, particularly television	.20

Source: Barry J. Fraser, Herbert J. Walberg, Wayne W. Welch, and John A . Hattie, "Synthesis of Educational Productivity Research," *International Journal of Educational Research* 11 (1987): whole issue.

Note: Estimates are calculated from data reported on p. 220. The ind exes in the table are on the same scale as the effect sizes in Table 3 but are not necessarily pure, one-way causal effects.

Chart 2.2.   Nine educational productivity factors.

The first factor is the ability or prior achievement. This year's achievement is going to be very predictive of how a child will do next. The reason it's so important is that a test that's given today has been influenced by all of the experiences that a child has had up until that point.

Age is obviously important. Other things being equal, children who are older are going to know more. Motivation is also important. I think of motivation as being a child's willingness to stick to a task even if it is difficult, and stick with it for a long time.

The next two factors, the amount of time and the quality of the teaching, are both important. I will return to them shortly after considering students' environments.

Large-scale sociological surveys show the linkage between achievement and exposure to television, which is the only negative factor. The more television the students watch, the worse they achieve. And it's a very consistent and alarming relationship, by the way, because the biggest study that I know of has estimated that children are watching 28 hours of television per week. And if you calculate five days of school and six hours a day, it's 30 hours of instruction. So, kids are watching almost as much television as they are in school. This is the hours within and outside of school. Chart 2.3 shows that kids spend roughly 10 times as much time outside of school as they do within school.

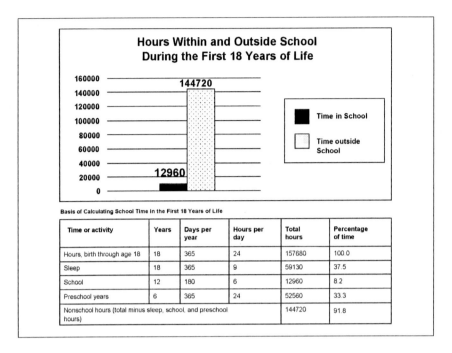

Chart 2.3.   Hours within and outside school during first 18 years of life.

I just completed a study a couple of years ago with two foreign students, one from mainland China and the other from Korea. We attempted to find every study that had been made of how children spend their time. And by the calculations, Chinese students in Hong Kong, Singapore, and mainland China spent almost exactly twice as many hours per school year as American students. Korean students spent 83% more time in school. *A Nation At Risk* pointed out that the United States has the shortest school year in the industrialized world, 180 days. It's more, like 200 or so in Europe; Japan, 240; and Korea, 260. Korea, as other Asian countries, typically topped the charts in science and mathematics, which arguably are the most comparable subjects across nations.

So we should not neglect time, and way of extending time. Chicago, for example, provides summer for children at risk of school failure.

Better teaching or more teaching? In my view, it's not a question of either/or, it's a question of both, and to systematically raise achievement.

We need also to consider social class differences in learning. Chart 2.4 is a close analysis of how parents in various levels of socioeconomic status speak to their children during their first four years of life. Professional parents have spoken roughly 45 million words to their children. In working-class homes it's more like 27 million and for homes on welfare it's only

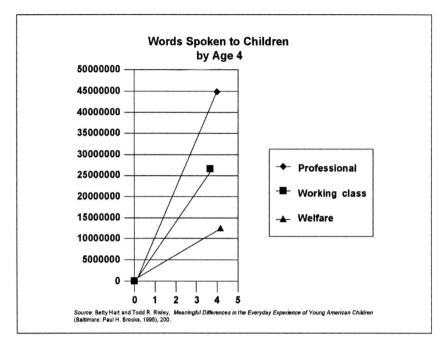

Words Spoken to Children by Age 4

Source: Betty Hart and Todd R. Risley, *Meaningful Differences in the Everyday Experience of Young American Children* (Baltimore: Paul H. Brooks, 1995), 200.

Chart 2.4.   Words spoken to children by age 4.

about 12 million. This is an index of how much children have been verbally stimulated. You could say that parents are the most powerful and profound teachers. Parents are with the children for those 18 years and especially for the first six years of the child's life, and if there are major differences attributable to poverty, then we're going to find these big difference when children actually enter school. It's tragic that we have not been able to figure out how to overcome these kinds of things, but much of the problem may be attributed to the small amount of time that children are actually in school.

We could talk about the quality of the home environment as well. The same study showed vast socioeconomic differences in encouragement and the complexity of sentences employed by parents.

Teachers would be familiar with these points on Chart 2.5. A number of studies have indicated that those kinds of teaching strategies that are highly effective and you have a numerical estimate of the degree of impact that they have on learning.

Chart 2.6 shows selected effects of quality instruction. I want to single out a couple of ones because I think that they are particularly valuable. One of the ones that I think is most important above all is the reading teaching. There's been a long, long debate about the best way to teach

Instructional Strategy Effects

Category	Average Effect
1. Identifying similarities and differences	1.61
2. Summarizing and note taking	1.00
3. Reinforcing effort and providing recognition	.80
4. Homework and practice	.77
5. Nonlinguistic representations (e.g., maps and other graphics)	.75
6. Cooperative learning	.73
7. Setting goals and providing feedback	.61
8. Generating and testing hypotheses	.61
9. Activating prior knowledge	.59

Source: Robert J. Marzano, *A New Era of School Reform: Going Where Research Takes Us* (Aurora, CO: Mid-Continent Research for Education and Learning, 2000), 63.

Note: The effects in this and other tables are generally ordered from largest to smallest as indicated by the effect sizes.

Chart 2.5.   Instructional strategy effects.

Selected Effects of Quality of Instruction

General Methods		Special Methods	
Instructional Elements		**Reading Teaching**	
Cues	1.25	Adaptive Speed Training	.95
Reinforcement	1.17	Phonemic Awareness	.86
Corrective Feedback	.94	Repeated Oral Reading	.48
Engagement	.68	Phonics	.44
Mastery Learning	.73	**Writing Teaching**	
		Inquiry	.57
Computer-Assisted Instruction		Scales	.36
For Early Elementary Students	1.05	Sentence Combining	.35
For Handicapped Students	.66	**Early Education Programs**	
		Preschool	.22–.50
Teaching		Full-Day vs. Half-Day	.48
Comprehension Teaching	.71	Kindergarten	
Direct Teaching	.55		
		Grouping	
Teaching Techniques		Acceleration of Gifted Students	.88
Homework with Teacher Comments	.83	Tutoring	.40
Graded Homework	.78		
Frequent Testing	.49	**Staff Development**	
Pretests	.48	Feedback	.70
Adjunct Questions	.40	Staff Development for Reading Teaching	.61
Goal Setting	.40	Microteaching	.55
Assigned Homework	.28		
Explanatory Graphics	.75		

Source: Herbert J. Walberg and Jin-Shei Lai, "Meta-Analytic Effects for Policy" in *Handbook of Educational Policy,* ed. Gregory J. Cizek (San Diego, CA: Academic Press, 1999).

Chart 2.6.   Selected effects of quality of instruction.

reading. The National Reading Panel filtered thousands of studies and came up with roughly about 100 that prove that Jean Chall was right. She wrote a book called *The Great Debate* about whether to teach reading by phonics or word attack skills versus whole word methods, and phonics is the clear winner in teaching the most essential of all things that children need to learn in school. If I drop down to the last one, staff development, I think the point has been made there in the numerical estimates of effects. Your education doesn't end when you get your baccalaureate. You could say that it begins. And so staff development and continuing education, indeed what we all are engaged in during this conference, is a critical element in teaching excellence is extremely important. Thank you very much.

Philip Bigler

It's really a pleasure to be here. When I was asked to be on this panel, it was such an honor to be back to the Milken Family Foundation's celebration of quality teaching. My recognition year was in 1999 and, as you all know, your life has changed dramatically and it's going to continue to change. I made the change to higher education and it's a real different experience. I am working now, as a director of a program at James Madison University working with the Constitution.

I'm also having the opportunity to actually work with our students who are going into education. I think that's really an important thing because I find so many of our young teachers go into schools and they come back discouraged because people are telling them the wrong things. One of my first words of wisdom is to stay out of the teacher lounge and you'll be a much better teacher.

I was a high school teacher for 23 years, so I guess that does make me an expert somewhat on education. Of those 23 years, four were what I refer to as "dog years." I aged seven to one so I actually taught the equivalent of 51 years. We all have a dog year every now and then, as you can imagine. Our topic today is "What makes a quality teacher?" And I see you all here having your coffee and dessert. My definition of a good teacher has always been a good teacher is a teacher who can drink three cups of coffee before 8:00 A.M. and hold it until 3:00 P.M. You all are doing very, very well. I'm proud of you, to say the least.

I've taught under seven Presidential administrations, from Richard Nixon to George W. Bush. I look at that and I realize that I've taught under 20% of all of our presidents. What has changed as an educator? How do you become a quality teacher? I had to become an educational statistic to become a good teacher. I had to quit teaching. I quit teaching after seven years. I was the statistic that you hear so much about. And why did that happen? Well, I'll tell you why. I wanted a job so bad as a young 22-year-old ide-alistic young man coming into education. My first job interview was at a small private school. It took me one year to get this interview. And this is what they offered me, $6,200 a year, five preparations, coaching football, and driving the school bus. We can't do that to teachers. That is not accept-able. My first real job was as was a long-term substitute at a place called Oak-ton High School and I was doing okay because I started off with these kids. The teacher who had been assigned these classes had an illness over the summer and I was asked to substitute for nine weeks with the understanding that he would come back. After about three weeks, they decided that they could hire me on as full-time teacher because the school was understaffed. We had too many kids in the class, 32, 33 kids. So they said would you like this job? And I said yeah, I would love this job. I wanted to be a teacher. And so they said well, you know, there is a problem—the problem is you're flexi-ble. I said okay, I'm flexible. What does that mean? They said well, you can teach anything; you're certified in social studies. You can teach history, eco-nomics, whatever. Now I really couldn't teach anything at that point, but I said sure, I can teach anything. You're right. Absolutely. And they contin-ued, these are really his classes. You've got to understand that he's coming back and you're really only a long-term sub. And he's only taught American history in his 30 years here. He's never taught anything else—that is all he ever teaches. So they really are his classes. They need to go back to him. What we're going to do is we're going to give you entirely new classes.

And what they did was ask all the social studies teachers to choose five students of their choice to give me for my classes. What an opportunity—to purge your class rolls of the most troublesome students. It comes once in a lifetime and you make the most of it. And they made the most of it. And so that was my first year as a teacher. I was rewarded with a layoff notice in April. I got laid off my first year. I got laid off my second year. We went through all sorts of budget crises, and other problems. By the time I got through seven years having worked in a trailer, taught history in a home ec room, I said, I'm quitting teaching because I am not a professional. So I left teaching and it was the best thing I ever did because I finally learned to appreciate what we do each and every day in our classrooms. Now, you want to talk about quality education. I'll tell you it's easy enough. I could have everyone of you come here and speak for one minute on the micro-phone and we would know what quality education is.

It is difficult trying to define quality education because there are so many characteristics, so many different ways of reaching the same result. I look at my own background and remember two teachers who made an impact in my life. Totally different teachers. One was a nun by the name of Sister Mary Josephine. My father was in the Navy so we traveled all around the country. I went to 12 different schools before I graduated from high school. I hardly even would get settled in a school before we were moving somewhere else.

Well, this sister who taught me in eighth grade basically gave me confidence as a young man. In many ways she changed my life. And three years later at another school I had a colonel who was a marine who had just come back from two tours of duty in Vietnam. Totally different personality. Rigorous. Kind of hard nose. But he really inspired me to learn history. So it's really going to be a challenge to make generalizations but I'm going to go through some of the things I think contribute to making a quality teacher.

It is critical that we start talking about this because we are near a teacher crisis. *Teacher* magazine ran a survey (Chart 2.7) just a little while ago about where we are in education and found that the average teacher right now is 44 years old. That means that in the next nine years, about 50% of our teaching staff is going to retire. You cannot have that kind of attrition without getting more people into this profession. I am a firm believer that a rising tide floats all boats. And I firmly believe that we have to raise teacher salaries across the board, because in America the way that we can truly show that we value education by paying people a decent wage.

And we have to start there. We have to raise teachers' salaries. Eighty-two percent of teachers right now have at least one student on an IEP Program.

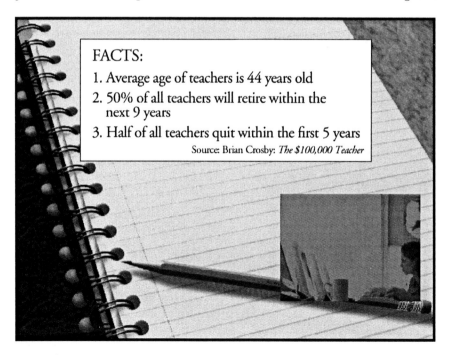

FACTS:
1. Average age of teachers is 44 years old
2. 50% of all teachers will retire within the next 9 years
3. Half of all teachers quit within the first 5 years
Source: Brian Crosby: *The $100,000 Teacher*

Chart 2.7.

That is something that has changed in my career. Today most of you probably have two, three or four kids on an IEP Program. Ninety-nine percent of all teachers are going to hold bachelor degrees; 46% hold master's degrees, so we are becoming better educated. But a statistic that stuns me is that only 40% of teachers said they would choose teaching again as a career. That's something that we really have to address.

Now, what does makes a good teacher? Take a look at Chart 2.8. The first thing that a good teacher has to do is have the ability to change. You must be able to change. That means that you're not going to be the same teacher at the beginning of your career that you are at the end. If you are, shame on you. Because quite frankly I've seen people in a classroom who are using the same notes that they used in 1975. And they're about ready to deteriorate and fall apart. They're even using dittos still from the old days. They haven't come along and changed. Change is something that is part of education and good teachers are always looking for a way to become better teachers.

You need to look at technology. You need to look at all of the exciting new things that are coming every year. In my own lifetime the major changes as a social studies teacher that made my life different was first when the ditto machine was replaced by the Xerox. Now most of you are younger than I am, so I'll have to give you a little bit of background, but in

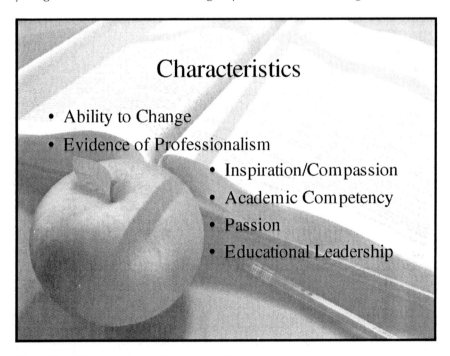

Chart 2.8.   Characteristics of a good teacher.

the old days we used to run dittos. A ditto was basically a kind of stencil that you would type up and then you would run it off on a ditto machine the next morning. The way you corrected these dittos was to take them out of the typewriter and take a razor blade and scratch off the back and then put it back and type over. You did that two or three times and that was about it. The next morning you ran it off and when you pass the papers out to the kids the first thing they did was smother their face into the ditto to inhale the ditto fluid. It had a wonderful smell, but said a lot for our drug policies in the 1970s and 1980s! So when I got my first Xerox machine, I said this has transformed me as a teacher because now my handouts look good. I can basically do political cartoons, all sorts of wonderful things. The same thing happened when film was replaced by videotape. We social studies teachers love film, and videotape certainly transformed us because when I began my teaching career, I used to have to go down and sit in the library the first day of school to order films for the entire year because everybody in the county was doing the exact same thing at that exact same moment and I was trying to get my films for the year. Inevitably, what would happen was I had to try to figure out what the schedule was going to be and I couldn't figure out field trips, snow days, assemblies, all the other kind of interruptions that we have, so that the time we got to January, I would tell the kids we're in the Civil War, but Teddy Roosevelt The Movie is here. So we are going to watch Teddy. And, of course, the kids were kind enough because they said well, that's great, it's something different. But now with videotape you can go and get high-quality documentaries and you can really stimulate these kids and give them a wonderful experience because it actually makes sense at the time of your curriculum. Computers, Internet technology, what an exciting time to be a teacher! This technology is transforming the way we do our business.

The next thing that I think a quality teacher should have is a sense of professionalism. This is something that I think teachers kind of take for granted but we need to pay more attention to it because we have to have pride in being educators. The problem with us as a profession is that we're humble people. We have to realize that teaching is a skill and that most people cannot do what you do everyday of your life. And if you don't believe me, come to Washington, D.C., and I'll bring in a $500/hour K Street lawyer into my classroom and we'll watch 14-year-olds turn him to mush. You are talented, rare people and we have to tell the public that. When you're at the grocery store and someone asks you what to do, you can't bow your head and say I'm just a teacher. Get rid of the just. Say, I'm a teacher and I teach kids. That is something we have to do. And you are role models. Look what else is out there: watch television for just one week this year, and see what these kids see everyday. You are their best role models. You are the ones who show them what is possible, you are the ones who give them something to aspire to. And that is part of being a professional, of being aware of what you can do for kids.

The other thing, and I have no idea how to measure these things, is you have to have inspiration and compassion. You've got to be able to care. You cannot reduce kids to educational statistics. It bothers me because I see kids all the time, and you know what it's like. That third grader or fourth grader who is crying in your classroom is your major responsibility and it doesn't matter what statistical category they fall into. We've got to help these children and that's something I think that the world needs to understand. We're all committed to helping children, children as individuals, and that's a powerful responsibility. When I was named National Teacher of the Year in 1998, I got 63 e-mails the next morning. I got e-mails from kids I didn't even remember. And you know what some said? "Mr. Bigler, I remember when you did this." I couldn't even remember this student, it's kind of scary. It means that the right word can change a child's life and conversely, the wrong word can do the same thing in an adverse way. You must be real careful about what you say. One of my colleagues keeps telling a story about me: that one day we had a child whose cat died and I wrote the kid a sympathy card. It meant so much to that child because that cat was very much part of her life and it helped her get over her grief because an adult made a simple gesture of understanding. So remember that we are role models.

You have to be an optimist to be a teacher; you have to believe that what you're doing each and every day of your life is important. And that means you have to have passion for what you're doing. Now, you are recognized leaders. What does that mean? That means that you are the face of education. People are going to look to you, they are going to ask you questions, and all of a sudden you are credible because you are a Milken Educator and you represent all of the people in our profession. First off, let me commend you for everything you're doing and congratulations.

Lewis C. Solmon

What I would like to do is give each of you an opportunity to either say something for one minute, ask somebody else a question, or pass.

Eric A. Hanushek

Well, the one thing that I would emphasize here is that I agree with my colleagues about what goes on in the classroom, and what makes a good teacher, the question is how do you ensure that there's somebody like that in the classroom at all times? And that's the policy question. We have found that we have done it very poorly by just regulating teachers at entry and then letting the system fly. And so we have to have other ways to identify the people who have these traits and to make sure that they're the ones that stay in the classrooms and that's the challenge.

Lewis C. Solmon

People now agree that value-added or the growth of test scores is the way to measure teacher impacts on student learning. We took that advice with TAP and are trying to do it in the schools that we are working in. But what you find is you say you're going to do it, it's a great theory, people write papers on it, and people get publications and all that. But then you try to do it, and they say well, you can't really use tests in K–2, test scores aren't stable there. And really there aren't tests in high school, but you should use value-added. There's a big difference between being a researcher or a theoretician, and actually trying to apply some of this. So I'd like to hear how do you do it when it's not stable in a third of the grades, and in half the grades there aren't tests. What do you do?

Eric A. Hanushek

Let me be very clear about what I was talking about when I put up some of the information on the research that's been done. That research has in fact tried to use complicated statistical models to estimate the value-added of teachers. They're based upon a range of test information that has been available. I think it'll be a disaster to try to actually run a personnel system based upon the tests that were given to the kids and the value-added that is subsequently estimated. We all know the properties of that system and they aren't pretty. On the other hand, what we do know also is that when somebody has high value-added as shown in these statistical models, it's something that other people can identify. Principals can identify the teachers that provide a high value-added, that are not the ones just with the high-scoring kids, but the ones adding the most, even if they start at a low level.

I actually think that this goes much further and that all of the teachers in a school know at least who's at the very top of the school in terms of their value-added and who's at the very bottom of the school in terms of value-added. I don't think the opinions on the ends of the distribution differ at all. There's a lot of confusion in the center of the distribution. But what I would think and it's something along the lines of what TAP actually proposes, trying to work on developing systems of peer reviews. You would have other teachers, principals in the school, maybe some parents involved in evaluation, and have systems that are designed really to try to keep the really good teachers and to get rid of the really bad teachers. That would have a huge impact on the performance of our system. Just working on the extremes and not getting confused about the middle by trying to decide between the 12th and the 13th best teacher in the school, that's not what you want to do.

Lewis C. Solmon

And that's what we actually do. We actually set the probability of a gain at a 70% probability level because we'd rather err on the side of being positive, right?

Lee S. Shulman

I think Phil has reminded us of all of the things that we all take seriously, that even if we solve all the technical problems associated with making meticulous comparisons of value-added, we will still not have addressed. And, when we get upset about America, it's usually not because we came in 14th and the Hungarians came in 12th in social studies. It's because it looks like we haven't educated people who care enough to vote. You know, why do we have the lowest voting rate in the free Western world? Why are people not more civically engaged? Why are they not more caring for their neighbors? I mean, there's a whole set of other goals of education that I feel terrified that we're going to lose sight of because it will be so much easier to measure academic achievement. I value academic achievement as much as anyone. I've devoted the last 20 years of my career to a focus on what it means to understand mathematics and science and history deeply. But I don't delude myself into thinking that's all that's involved and I worry that we're going to lose sight of the other goals of education. That's my big worry right now.

Lewis C. Solmon

You would probably argue that this would be a bad question or an unfair, silly question to ask: if a genie came out of a bottle and said you could either raise reading scores or raise the voting rate in your school district, which would you do? I mean, that you would probably say that's a bad question.

Lee S. Shulman

Oh yeah. But that would be like asking me if I wanted my children as I was raising them to be able to support themselves or to be good human beings. That's not a good question.

Lewis C. Solmon

I knew you were going to say that.

Herbert J. Walberg

I think that Phil's salary should be multiplied by a factor of five or ten. But, I take exception to Phil's point about blanket increases in salaries. First, I think the point was made in our early discussion this morning, the country doesn't have the money to do that. The country doesn't have the inclination to do it. I think that there's a strong need to reward and give incentives for higher performance. In many other fields there are vast differences in the pay that people get. Look at the celebrities of our society: Hollywood movie stars, basketball players, high-powered attorneys, people make huge amounts of money and some are, you might call them, journeymen. They just are not at that level. And I think that there has to be, to use a dirty word in education, merit pay. I think general infusions of money is not the solution. You heard that educational expenditures on a per-student basis had been rising steadily for a half century. And yet test scores have been low and stable. In addition, you look at the comparisons of the cost of education in other countries despite the fact that U.S. students start off as bright as any students in the world in the beginning. The longer they stay in American schools, the lower their rankings by the standards of other countries and an objective measures of their knowledge of science and mathematics. And yet the United States is third highest in expenditures per student in the world. So the fact that we are enormously efficient and productive in many industries should lead us to think about new ways of doing things. And I think that some sort of salary differential should be important.

But we ought to rethink all the detailed federal regulations in special education, bilingual education, and many mandates that come from states and the federal government that require many kinds of forms to be filled out and the distraction that causes for many superintendents, teachers, and principals. By the international standards of comparison, it's amazing to me that only roughly half of our expenditures go directly into instruction.

So if you subtract out what's sometimes called, Bill Bennett used to call, the blob, that is all the administrative bureaucracy and things of this nature by saving on some of those things and having less detailed regulations as Jeanne Allen was suggesting earlier today, I think that there are ways that we could save money. But I think that that money that is saved ought to go to teachers that indeed are doing a good job.

Philip Bigler

I don't disagree with you at all on that. We're really going to have to go to a differentiation in staffing either through licensure or whatever to recognize those teachers that do go above and beyond. I know in Virginia we're having that conversation right now and that's something that's been on going in a lot of different states. The problem I found was that when Fairfax County adopted a merit pay program, it was the best evaluations that we ever had during that period of time. It was also the most expensive evaluation program. You had peer evaluators coming into your classroom. You had your principal working with you. They wrote these incredibly lengthy and very productive evaluations.

The first budget cycle that we had a problem, guess what went, merit pay bonuses. And that's what ends up happening in education and it's very frustrating because when you buy into something, you really would hope they would follow through. But I fully agree that we have to start seeing that number one, that not all teachers are equal. We have to get over the mentality in education that we're all interchangeable parts. That you can plug any teacher into a classroom, and it doesn't make a difference who that person is. You all know that there are certain people that you want your kid to have as a teacher and there are others that you don't.

Lewis C. Solmon

Does it seem to anybody else that not doing something because there might not be money in the future is like not getting married because there's a possibility that you might get divorced some day?

Audience Question

Right now the No Child Left Behind Annual Yearly Progress (AYP) in our state, California, is the Academic Performance Indicator (API) for each school. We look to high-stakes testing to measure the effectiveness of our school. My question is what are other ways to look at effective schools other than high-stakes testing if we know that quality education depends on quality teaching and we know that collegiality is important and we know that small learning communities are important. Are there ways to measure those aspects of a school and then in turn as a by-product, wouldn't student achievement rise?

Eric A. Hanushek

I can say a little bit about high-stakes testing. I think that right now we're struggling to find the best way to measure performance and to rate schools and student outcomes in that we haven't got there yet. But the thing we know is that during the 1990s when states first started putting in accountability systems, the states that put in accountability systems had better gains on NAEP performance than the states that did not put in accountability systems.

There's a whole large set of questions of refining what we do with accountability measures and how we reward or punish schools and in what dimensions. I personally believe that the things we should pay most attention to are student performance measured in a variety of ways. I don't think we should slight community involvement. But I think that we found that performance in reading, math, and science have such a long-lasting impact on the students themselves and on society in general that we have to pay a little more attention to that.

Herbert J. Walberg

I'd like to question the premise about why we need something aside from standardized tests. I think there are four good reasons to take them very seriously. In the first place, our elected representatives in this country, both in the states and Congress in both political parties, are very much behind accountability. In a sense we are working for the public and the public is represented by our elected officials. That doesn't make it right, of course, but it certainly needs to be taken seriously. Second, in my view kids are going to have to take standardized tests. If they want to get into the police force in Chicago or if they want to get into law school at Harvard or many other places, they're going to have to do well on standardized tests. If our kids were doing well on standardized tests compared to those in other countries, then we could be much more relaxed about it. I also think that these tests have good scientific qualities that are not always recognized. They have the features of reliability and validity. We could use portfolios but they are very expensive to use and they're often very unreliable because what I think is a good essay may differ wildly from what someone else thinks. So these tests are not a conspiracy against good education, they're an effort to move things along.

Now in answer to your question, however, what are the alternatives? Jeanne Allen, in my opinion, emphasized an interesting point, as did Nina Rees. And that is when parents have the capacity to choose another school, they can weigh intangibles that are not represented in those tests. We could say that there are different tastes in education. Some parents might like to have a vocational program for their kids. Others might like Latin and Greek and a classical education. There's just a wide variety of proficiency. Although there may be a common core that all students should know, there are other kinds of preferences for the type of teaching that goes on as well as the subject matter. So I think choice should be welcomed, and particularly as several people have emphasized, for poor kids in failing schools. If they have the capacity to go to other schools, it introduces another kind of accountability.

And finally, there have been several studies in addition to what Rick mentioned. Suzanna Loeb and Martin Carnoy of Stanford University have done, in my opinion, one of the finest studies and Rick himself has done work, important work, in this area that suggests that if you pay attention to test scores, particularly those of minority groups and kids in poverty as No Child Left Behind emphasizes, you do in fact get better performance. Can the tests be abused? Of course, there can be cheating and things of that nature. But there can be cures to that as well.

Lee S. Shulman

What Herb has said is one of the reasons why we have to be careful about what he's arguing for, because the argument was that Congress favors these things and they're reliable and valid and they give us real numbers. Well, the reason Congress favors them is they like things that can be put in simple numbers. And there's a kind of circularity there. When I was working on the National Board development almost 20 years ago, I had the great pleasure of having probably the century's finest psychometrician, Lee Crohnbach, as my colleague and assistant in this work. And yes, he called himself my assistant. And what he told me was, you figure out what matters so much that we ought to be able to measure it and then give us who do psychometrics the challenge of figuring out how to measure it. I think that portfolios of various kinds are much more powerful approaches to try to capture the full qualitative and quantitative range of things that happen in a school that makes it a good school.

That if we reduce our measures immediately to those things we can measure, that's all that will matter. And I think we've got to turn this around. We've got to ask the educators in the states what really counts as evidence for whether your school is doing its work. Let's put together the artifacts and then let's ask the people who understand psychometrics for ways of quantifying those artifacts. I think we're going in the wrong direction now.

Audience Question

I teach in a state, California, that has teaching standards for the profession and I was wondering if anybody on the panel knows if any other states in the United States, any other states also have teaching standards for the teaching profession. Having gone through the National Board certification process, I am aware of the National Board standards, but I don't think they are mandated across the United States per state. So the first question is, do other states have teaching standards that they hold teachers accountable for? And the second question I'd like to address to Dr. Walberg, you mentioned another process in assessing teacher quality, the American Board. And I was wondering if you could go into that a little bit because I'm not familiar with that one.

Lee S. Shulman

Other states do have standards. One of the most widely used set of standards are what are called the Interstate New Teacher Assessment and Support Consortium (INTASC) standards, which dozens of states are using. Those were closely aligned with National Board standards but they're for entry. But what has happened is the sort of thing that that Phil described. Right here in California we establish standards for exit from teacher education programs. In the recent budget crunch the first thing that happened there was that they were indefinitely deferred. And so we have this funny thing that happens in California and in other states is on the one hand you raise the formal standards for teaching significantly. On the other hand, you open up all the rear doors for emergency credentials. Well, ask Rick what the incentive there is. So it's a bait and switch, if you will.

Herbert J. Walberg

The American Board for the Certification of Teacher Excellence is a new program and it's now being developed and probably will be ready in about a year or so from now. But it's based on the premise or the research largely done by economists about the things that are predictive of how well a teacher's students will do. It's been found consistently that the amount of education and the amount of experience are very inconsistent correlates. What are the stronger correlates are knowledge of the subject matter or having taken a lot of courses in the subject so that it's a teacher of high school that's had, let's say, 10 courses of mathematics beyond calculus, can be expected to know that subject extremely well. So the first consideration is knowledge of the subject matter and that can be tested. That's what the first part of the test is based upon. The second part of the test is professional teaching knowledge and it's based upon the research that's been done on what leads to the teaching acts and behaviors that are associated with higher levels of achievement. It doesn't guarantee that a teacher is a good teacher, but it does guarantee two things. They have the subject-matter knowledge and they have at least the knowledge of good teaching practices.

Audience Question

My question is to Mr. Hanushek. You were talking about testing of teachers. I think you said something about testing as far as minority teachers are concerned. Have studies been done to show that minorities score lower?

Eric A. Hanushek

What we found in terms of the people who are willing to go into teaching is that the more testing and the higher the standards for testing, the fewer the people willing to enter into teaching. But past research has suggested that minority teachers respond even stronger than nonminority teachers so that the supply of minority teachers drops more precipitously for any ratcheting up of test requirements.

I'm not saying that minorities score lower. I'm just trying to indicate that if a state institutes a higher test standard, it cuts down on the number of people who are willing to apply for certification and enter the teaching profession. If the potential teachers are required to take a test for entry, and if the state increases the scores on that test that are required for satisfactory entry or credentials, even fewer will agree to stand for certification and enter the schools. Research has indicated that the potential minority candidates for teaching respond more negatively than non-minorities to testing. Consequently, making the tests more rigorous has a stronger deterrent effect on minorities. That's what I was trying to indicate. That's what the studies that have looked at the entry into teaching and what happens with tests show.

Audience Question

Okay, thank you. I just wanted to tell you a little story. I have a friend who's a really good teacher. The reason why I know is because she was in a teaching classroom, sixth grade last year. Well, this past year she is an aide in the preschool of our school. She's a wonderful aide, but she's an even better school teacher, a special regular classroom teacher but because she's not passed her test for the last three times, she has not been able to go back in the classroom.

Eric A. Hanushek

Well, I completely agree with that. I think that we ought to make a lot more judgments on the basis of how people do in the classroom as opposed to these credentialing requirements, because they are not a very good screen about who does well in the classroom.

Audience Question

This comment is mainly for Dr. Shulman. I feel like you have read my mind. I was one of the first 13 teachers in the state of Maryland to pass the National Board. It changed my teaching forever. And I kind of feel that way about the Milken award. I think it's going to be changing my career forever, but it's not just the teaching in the classroom. I think it's given me a broader perspective. One comment I might make is that when you're considering the characteristics of what an effective or an excellent teacher will be, one of the things to think about or that I've been thinking a lot about is knowledge of your students, not just knowledge of your content. One of the things I do when I'm mentoring other teachers or new teachers is I say to them, listen to the kids. Watch the kids. They will teach you how to teach them. And I just thought maybe you'd like to comment on that.

Lee S. Shulman

I agree entirely. And I think one of the things we've been doing in studying how people learn in other professions like law, medicine, nursing, and the clergy is part of the training is to do an unnatural act, which is to listen to other people very, very carefully. Teaching in that sense is an unnatural act because you've got to keep your mouth shut, listen to the kids, watch them, and you've got to understand a lot about their development, about what it means when they say certain kinds of things. And this is another reason why I'm a strong advocate for very, very powerful forms of professional preparation for teachers. It's not enough to say to teachers, hey, you listen. We say that to our kids for years, don't we? You've got to learn how to listen like a teacher. And I agree with you entirely. It's enormously important and it's not something people who have not been well trained do intuitively. They do the opposite. They keep talking like I do.

Philip Bigler

I'd just like to add one more point. One of the things that seems to be missing from all this discussion about assessment is that the teacher is the best assessor of student progress. For some reason or the other we've lost the sense that a teacher has a grade and a credibility beyond anything that any test or standardized performance assessment can give. Teachers are the best experts on what's going on in a classroom.

Audience Question

What I've heard here in the last two days makes me remember something and I'll bring President Reagan up again, he's been mentioned so many times today. When he ran for president in the first instance he said are you better off now then you were four years ago and that was sort of the thing he asked people to assess where they were after four years of the previous president. And I would like to throw this question out to this audience. I've heard said, mostly by the people who stood up and made comments about the situations they find themselves in, a lot of very heartbreaking comments about how people can't function in the systems that they find themselves in. How frustrated they are. They have to move to different places because they can't do what they really want to do and the kinds of things that they encounter. And I would like to ask the panel and everybody here if you were to invent from scratch an education system for a country like ours, would you invent one that looks like the one we've got? Would you have the kinds of problems that constantly come about money, about cycles, about getting rid of the good things when the money runs out? Would that be the way you would create a system? Think about that. I'd like the panel to comment.

Philip Bigler

One of the greatest strengths of the American educational system is that we have a forgiving system. Everybody has an opportunity and quite frankly, you don't get stereotyped into being sent into vocational ed or whatever. I've seen a lot of students and I've failed with kids, and I won't deny that. I've had my failures. But I've seen the ability of the resiliency for kids to go on. This has been the great leveling aspect of America. Someone pointed out that this is our Statue of Liberty in a lot of ways—the educational system. It has made this country a nation of immigrants, a nation of opportunity for young people. And, I think the greatest strength this country has is the democratic nature of our educational system.

Lewis C. Solmon

Why don't we actually let the teacher have the last word. Let's thank the panel, and thank you very much for your attention.

PANEL CONTRIBUTIONS

CHAPTER 3

FORGIVE AND REMEMBER

The Challenges and Opportunities
of Learning from Experience

Lee S. Shulman
The Carnegie Foundation for the Advancement of Teaching

Recently, I was in Washington D.C. to meet with a group from the National Academy of Engineering (NAE). They plan to create a national center for research on how people learn to be engineers.[1] I was helping them think about ways we can study how people learn a profession, in this case, engineering. How can you get people—in this case, faculty members—to move from the findings of research to actually applying it in practice? They said, "You know, professors of engineering don't have a lot of time to lead educational research. They think they know how to teach engineering—the way they were taught. How can we get them to do something different?" This may sound familiar to those of us who work in teacher education or teacher professional development.

Three things struck me while I was working with the NAE, and these three are relevant to today's topic. First, what engineers do is design and

Talented Teachers: The Essential Force for Improving Student Achievement, pages 87–95
Copyright © 2004 by Information Age Publishing

Reprinted with permission from the New Teacher Center at the University of Santa Cruz. Keynote address originally presented at the 2002 New Teacher Center Symposium.

create artifacts like bridges or tall buildings. All of us are sitting very comfortably in this room because we have implicit faith in the engineers who designed this hotel. We trust that this ceiling will not fall on us, and that the floor will bear our weight. And you can hear me because other engineers designed sound systems to make it possible for me to speak very softly and still be heard. All these are artifacts, tools, instruments designed by engineers.

Second, I saw that the National Academy of Engineering is concerned with a problem common to all professional training: how can we teach engineering students how to engage in engineering practice without subjecting clients to undue risks? If a student engineer had the last word in designing this ceiling, would you feel just as comfortable sitting there as you do now? And what is your feeling about having a first-year surgical resident be the person who will make the incision during your surgery? But how else can they learn? This is a dilemma common to all the professions.

My third insight has to do with realizing how much more complicated the job of a teacher is than the job of an engineer. All that an aeronautical engineer has to do is design a plane. Other people test it, yet others pilot it, and still others repair it and are responsible for its upkeep. In teaching, we are responsible for preparing people who must not only design the plane but also fly it, serve the drinks, and be prepared to evaluate how well the plane performed. Teaching is much more complex, and it is also more lonely. You close the door, and you're the only one. In engineering, there is a great deal of modeling that goes on and then collaborative review of the models. It's very rare for an engineer doing complex design to ever be truly flying solo.

I mention these three things because my topic this morning is the universal use by the professions of a somewhat protected experience for novices. Whether it is teacher induction, medical residencies, clinical experiences for lawyers, or engineering internships, this strategy is part of the system of educating professionals, and it gives rise to a couple of important questions. The first question is: How is learning from experience possible? If you think about it for a moment, it's a miracle; odds are that only a tiny minority of experiences are really learned from. Therefore, what is the essence of learning from experience? The second question relates to the problem I just alluded to: How do we deal with the fundamental ethical and moral question of what entitles us to expose children, hospital patients, or clients to the services of someone who is, by definition, not yet ready to practice? How do we justify that? Do we simply say, "Well, it's the only way they can learn." That may be part of it, but it is a little more complicated than that.

I should also say that in this talk I'm drawing quite consciously on some things we are now doing at The Carnegie Foundation for the Advancement of Teaching. We are studying how people are prepared for a variety of professions—as lawyers, engineers, teachers, and members of the clergy. There are some fascinating parallels and some delicious contrasts among these fields. This work continues to remind me of what an extraordinary challenge it is to help new teachers learn to teach. It also shows me that we are not alone; in every one of the learned and service professions, similar problems are encountered.

This brings me to the title of this morning's talk, "Forgive and Remember." *Forgive and Remember* is the title of a book written more than 20 years ago by a sociologist named Charles Bask. Bask's book is a study of the surgical residency, and its focus is on the management of error in that residency. He begins with the observation and recognition that in a residency (which can include any form of professional residency) errors, surprises, and mistakes are inevitable. He doesn't actually go so far as to make the assertion—which I would make—that if you structured the experience during the residency period so tightly that there are no errors, you also structured the experience to guarantee that there will be little or no learning.

This is the dilemma. How do you manage the inevitability, and even the necessity, of error in the surgical residency—or in any other protected professional learning experience? One of the questions Bask asks is what kinds of errors can be forgiven. He has the basic insight that errors due to gaps in knowledge are forgivable—if you don't forgive and forget, but rather you forgive and remember. His rationale is that in this situation you concurrently serve clients and serve society by educating the next generation of those who will be able to provide professional service. And, since error is inevitable, its expiation rests in being able to learn from the experience. I'm going to propose the general argument that learning from experience is justifiable, if what accompanies it is real memory, real learning, real understanding, and real commitment.

Consider the character of the induction experience, whether you think of it as part of student teaching, in a traditional sense, or as a residency or induction year. Think about not only the inevitability, but also the necessity, for error—and also for surprises, some of which may be pleasant. In this light, what kinds of experiences are most likely to be learning opportunities?

One reason why error is so critical for us to understand is that it relates to the broader notion of surprise—the unexpected or the unpredicted. While predictability may be a highly desirable condition in which to operate, learning begins with accidents. It's fascinating to think about how in our earliest days of life surprise is one of the developmental challenges we learn to deal with. Think about playing peek-a-boo with a four-month-old baby. What happens? You do your initial peek-a-boo, and the baby cries. The baby is frightened, but nevertheless signals through the tears, "Do it again!" You do it again, and the baby cries some more. By the third or fourth time, however, the baby is inducing surprise, and you notice that the tears are punctuated with little giggles. Talk about the management of surprise! The baby has started doing what we as a species do when we are working at our best—to seek surprise, to seek uncertainty, to seek complexity, and even though it is initially terrorizing, to figure out a way to manage it. We don't do away with the surprise; we learn how to deal with it, and we develop a variety of strategies. What better description can there be of learning to teach?

I will lay odds that the overwhelming majority of teachers in this room probably prefer forms of discovery learning, project-based learning, and problem solving by groups over a highly structured, highly scripted curriculum. Novice teachers do the same thing; they want to do the most complex, group-based, problem-solving discovery learning, and they want to do it right away. Teachers who teach in that manner are guaranteed surprise. If you want to teach in ways that ensure you will know where the kids will be and what they will know at the end of the day or week, you teach a highly-controlled curriculum. It's often a good idea, but if you want to ensure that life will be filled with surprises, keep teaching open-ended kinds of curricula in rather unstructured ways.

The quest for surprise, the valorization of surprise over the predictable, is really central to what we do as professional teachers and teacher educators. And we do it in large measure because we intuitively understand that this is a fine way for the kids and for us to grow. We know that growing in understanding entails becoming ever more capable of dealing not with the predictable—we can design macbilles to deal with predictables—but of dealing with uncertainty and the unexpected. It's also why jokes are one of our favorite forms of communication because a joke is a peek-a-boo with words. Funny stories delight us because they contain surprises.

One indicator of your teaching going well is that you surprise the students and they surprise you. And the delight in each of your surprises is what propels the learning forward. Good research always has some form of surprise in it; nothing is duller than a study that confirms what everybody already believed. Good research, good jokes, and good learning experiences have the unpredictable at their centers.

ARTIFACTS SUPPORT LEARNING FROM EXPERIENCE

Let's keep that in mind as we consider what makes learning from experience difficult. One thing that makes learning from experience terribly difficult is that experience is like dry ice: it evaporates at room temperature. As soon as you have it, it's gone. So, one of the big problems in learning from experience is that we need to be able to examine, to analyze, and to reflect on experiences—but experiences fade. And they not only fade, they get distorted. How many times have you been in a situation where you were absolutely sure you did something, and it turned out you didn't? Why don't we think that happens when we are learning from experience as we learn how to teach? Even if we know what we did, it's very hard to know what the consequences were for the students. But learning from experience implies that we not only have a way of looking at what we did, but also at what the students learned. Too often what the students experience and learn is more invisible to us than our own ability to recount what we did. My question to you is how we can be reflective practitioners if the experience from which we're supposed to be learning disappears from view as soon as it happens. I think an answer to this question is contained in a word that engineers use all the time. The word is "artifacts." Artifacts are things—objects, tools, instruments—that human beings construct because they are needed but don't exist in nature. Constructing an artifact is by definition an unnatural act. And yet, I would argue that artifacts are the key to learning from experience.

One of the most vivid demonstrations of the importance of artifacts was a study by Anna Richert of Mills College in Oakland. Anna explored the conditions under which the reflections of people learning to teach become most vivid, most powerful, and most fruitful. She found two conditions were important, if not necessary, for good reflection to happen. The first condition is that the richer the set of artifacts that represented the practice of experience undertaken, the more powerful the reflection, and the second condition is that having a partner to reflect *with* you significantly increases the efficacy of reflection. These two conditions are related, because if all the partner has to work with is the dry ice of memory—and it's *your* memory, not the partner's—it's a much less powerful experience than if you were sitting there with a video of the class, with samples of student work, or with a piece of the journal you wrote immediately after the class. Suddenly reflection becomes not grasping for the fading wisps of memory, but instead working together on the shared artifacts available to all members of the conversation. And I guess I would argue that these principles can be generalized, that learning from experience almost always entails learning from, with, and through the artifacts that are generated to capture, display, and preserve the experience. If you do artifact construction self-consciously, learning is much more likely to occur in the conversations that follow. And if the reflection is conducted collaboratively, the process is further amplified, clarified, and sustained.

SECOND-ORDER ARTIFACTS:
BEYOND REFLECTION AND CONVERSATION

But I am not prepared to stop there, because we still have to address the moral or ethical question of professional training that I raised earlier. Let's say the artifacts capture a really messy bit of teaching in which you engaged. Is the fact that you can learn from those artifacts sufficient moral justification for your students and you to have undergone that experience? I would argue, "Not quite." There is one more piece of the puzzle that must be filled in, and it rests on the notion that learning from reflection on your own practice cannot possibly be the major source of professional learning.

Think about it for a moment. You are one teacher, and you teach one classroom at a time to a particular group of students. If your professional development were wholly dependent on what you learned from your individual experience, who would ever be prepared to trust your professional wisdom? Would you like to go to a physician who only knew what he was able to learn from his own experience, or to a surgeon who only knew what she knew from the mistakes she had made? Don't you have to go further? I would say "yes." For us to justify learning from experience as an explicit strategy of professional education, those experiences not only must be educative through reflective analysis and conversation; they also must be transformed into a second-order artifact, an artifact of scholarship.

What is scholarship? Scholarship is what human beings do in order to create organized ways to learn from one another. Scholarship is a communal activity that rests on the fundamental premise that what we can learn as individuals is only a tiny sliver of what we need to understand as a community. Therefore, we must create new artifacts that represent, explain, and project what we have learned in ways from which others can learn. In the sciences, there are research papers, and in teaching, those could be cases, teacher portfolios, or videos. If our experience begins as a benign surprise or an embarrassing error, whatever we come to understand through looking at first-order artifacts can, in turn, be transformed into second-order artifacts. Only then are we in the realm of "forgiving and remembering."

People make fun of the practice of scholars who pepper their manuscripts with footnotes and references, but each footnote and reference reminds us that our piece of individual writing or learning could not have happened were it not for the efforts of others. Madelyn Grumet has reminded us that the word "acknowledgment," which so often goes in the beginning of the book, is a pun because to "ack-knowledge" is in effect to remind the reader that the knowledge in this book could not have occurred without the knowledge of others, that we stand on the shoulders of a community of giants whenever we do our work. It means that we need this coral reef of small contributions in which others—teachers and teachers educators—decided not to keep their mistakes private, not to keep their surprises to themselves but to make them public, to subject them to peer review and evaluation, and to display and communicate them in ways that make them building material for others in the profession.

Then and only then are we moving from what is fundamentally a selfish act of using our own experience and sometimes the sad experiences of our clients so that we might learn, to the point of making a contribution that is indispensable in our profession—making our work public so that others don't have to undergo one of those experiences in order to learn. All the professions do that, and we in teaching are finally beginning to do it, but we've got to do it more.

Judy Shulman's work with teachers writing cases and producing casebooks exemplifies this principle. Every one of those teacher-writers not only learned from having reflective conversations about his or her practice, but the very doing of the case produced an artifact that others learn from. That's an example of forgive and remember. (A group of teachers from the New Teacher Center in Santa Cruz came together to write the casebook *Using Assessments to Teach for Understanding*.)

One thing that creating an artifact does is force us to interrupt our work; that's why it's so annoying at times. Nurses are often utterly annoyed by the necessity of entering all that stuff into a patient's chart, but wouldn't you love it if all the teachers who served the children you are teaching entered onto a common chart what they had done and what they observed during their time with the students? But it's annoying; you have to interrupt your "real work" to do it.

The anthropologist Elinor Ochs at UCLA studied a group of experimental physicists, and what surprised her was how annoyed these physicists were to have to "stop doing physics" because it was time to prepare a paper for the next national meeting. In order to make their presentations, they had to stop and review and ask themselves what they had really learnt, and how to represent what they learned in a more compressed, elegant and economical fashion? They almost always had to invent new artifacts—slides that compared things they had done, figures that summarized what they had learned. Ochs reports a fascinating finding—they don't stop doing physics in order to prepare their paper, they stop doing one kind of physics in order to do an absolutely necessary other kind of physics. They start asking themselves, "What have I really learned, and how can I talk about it in ways that will educate the rest of my community?" By stopping and creating new artifacts that didn't naturally emerge from what they were doing, they ratcheted up their understanding an order of magnitude. Simultaneously, they learned, and thus their community learned. But again, this happens only if they're prepared to stop. So in a very paradoxical sense, you can only make progress by interrupting your progress.

VISUAL METAPHORS FOR BUILDING
"PEDAGOGICAL CAPITAL"

At The Carnegie Foundation, we think about what teachers learn from their own practice. We have been working with elementary and secondary school teachers, as well as with teacher educators, but by far the largest number of teachers with whom we've worked are university and college professors. This may seem like an unlikely group of folks to engage in a study of their own practice, but they are increasingly doing it with excitement. Over 200 postsecondary institutions nationwide have now developed forms of teaching academies so their faculty can get support in studying their own practice. I was at Illinois State University just a couple of months ago to help in the endowment of a chair, based on a $2.5 million gift to appoint a professor of the scholarship of teaching in one of the disciplines. People are now being recruited to other universities because they have the capacity to study their own practice!

In order to talk about this work, we at Carnegie have been using a set of visual metaphors: mirrors, lenses, windows, and projectors. The mirror is often used as a metaphor for reflection on one's own practice. Simply holding up a mirror is in and of itself an obstruction that initiates new kinds of analyses that would otherwise not occur. The variety of ways in which we can hold up a mirror to practice makes it a powerful tool. Think about those three-way mirrors that you look at in the department store; they give you the chance to see what you look like as you walk out of the room, as well as how you appear when you walk in, and that's a good analogy for using artifacts that can be more powerful than simply jogging our memory. And recall how indispensable the mirrored wall becomes for serious dancers. Artifacts can present angles of vision that aren't normally available to us.

But that is still not enough. The instrumentation that adds to what the mirror can do is the lens. The lens is what we add by having our conversation partners apply analysis to what we see in the mirror. This makes it possible for us to see things we wouldn't otherwise see. Who can forget the first time they looked at their own teaching after they learned about Mary Budd Rowe's concept of "wait time"? Wait time is a conceptual lens—suddenly, you see things you didn't see before. I could argue that one of the most important things we do in the educational research community is to offer lenses, both analytic and perceptual, which make the invisible visible, which make the hidden apparent.

So we need mirrors, and we need lenses, but so far we're still engaging in a solitary act. We also need windows to look through. We need windows into our neighbors' classrooms to see what they are doing, to learn what they are learning. They, in turn, must be able to look at us. This means that in order to see, we have to be prepared to be seen.

And finally, we need projectors. I don't think it's enough to peek into our neighbors' windows. We've got to figure out ways to project those visions, those artifacts, those analyses, in ways that can educate the larger community—people we have never met or may never meet.

We need to confront the inevitability of this technical and moral challenge. We have to learn from experience, which means we have to self-consciously construct artifacts that make learning from experience possible and to have the professional conversations that make them powerful. We have to build what I'll call "pedagogical capital" in the form of such artifacts of learning. Only then will we be able to say in good conscience that in educating teachers we forgive and remember.

NOTE

1. The Center for the Advancement of Scholarship on Engineering Education (CASEE) has since been established.

REFERENCES

Bask, C. L. (1979). *Forgive and remember: Managing medical failure.* Chicago: University of Chicago Press.

Ochs, E., & Jocoby, S. (1997). Down to the wire: The cultural dock of physicists and the discourse of consensus. *Language in Society, 26*(4), 479–505.

Richert, A. (1987). *Reflex to reflection: Facilitating reflection in novice teachers.* Unpublished doctoral dissertation, Stanford University.

Rowe, M. B. (1974). Wait-time and rewards as instructional variables, their influence on language, logic, and fate control: Part I-Wait-time. *Journal of Research in Science Teaching, 11*(2), 81–94.

Rowe, M. B. (1974). Relation of wait-time and rewards to the development of language, logic, and fate-control: Part II-Rewards. *Journal of Research in Science Teaching, 11*(4), 291–308.

Shulman, J. H. (Ed.). (1992). *Case methods in teacher education.* New York: Teachers College Press.

Shulman, J. H., Whittaker, A., Lew, Michelle (2002). *Using assessments to teach for understanding: A casebook for educators.* New York: Teachers College Press.

CHAPTER 4

MAKING DIFFERENCES

A Table of Learning

Dr. Lee S. Shulman

At the beginning of God's creating of the heavens and the earth, when the earth was wild and waste, darkness over the face of Ocean, rushing spirit of God hovering over the face of the waters—God said: Let there be light! And there was light. God saw the light: that it was good. God separated the light from the darkness. God called the light: Day! And the darkness he called: Night! There was setting, there was dawning, one day.

—Genesis I, Verses 1–5; Everett Fox (1995 translation),
The Five Books of Moses, Schocken Books, Inc.

Some things exist by nature, some from other causes. Animals and their bodily organs, plants, and the physical elements—earth, fire, air and water—such things as these we say exist "by nature."

—Aristotle, Physics, Book 2

Talented Teachers: The Essential Force for Improving Student Achievement, pages 97–113
Copyright © 2004 by Information Age Publishing
All rights of reproduction in any form reserved.

This article was originally published in *Change*, November/December 2002. Volume 34, Number 6. Pages 36–44. Reprinted with permission of the Helen Dwight Reid Educational Foundation. Published by Heldref Publications, 1319 18th Street, NW, Washington, DC 20036-1802. Copyright © 2002.

> *All the world's a stage*
> *And all the men and women merely players;*
> *They have their exits and their entrances,*
> *And one man in his time plays many parts,*
> *His acts being seven ages....*
> *That ends this strange eventful history,*
> *Is second childishness and mere oblivion,*
> *Sans teeth, sans eyes, sans taste, sans everything.*
>
> —"As You Like It," 2.7. 139–167

One of the central ways we make sense of experience is by making differences. The world presents itself without inherent order, and our impulse is to place things in piles, count them, and name them. In the act of creation, day is divided from night. Aristotle classifies just about everything. Shakespeare gives us the seven ages of man, Dante maps the circles of hell, Burton anatomizes melancholy.... In ways that Kant never intended by the phrase, we are driven by a "categorical imperative," the irresistible impulse to place things in categories.

This is not an irrational impulse. Distinctions and taxonomies are tools for thought. We make distinctions for the same reasons we carve a turkey or write our books in chapters—to make the world more manageable. And it's only natural that we further order our distinctions and categories into systems, tables, and taxonomies.

The systems sometimes entail stages or hierarchies that imply a sequence of merit or maturity (for example, the biological phyla progressing from single cells to human beings). Sometimes there is no implied hierarchy (as in libraries, university catalogues, and the four basic food groups). We may propose systems that look like a call for balance and new priorities, as in Ernest Boyer's four scholarships.

Categories and distinctions also can call attention to ideas, principles, or values that hitherto have been ignored. In my own work on knowledge for teaching, for example, I once argued that it was insufficient merely to distinguish between content knowledge and pedagogical knowledge of teaching methods. I proposed a new category, *pedagogical content knowledge*, as a way of signaling that there was a missing component in our theories of teaching.

That concept, often called PCK, became a tool for thought, an analytic category, a mnemonic, and even a call to action. As a new category, it was like a new piece of furniture in the living room. It changed the landscape and created both new opportunities and new barriers. In short, for all the postmodern criticisms of distinctions and taxonomies, they sometimes come in quite handy. Indeed, as educators, one of the ways we can make a difference is by making distinctions.

A NEW TABLE OF LEARNING

There is no such thing as a "new" taxonomy; all the likely taxonomies have been invented, and in nearly infinite variety. Probably the single most famous list in the world of educational thought is the Taxonomy of Educational Objectives devised by my one-time teacher Benjamin Bloom. I can't begin to talk about a new taxonomy without acknowledging the invaluable contributions of Bloom and his colleagues—as well as other taxonomic pioneers including William Perry, Lawrence Kohlberg, Grant Wiggins, and many others who have attempted to create some system for classifying the kinds of learning we seek for our students. Here then, stark and unadorned, is what I will call Shulman's Table of Learning:

Engagement and Motivation
Knowledge and Understanding
Performance and Action
Reflection and Critique
Judgment and Design
Commitment and Identity

That's all there is. If you ask what comes after commitment and identity, I will suggest it is new engagements and motivations. Like the brave souls whose job it is to paint the Golden Gate Bridge, when you reach the end you return to the beginning. The table meets the mnemonic criterion of seven items plus or minus two, so it's a list you can probably remember without notes. It's also a list you can forget when forgetting, as I'll suggest later, is appropriate.

In a nutshell, the taxonomy makes the following assertion: Learning begins with student engagement, which in turn leads to knowledge and understanding. Once someone understands, he or she becomes capable of performance or action. Critical reflection on one's practice and understanding leads to higher-order thinking in the form of a capacity to exercise judgment in the face of uncertainty and to create designs in the presence of constraints and unpredictability. Ultimately, the exercise of judgment makes possible the development of commitment. In commitment, we become capable of professing our understandings and our values, our faith and our love, our skepticism and our doubts, internalizing those attributes and making them integral to our identities. These commitments, in turn, make new engagements possible—and even necessary.

THE ROOTS OF THIS WORK

About five years ago, when Russ Edgerton was serving as education officer for The Pew Charitable Trusts, he produced a terrific white paper, which has propelled many of the most interesting initiatives in higher education today. One of Russ's arguments focused on something he called "pedagogies of engagement"—approaches that have within them the capacity to engage students actively with learning in new ways. He wasn't talking only about service-learning, though service learning was an example; he was talking about an array of approaches, from problem-based and project-based learning to varieties of collaborative work and field-based instruction. Russ used the rubric "pedagogies of engagement" to describe them all.

For me, there was an intriguing ambiguity associated with Edgerton's phrase, and the claims implicit in it. Is engagement a means to an end, a proxy, or an end in itself? Are pedagogies of engagement a way to involve the minds, the hearts, the hands and feet, the passions and interests of students who are otherwise inclined to learn passively? Is the hallmark of these pedagogies the fact that they grab the student's interest? Or is their purpose not only to grab but to hold that interest, not only to entice but to instruct?

Or—a third possibility—did Edgerton intend to claim that engagement is a worthwhile end in itself, and that often an educator's responsibility is to make it possible for students to engage in experiences they would never otherwise have had? After all, we attend a chamber music concert as an end in itself, not as a means to some other end. These questions in response to Edgerton's discussion of pedagogies were one source of my thinking about the relationship between engagement and other dimensions of learning.

A second stimulus for the taxonomy was the study of professional education that The Carnegie Foundation is now undertaking, looking concurrently at preparation for law, engineering, teaching, and the clergy. One emerging theme in this work is that learning to be a professional isn't a purely intellectual endeavor. To become a professional, one must learn not only to think in certain ways but also to perform particular skills, and to practice or act in ways consistent with the norms, values, and conventions of the profession. Thus, to learn to be a lawyer, one needs to *think* like a lawyer, *perform* like a lawyer, and *act* like a lawyer.

Acting is more than knowing something or performing well; it seems to involve the development of a set of values, commitments, or internalized dispositions. It reminds me of what theological educators talk about as *formation*—the development of an identity that integrates one's capacities and dispositions to create a more generalized orientation to practice. Moreover, professionals cannot, in principle, learn all that they will need while they remain in school. Professional education must have at its core the concept of ongoing individual and collective learning, because the experiences of engaging, understanding, and acting must become the basis for subsequent learning and development.

These and other reflections about Carnegie's work on professional education triggered a "categorical imperative," and I responded by trying to invent a more ordered system, a table of learning or a taxonomy of educational ends.

WHAT ARE THE USES OF TAXONOMIES?

To answer this question, and to say something about the history and nature of taxonomies, I want to return to the work of Benjamin Bloom. What motivated Bloom and his colleagues to create taxonomies in the first place?

It was the late 1940s, and, partially in response to the needs of veterans returning from World War II eager to get a superb education, undergraduate liberal education was experiencing yet another renaissance (they occur rather regularly). "General education" was the mantra of the day, and it posed interesting problems for practitioners. One problem was that everyone agreed that general education should be about more than putting discrete items of knowledge into students' heads, that knowledge wasn't enough; the question was, "What more is there? Knowledge and *then what?*" Educators needed a language, a set of terms for making sense of the general education world.

About the same time, some campuses that were developing new general education programs made the very interesting decision to distinguish the roles of teacher, mentor, and instructor from those of evaluator, judge, and grader. The result was an arrangement such as I encountered as a student at the University of Chicago—the Examiner's Office, directed by Bloom, designed to develop assessments that would measure and evaluate how well students had learned what the general education program intended to teach.

The challenge was to ensure that what was assessed was compatible with what was taught. It made no sense at all to have instruction and assessment marching to different drummers (even though we now do that as a matter of public policy in K–12 and are in danger of doing so in postsecondary education). Educators needed a new language, a lexicon, to connect and align teaching and assessment. Bloom and his colleagues spent a number of years developing this common language, and because the concern for its existence was shared across institutions, dozens of institutions collaborated.

So what did this common language look like? Many educators across the world know the six categories of Bloom's *Taxonomy of Educational Objectives* by heart: knowledge, comprehension, application, analysis, synthesis, and evaluation. Complicating things further, Bloom recognized that the cognitive domain was only part of the picture, so, several years later, the *Affective Domain Taxonomy* was added by Krathwohl, Bloom, and Masia. It depicts how learners move from a willingness to receive an experience, to beginning to respond to it, to valuing what is taught, to organizing it within their larger set of values and attitudes, and ultimately to internalizing those values such that they no longer need an external stimulus to trigger the associated affective and emotional responses.

The Cognitive Taxonomy	The Affective Taxonomy
Knowledge	Receiving
Comprehension	Responding
Application	Valuing
Analysis	Organizing
Synthesis	Internalizing
Evaluation	

What can we learn from Bloom about the uses and perhaps abuses of taxonomies? One thing that happened is that the categories quickly became far more than rubrics for assessment. Taxonomies exist to classify and to clarify, but they also serve to guide and to goad. People rapidly began to use Bloom (and related schemes) as frameworks for designing courses and programs. They used the taxonomies to determine if they were putting too much emphasis on knowledge; if they were teaching for comprehension; if they were teaching for analysis or synthesis; if students at the end of a course were able to evaluate and make critical judgments about the relative value of alternative ways of making sense of the world.

Quickly, then, the taxonomies moved from being a scoring rubric and vehicle for communicating about test items, to being a heuristic for instructional design. (It's worth noting that although William Perry's model became as central to discussions of higher education and its goals as Bloom's has been in elementary and secondary education, the two literatures have developed quite independently.)

Moreover, we see that these heuristics are not value-free; indeed, they rapidly become ideologies, a form of collective conscience. Disciples of Bloom soon switched from asking, "Do we have the right balance between higher- and lower-order thinking in the design of our course?" to asking, "Shouldn't we be teaching more higher-order thinking?" A moral obligation to teach synthesis (not to mention evaluation) was created, and the taxonomies evolved from an ostensibly dispassionate framework into ideologies that had real, normative implications (though not necessarily bad ones). This is how taxonomies often work: They become ideologies. A taxonomy's rapid progression from analytic description to normative system—literally becoming a pedagogical conscience—warrants caution.

Another thing that happens to taxonomies, and it happened to Bloom's, is that they come to be understood as making a theoretical claim about sequentiality and hierarchy, suggesting that the only legitimate way to learn something is in *this particular order.* The implication of sequence and hierarchy within taxonomies obscures their true value, because taxonomies are not and should not be treated as theories. They are *certainly* not grand theories. At their best, they are what Robert Merton has called, coining a very useful concept, "theories of the middle range."

A theory of the middle range can be thought about in many ways: as an extended metaphor, a limited explanatory principle, or even a story. Thus, Bloom's cognitive taxonomy tells the story of education beginning with the acquisition by rote of facts that someone else has taught you and which you are only expected to reproduce or repeat. The story becomes more exciting as knowing matures into understanding and application, and then even more adventurous as ideas are subjected to analysis, as new ideas can be created and synthesized, and finally, at the highest level, as the learner becomes capable of judging and evaluating the truth or usefulness of the ideas themselves. That's the narrative version of Bloom's taxonomy.

Here then (I cannot resist) is a possible taxonomy (or is it a typology?) of the uses of taxonomies:

Uses of Taxonomies

Lexicon; working vocabulary; language
Classification (library, catalogue, Carnegie Classification)
Elements to be balanced (food groups; Boyer's scholarships)
Assessment and design framework; protocol for analysis
Middle-range theory
Master narrative
Mnemonic; checklist; heuristic
Ideology; conscience; moral code
Elements to be played with

A TABLE OF LEARNING: ELABORATING THE ELEMENTS

Now let us return to the Table of Learning, which I introduced earlier as a taxonomy of liberal and professional learning. What do its six elements mean, and how are they related?

The first item on the list, *engagement,* is one of the most interesting and important aspects of learning. We rarely paid enough attention to it in the past, but higher education is now much more focused on "active learning" and on evidence that students are engaged in worthwhile educational experiences. Indeed, it's interesting that one of the instruments receiving the most attention in the last couple of years has been the National Survey of Student Engagement (NSSE)—another product of Russ Edgerton's work at Pew and an intended antidote to the reputational ranking systems that many of us find so infuriating.

The argument NSSE makes is that we want to know about student engagement because it serves as a proxy for learning, understanding, and post-graduation commitments that we cannot measure very well directly, or that we would have to wait 20 years to measure. As noted earlier, however, I would argue that engagement is not solely a proxy; it can also be an end in itself. Our institutions of higher education are settings where students can encounter a range of people and ideas and human experiences that they have never been exposed to before. Engagement in this sense is not just a proxy for learning but a fundamental purpose of education.

Understanding is the category we spend most of our time as educators worrying about, as well we should. It includes knowledge, and it includes the ability to restate in one's own words the ideas learned from others. In fact, one way of putting it is to say that understanding means knowing the difference between paraphrase and plagiarism. It also means knowing when we can claim an understanding for ourselves, when we can claim an understanding of the work of those whose sources we acknowledge, and when we can say, "I didn't know this, but somebody else did and here it is." In contrast to knowledge and information, understanding connotes a form of ownership.

Next we come to *performance, practice,* or *action.* For me the difference between understanding and practice lies in the fact that acts of understanding are always based on what's in our heads. Even performances of understanding, such as writing an essay, are still about the ideas themselves. But as we move toward performance or practice we start to act in and on the world, to change things in it, and therefore a different set of consequences are associated with performance than with understanding.

We in the academy would love to believe that one can't practice or perform without first understanding. Alas, we all know that's not true (those of us who've raised children certainly know it's not true, neither for the raiser nor the raisee). During my decade of work on medical diagnosis, I studied gifted internists to understand how they made diagnostic judgments. A good friend, the Australian surgeon Ken Cox, came to me one day and said, "Lee, you're doing pioneering work on internists, trying to learn how their diagnoses lead to courses of action, but there's a big difference between internists and surgeons."

"Internists," he said, "make a diagnosis in order to act. Surgeons act in order to make a diagnosis." That may be a frightening thought for anyone facing surgery, but if you're wheeled into the emergency room with severe abdominal pain, and the physician treating you says he needs to do three days of tests before he acts, your family may want to begin saying their farewells to you. There are times when action is absolutely necessary in order to figure out what's going on, rather than waiting to figure out what's going on in order to act. My point is that the directionality of the taxonomy is situational; it isn't always the same. Practice may be the crucible in which understanding is tested, or in which commitment is affirmed; it's the pivot point, one might argue, around which most of education revolves.

I've already commented on the relationship between critical reflection and action. But let me add that the connection between *critical reflection* and action is in some ways a paradoxical one because in order to act in the most effective ways, we sometimes must cease action. Eleanor Ochs, an anthropologist, studied a team of physicists working on a large-scale collaborative research project. It was, she found, when they had to stop their research in order to prepare papers for a conference (which felt to them like an interruption) that they made important discoveries about how to move forward with the next stage of research. At The Carnegie Foundation, we often talk about our work as attempts to provide mirrors and lenses that can assist others to pause, reflect, and see their work differently as they move into a next stage of activity. Thus, action without reflection is unlikely to produce learning.

Judgment and design are like understanding—only different. They're what happens when understanding meets the constraints and complexities of a world with respect to which we can no longer say (as we might in a world of ideas alone), "all other things being equal...." When I design a home, I work within constraints of budget, terrain, and lifestyle of the person for whom I'm designing it. I'm limited, too, by codes and regulations of the county in which it's being built; a home will look different in a tectonically challenged part of the world like Palo Alto, California, as opposed to one that is challenged by tornadoes, like East Lansing, Michigan. Design is a matter of exercising understanding, as well as applying skills, under a variety of constraints and contingencies.

By the same token, when we're asked to exercise judgment—and I think this is why Bloom put evaluation so high on his taxonomy—we are being asked to take into consideration multiple factors and constantly to compare those factors to values and standards that may themselves be shifting, in order to make some evaluative judgment about quality, courses of action, or people. So, while judgment is like understanding, it's also *not* the same, and as educators, we need to go beyond teaching and assessing for understanding in order to foster judgment and design. Of course, the training of engineers is mostly about design, and education in areas like law, music, and art is often about judgment. There's much to be learned from these disciplines.

Finally, we come to *commitment*. As noted earlier, we experience commitment as we internalize values, develop character, and become people who no longer need to be goaded to behave in ethical, moral, or publicly responsible ways. We also commit ourselves to larger groups, larger communities, larger congregations, and professions at large—and by doing so, we make a statement that we take the values and principles of that group seriously enough to make them our own.

Therefore, commitment is both moving inward *and* connecting outward; it is the highest attainment an educated person can achieve, and it is also the most dangerous—I don't think I have to explain why, given the state of world affairs these days. An educated person, I would argue, is someone whose commitments always leave open a window for skeptical scrutiny, for imagining how it might be otherwise.

So, what does the Table of Learning look like with all of its elements working in concert, as a narrative? I proposed one for Bloom earlier, and here is mine.

Once upon a time someone was engaged in an experience of learning. And that engagement was so profound that it led to her understanding things she didn't understand before, and therefore gave her the capacity to practice and to act in the world in new ways. But once she starting acting in the world, she realized that action doesn't always work out the way you intend, so she had to start looking at what she was doing and the consequences of her actions. This meant re-examining her actions to see whether she might want to act differently.

Through that kind of reflection on her own performance and understanding, she became wiser and capable of making judgments and devising designs in situations that were progressively more uncertain. And as she did so, she began to internalize the values that she had been exposed to, at which point she was no longer merely engaged but truly committed. Those commitments, in turn, disposed her to seek out new engagements, which led (of course the story is a circle) to new understandings and practices....

Isn't that a lovely story? Well, we can tell a similar story using Perry's Model, Kohlberg's Stages of Moral Development, or the levels of Dante's Inferno (indeed, learning is what Dante's epic poem is all about). And again, these are not trivial narratives because they offer us coherent ways of thinking about why we do what we do, where we're coming from, and where we're going as educators.

What is important about these taxonomies is that they are indeed heuristics. They help us think more clearly about what we're doing, and they afford us a language through which we can exchange ideas and dilemmas. They point to the mutually interdependent facets of an educated person's life of mind, of emotion, and of action. They are powerful in these ways as long as we don't take them too seriously, as long as we don't transform mnemonic into dogma or heuristic into orthodoxy.

SHUFFLING THE DECK: PLAYING AT THE TABLE

One way to forestall premature hardening and misuse of the categories is to recognize from the beginning that there is no single "first stage." For example, while the Table of Learning lists *commitment* as the terminal stage of a sequence, the closing chapter of the narrative as it were, it's possible to imagine a situation in which commitment is itself the starting point for new learning.

Several years ago, I had the wonderful experience of visiting Messiah College as part of The Carnegie Foundation's work on moral and civic education. One thing that struck me was that Messiah's students arrive already committed. As a faith-based institution, the college naturally attracts students from religious families—students who are members of congregations and who already have a deep-seated set of commitments.

Our site-visit team talked to students about the goal of the first-year experience at Messiah, and they said, as with one voice, "The faculty is out to challenge our faith." And the reason, as our interviews with faculty made clear, is that students' prior commitments need to be exposed to the crucible of engagement with texts and people with different views. Only then, only through new engagements, can stronger commitments be formed. For Messiah, therefore, the table of learning might well look like this:

Commitment (to religious beliefs and practices)
Performance (of rituals and prosocial actions)
Engagement (with new texts and ideas)
Understanding (of new ideas and doubt of certainty)
Reflection (on tension between faith and "reason")
Judgment (deliberations, dialectics, debates)
New Commitment (to beliefs, practices, faith, and reason)
New engagements...

What's interesting is the cyclical quality of all this. Successfully committed people are more disposed to engage—they don't just sit home and feel committed (although that depends on whether it's an intransitive or transitive verb, doesn't it?). Commitment is a powerful stage in the learning process because it engenders new engagements, which in turn engender new understandings, and so forth (see Figure 1).

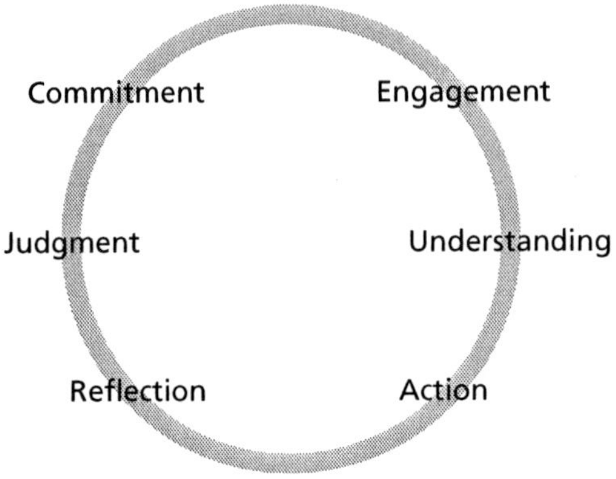

Commitment   Engagement

Judgment   Understanding

Reflection   Action

Figure 4.1.

If commitment and engagement have a potentially paired relationship with one another, might this be the case for other pairs as well? For example: How do we get understanding to lead to the capacity for judgment and design when the conditions under which understanding can be displayed become fuzzier, more variable, more ambiguous, less readily controlled? And how, once we have engendered in people the disposition to act in the world, do we get them to stop acting and step back in order to think about what they're doing? Figure 2 emphasizes those particular pairings within the cycle of learning.

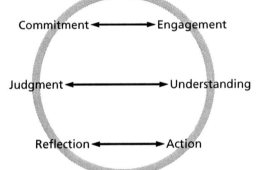

Commitment ←——→ Engagement

Judgment ←————→ Understanding

Reflection ←——→ Action

Figure 4.2.

Which leads me to another observation about these taxonomies, which is that taxonomies exist to be played with, not to be read devotionally. Let me give you an example of playing with a taxonomy (see Figure 3).

Figure 4.3.

What this version of the table suggests is that knowledge, understanding, analysis, and design each need, on the one hand, to be worked upon in a critical and reflective manner via judgment, and on the other hand, to be enacted in practice as a crucible or reality-test for the ideas. You may think of yet other ways to relate the central terms. My point is that once we feel comfortable with a set of terms, we can begin to play with them. They are, after all, propositions, and not received wisdom; they are ideas that become useful when we treat them seriously and yet with a bit of skepticism, disrespect, and playfulness—which, interestingly, is an attitude that we try to foster in our students, as well, with regard to much of what we teach them.

In short, I propose the Table of Learning not because it's theoretically valid or true—no taxonomy is—but because I find it practically and theoretically useful, conceptually robust, and fun. (My categories are evocative of the classic Greek standards of good architecture: commodity, firmness, and delight.) Having these terms and ideas in front of me, in a small enough number so that I can actually hold them in my mind (which gets harder as I get older), is helpful because they serve as a mnemonic, a heuristic, a way of helping me think about a wide range of educational conditions and situations.

I find the taxonomy valuable, as well, because I can use it to think not only about students but also about *institutions.* NSSE is relevant here again because it recognizes that engagement may apply not only to individual students but to their institutions. One now regularly hears the phrase "the engaged university." It rolls trippingly off the tongue, but it's important to begin defining more precisely what it means.

Is an engaged university one where certain patterns of engagements are characteristic of individuals or groups of students? Or is an engaged university one where students are highly motivated to engage with the texts and experiences that the institution deems valuable? Of course these are not mutually exclusive meanings. And one might ask the same question about other elements of the taxonomy. For example, what might it mean to be an "understanding university"?

With respect to "commitment," can we speak of an institution that matures from being merely engaged to one that is committed—and how would we know the difference? Here's one possible basis for knowing: If an institution becomes engaged because of its leadership and key people, from the president's office to the faculty, then what happens to the institution when those key people leave?

I might argue that at an engaged institution one would rapidly see a return to what was happening before, but at an institution that had moved from engagement to commitment, the culture of the place would remain changed. A committed institution's culture has been internalized in some fashion, so that even when the original perpetrators move on, the institution remains committed to continuing engagement. One of the great challenges for leadership is how to create this kind of committed institution, and it's one of the great challenges for us as teachers.

I can also use the Table of Learning to think about myself. A framework that leaves no room for describing the work of the person who created it should make us suspicious. This is what Merton meant when he talked about the need for theories to be "self-exemplifying." Similarly, Joseph Schwab, my teacher at the University of Chicago, once left us on a Friday with this little question: "And where is Plato on Plato's divided line? Where is Plato sitting in the cave when he is thinking about the cave?" It *killed* my entire weekend. And so the Table of Learning invites me to think about my own learning as a teacher and a scholar. Indeed, I would argue that it can, in some ways, serve as a model of faculty development across the career, reminding us that all education is continuing education.

ANTINOMIES AND THE CONCORDANCE OF OPPOSITES

Nancy Cantor and Steven Schomberg have written eloquently (in this issue) about their concept of education, and they pose a couple of intriguing antinomies. One is that undergraduate education involves a critical balance between playfulness and responsibility. On one hand, students come to our campuses to learn to play with ideas, which, paradoxically, means that they must take ideas seriously enough to consider playing with them. On the other hand, students come to our campuses to learn that education is also about developing a sense of obligation and responsibility to the society that will benefit from their capacity to play with ideas ever more creatively and insightfully. In a similar vein, they see the university as simultaneously a place apart—the ivory tower is needed because it's hard to play in the middle of Times Square—*and* a place connected to communities and to society.

As we look at our purposes for education, and at the taxonomies that aim to give language and shape to those purposes, we need to keep front and center our recognition of the contrasts, the tensions, the antinomies—

seeing them not as problems but as opportunities to define our roles. Engagement on the part of students is a goal, and we ought to stipulate it and measure it and take responsibility for it, but there are times and purposes for which we will instead seek *dis*engagement.

These are not contradictions; they are mutually supportive, compatible, and interdependent. We seek understanding for the pleasure and confidence it brings, and we seek puzzlement or self-conscious ignorance for the mental itching and scratching it engenders. We want students who will leave our institutions deeply committed to values and civic and moral responsibility; yet we must never forget that they must also be committed to skepticism and doubt. We foster the transformation of thought into action, but we also strive to educate for delay, self-criticism, and reflection. These equally important goals must be taught and assessed in ways that taxonomies, properly understood and used, can help us do in powerful ways.

A LOOK IN THE MIRROR

In the spirit of self-critical reflection, I want to conclude by expressing some misgivings I have about the elements that appear in the Table of Learning—and about what's missing. In particular, I'm sensitive to the potential or apparent absence of emotion, collaboration, and the centrality of trust.

Although engagement and commitment are certainly constructs intended to convey a strong component of emotion and feelings, I worry that the table as a whole feels overly cognitive. How might it be revised or interpreted to remind those who use it of the centrality of the emotions in the motivation to learn, the exercise of reason, and the development of character—all legitimate and necessary aspects of any vision of the well-educated person? This is something I will continue to think about.

The table may also seem to convey a strongly individual orientation. Yet engagement is often collaborative with others, and commitment frequently involves the development of, and membership in, communities. Moreover, the exercise of understanding, practice, reflection, and judgment or design is increasingly collaborative in character, drawing upon distributed expertise adroitly combined, rather than on the power of solo performances.

In both the emotional and collaborative aspects of learning, the development of trust becomes central. Learners must learn both to trust and to be worthy of trust. If learners are to employ their achievement of the goals of liberal and professional education to take on the responsibilities of leadership in a democratic community and society, their good judgment needs to be exercised in a context of trust and interdependence. Are these perspectives utterly missing in the table? Or are they embedded in the ideas, if only those who use them are conscious of them?

Taken together, these concerns about missing or under-emphasized features of the table remind us that although a taxonomy is not a theory, it shares many of the virtues and liabilities of theory. A system of categories is an attempt to simplify and order a complex and chaotic world. The unavoidable price of simplification is to make some views salient while others fade into the background. That is why all such systems need to be used with a combination of reverence and skepticism.

What then do I hope for this Table of Learning? I hope it will be useful precisely because its parts are so familiar. It offers us familiar blocks to rearrange, with its echoes of Bloom and Perry, of Krathwohl and Kohlberg. I hope that it will serve as a set of heuristics, as a stimulus for thinking about the design and evaluation of education, and as the basis for creative narratives about the learning process. Indeed, I hope it will variously contribute to all the functions I described earlier as the uses of taxonomies. I hope it will guide and inform both invention and critique. And I certainly hope that it will be used playfully rather than devotionally or dogmatically.

When speaking of the goals of science, Alfred North Whitehead once declared, "Seek generalizations—and distrust them!" In the same spirit, I urge you, "Seek taxonomies—and play with them!"

RESOURCES

Anderson, Lorin W., & David R. Krathwohl, Eds., *A Taxonomy for Learning, Teaching and Assessment: A Revision of Bloom's Taxonomy of Educational Objectives*, New York: Longman, 2001.

Anderson, Lorin W., & Lauren A. Sosniak, Eds., *Bloom's Taxonomy: A Forty-Year Retrospective, Ninety-third Yearbook of the National Society for the Study of Education*, Chicago: University of Chicago Press, 1994.

Bloom, B. S. and collaborators. (1956). *The Taxonomy of Educational Objectives: Cognitive Domain*. New York: David McKay.

Krathwohl, Davis R., Benjamin S. Bloom, and Bertram B. Masia, *Taxonomy of Educational Objectives: Affective Domain*. New York: David McKay, 1964.

"National Survey of Student Engagement: The College Student Report," www.indiana.edu/~nsse/

Perry, William G., Jr., *Forms of Intellectual and Ethical Growth During the College Years: A Scheme*. New York: Holt Rinehart and Winston, 1970.

Rhem, James, "Of Diagrams and Models: Learning as a Game of Pinball," *National Teaching and Learning Forum*, Vol. 11, No. 4, http://www.pitt .edu/AFShome/n/t/ntlforum/public/html/v11n4/diagrams.htm.

Wiggins, Grant, *Educative Assessment: Designing Assessments to Inform and Improve Performance*. San Francisco: Jossey-Bass, 1998.

CHAPTER 5

TEACHER QUALITY

Eric A. Hanushek

School reform is a topic on many people's minds today, and the air is full of advice and recommendations. Unlike many policy areas, the vast majority of people have strongly held opinions, mostly arising from their own personal experiences in school. As a result, much of policymaking involves walking a line between research findings and popular views.

Unfortunately, these popular views frequently are not the best guide for decision making.

This discussion begins with some evidence about the importance of teacher quality and moves to ideas about how the quality of teachers can be improved. Central to all of the discussion is the relationship between incentives and accountability. In simplest terms, if the objective is to improve student performance, student performance should be the focal point of policy.

From a policy perspective, although the proper role for different levels of government has been controversial, I believe that there are important things to be done by the federal government. These things are, nonetheless, quite different from both the current activities and many of the things that are being discussed.

Talented Teachers: The Essential Force for Improving Student Achievement, pages 115–123
Copyright © 2004 by Information Age Publishing
All rights of reproduction in any form reserved.

THE IMPORTANCE OF TEACHER QUALITY

Starting with the Coleman Report, the monumental investigation in 1966 by the Office of Education, many have argued that schools do not matter and that only families and peers affect performance. Part of this view is true, and part is quite wrong. This report was the most extensive investigation of schools *ever* undertaken. Unfortunately, that report and subsequent interpretations of it have generally confused "measurability" with true effects. Specifically, characteristics of schools and classrooms, like the teacher having a master's degree or the class size being small, did not show any effect on student performance—leading to the conclusion that schools do not matter. This conclusion, probably more than anything else, led to a prevailing view that differences among schools are not very important.

The extensive research over the past 35 years has led to two clear conclusions. First, there are very important differences among teachers. This finding, of course, does not surprise many parents, who are well aware of quality differences of teachers. Second, these differences are not captured by common measures of teachers (qualifications, experience, and the like). This latter finding has important implications that I sketch below.

The magnitude of differences in teachers is impressive. Let me provide two different indications of teacher quality. For these measures I use a simple definition of teacher quality: good teachers are ones who get large gains in student achievement for their classes; bad teachers are just the opposite.

Looking at the range of quality for teachers within a single large urban district, teachers near the top of the quality distribution can get an entire year's worth of additional learning out of their students compared to those near the bottom. That is, a good teacher will get a gain of one and a half grade-level equivalents, whereas a bad teacher will get a gain of only half a year for a single academic year. Alternatively, if we look at just the variations in performance resulting from differences in teacher quality within a typical school, then moving from an average teacher to one at the 85th percentile of teacher quality would imply that the better teacher's students would move up more than 7 percentile rankings in the year.

We can also return to the popular argument that family background is overwhelmingly important and that schools cannot be expected to make up for bad preparation from home. The latter estimates of teacher performance suggest that having three years of good teachers (85th percentile) in a row would overcome the average achievement deficit between low-income kids (those on free or reduced-price lunch) and others. In other words, high quality teachers can make up for the typical deficits that we see in the preparation of kids from disadvantaged backgrounds.

Unfortunately, the current school system does not ensure any streaks of such high-quality teachers. In fact, it is currently as likely that the typical student gets a run of bad teachers—with the symmetric achievement losses—as a run of good teachers. Altering this situation is the school policy issue, in my mind.

CERTIFICATION AND OTHER CENTRAL APPROACHES TO QUALITY

In recognition of the importance of quality teachers, a variety of recommendations and policy initiatives have been introduced.

Unfortunately, the currently most popular ones are likely to lower teacher quality rather than improve it.

The idea that has been picked up by policymakers at all levels is to increase the requirements to become a teacher.

The idea is simple: if we can insist on better prepared and more able teachers, teacher quality will necessarily rise and student performance will respond. This argument—at least as implemented—proves as incorrect as it is simple.

The range of options being pushed forward include raising the coursework requirement for teacher certification, testing teachers on either general or specific knowledge, requiring specific kinds of undergraduate degrees, and requiring master's degrees. Each of these has surface plausibility, but little evidence exists to suggest that these are strongly related to teacher quality and to student achievement.

More pernicious, these requirements almost certainly act to reduce the supply of teachers. In other words, the proposed requirements do little or nothing to ensure high quality teachers, and at the same time, they cut down on the number of people who might enter teaching. Teacher certification requirements are generally promoted as ensuring that there is a floor on quality, but if they end up keeping out high-quality teachers who do not want to take the specific required courses, such requirements act more like a ceiling on quality.

The story on teacher certification initiatives is actually just a special case of a larger set of misguided policies that go under the name "input policies." These are attempts to specify pieces of the educational process. The recent craze for lowering class size—two years in a row the federal budget was held up until agreement could be reached on federal funding for hiring new teachers so that class sizes could be reduced—is the clearest example of an input policy: a variety of motivations have pushed this policy, which has little chance of success in terms of student achievement. This actually typifies the most common kinds of policies that we have been undertaking for the last three decades at least.

The Evidence on Inputs

The evidence on each of the input policy issues comes from a variety of sources but is very consistent. The simplest version is that we have been pursuing these policies for decades, and they have not worked. Table 1 shows the pattern of resources devoted to U.S. education since 1960. There have been dramatic increases in just the resources that people today advocate supplying.

Table 5.1.   Public School Resources in the United States, 1960–1995

Resource	Pupil–teacher ratio	Percentage of teachers with master's or other higher degree	Median years of teacher experience	Current expenditure/ADA (1996–1997 dollars)
1960	25.8	23.5	11	$2,122
1970	22.3	27.5	8	$3,645
1980	18.7	49.6	12	$4,589
1990	17.2	53.1	15	$6,239
1995	17.3	56.2	15	$6,434

If we concentrate on the period of 1970 through 1995 (because we have student performance measures for a comparable period), we see that pupil–teacher ratios have fallen by close to a quarter, the number of teachers master's degrees has more than doubled, and median teacher experience has almost doubled. Because each of these inputs costs more, average real spending per pupil has increased by more than 75 percent, that is, by three-quarters after allowing for inflation. But if we look at student performance on the National Assessment of Educational Progress, we see that performance is virtually unchanged in math and reading and has fallen in science. This is hardly what the proponents of increased resources suggest should have happened.

This evidence on resources and performance is supported by detailed econometric studies. These statistical analyses of what goes on in the classroom provide little reason to believe that input policies will systematically improve student outcomes.

While some studies suggest positive relationships with added resources, they are balanced by studies that actually show negative relationships. The existence of some positive findings allows advocates of specific policies to point to highly selective evidence supporting their cause, but it does not make for a different reality.

Similarly, with the recent push for class-size reduction, considerable attention has been focused on the Tennessee experiment of the 1980s,

Project STAR. A much larger amount of uncertainty surrounds the evidence from this than most advocates want to acknowledge. Without going too far afield here, suffice it to say that Project STAR has been hugely overinterpreted. The clearest indication from this experiment is that very large reductions in class size (from 23 to 15) lead to small effects on student performance in kindergarten—hardly the evidence needed to support small reductions in class size at all grade levels.

The Policy Implications

It is important to understand how pursuing the conventional input policies could actually hurt the situation. As pointed out, increasing the requirements for teacher certification could limit the supply of potential teachers and could thereby actually lower the quality of the typical teacher who ends up in the classroom. Similarly, lowering class size could hurt in two ways. First, it is very expensive, so it absorbs funds that could be applied to productive policies. Second, it expands the demand for teachers and can lower student achievement if the quality of new teachers ends up lower.

Note, however, that we do not know much about the overall effects. The California class-size-reduction policy of 1997 indeed drew in more teachers who were not fully certified, but whether they were lower quality is unclear because certification is not closely related to effective performance in the classroom.

The generic issue is whether or not higher levels of government can effectively improve schools through uniform funding or with rules for how education is to be conducted in local schools. Here the evidence is quite clear.

We do not know how to identify a well-defined set of inputs that is either necessary or sufficient for ensuring high-quality schooling. Finding such a set has been the Holy Grail of education research, and the search has been quite unsuccessful. Indeed, I do not believe that it is an issue of just needing more or better research. I simply do not think that we will identify (at least within our lifetimes) such a set with any clarity. I believe that the educational process is much too complicated for us to uncover a small set of criteria that are amenable to central legislation and control.

The evidence also underscores an aspect of the policymaking problem. Class-size reductions have been politically very popular. The federal government was merely mimicking the popular 1997 actions of the state of California. A large part of the political sentiment emanates from the commonsense arguments that persuade the general public that these are sensible policies. They just conflict with the evidence. And they imply that the policymaker must deal with political problems as well as policy problems.

PERFORMANCE INCENTIVES— AN ATTRACTIVE ALTERNATIVE

The simple position taken here is: *if one is concerned about student perfor-mance, one should gear policy to student performance.*

Perhaps the largest problem with the current organization of schools is that nobody's job or career is closely related to student performance. Relat-edly, popular input policies do nothing to change the structure of incen-tives. The key to effective policy is turning to performance incentives for teachers and other school personnel.

This is not to say that teachers or other school personnel are currently misbehaving. I personally think that most teachers are very hard working and that the vast majority are trying to do the best they can in the class-room. It is simply a statement that they are responding to the incentives that are placed in front of them (just as we all do). So when various deci-sions are being made, such as how to deal with added resources, the deci-sions may or may not be directed at the use that would maximize student learning. Instead, they might be directed at things that are publicly popu-lar or things that make the decision makers' job easier or more pleasant.

The problem that goes along with this position statement is that we do not know the best way to structure incentives.

We have not tried many performance incentive systems, so we have very little experience with or evidence from them. A variety of approaches have been suggested and have conceptual appeal: merit pay for teachers, rewards to high performing schools, and various forms of choice, includ-ing charter schools, tax rebates, and vouchers. Although evidence is slowly accumulating, the range of experiences is very limited.

There are nonetheless some things that we are quite certain about in the design of incentive structures.

Accountability and Value Added

One reason for general teacher resistance to incentive systems like merit pay is concern about what is being rewarded.

We know that families make a huge difference in the education of stu-dents. An implication of this is that we should not reward or punish teach-ers for the education they are not responsible for. If some students come to school better prepared than others, their teachers should not receive extra rewards. Similarly, if students come from disadvantaged back-grounds that leave them less well-prepared for school, we should not pun-ish their teachers.

We want to reward teachers for what they add to a student's learning, that is, for their value added to the education of the child. Rewards should be geared to what teachers control, not to the specific group of students that they are given.

Pursuing this approach requires an aggressive system of performance measurement. We have to be able to track the progress of individual students, and we have to be able to relate this progress to the teachers who are responsible for it.

This does not necessarily mean that we want a system of individual rewards as opposed to group rewards for teachers in a school, but it does mean that we have to accurately measure the performance of schools. This area—designing accountability systems—is an obvious area for federal leadership (although not necessarily for federal control).

Local Decision Making

It is also almost inconceivable that we could run a good performance incentive system from the national capital or even a state capital. If we try to devise the one best system and force it on local districts and schools, we will almost certainly fail. This statement really bites strongest when thinking about the limits of the federal government.

Whereas the federal government can help provide funding for and guidance on the use of performance incentives, it is not in a good position to determine the "how" of the performance incentives.

At the same time, we should not simply assume that local districts and schools are currently able to make good decisions. Personnel have not now been chosen for their ability to operate and manage different incentive systems. And, as mentioned, we do not have sufficient experience to provide any detailed guidance. Nonetheless, preparing local officials for performing these tasks is where we should be headed.

Neither should we assume that all policies that emphasize student outcomes and that provide performance incentives are altogether good. The design of incentives is complicated because many incentive structures lead to unintended and undesirable consequences. For example, if a move to broaden school choice led to complete racial or economic segregation in the schools, we would not think that it was a desirable policy. Therefore, we need to develop more experience with incentives and to evaluate these experiences. With incentive systems, the details generally prove to be critical.

LEARNING ABOUT INCENTIVES

In my opinion, one of the largest problems with education policy is that we never learn much from the policies we put into place. In fact, we frequently make policy decisions in ways that defy *ever* learning about their effects. The California class size initiative is a good example. All districts in the same state were simultaneously given financial incentives to reduce class size. Thus, even if one looks at student performance around the state, it is not possible to see what would happen in the absence of these incentives. Similarly, England recently introduced a broad policy of merit pay for teachers, but they did it everywhere at once. If student performance changes, is it because of the new incentives or because of other factors?

I realize that it is not the kind of policy that brings immediate political gratification, but I believe that nothing would have a more powerful influence on student performance ten years from now than a broad program of educational experimentation.

The parallel with medicine is painfully obvious.

In medicine, we are willing to admit that we do not know everything about different procedures or therapies, and we conduct random-assignment controlled experiments to identify the effectiveness of different approaches. The results of this on the overall health of our population are clear and obvious.

We also have a long history of social experimentation in health, welfare, and housing. We have learned an enormous amount over time that has helped to improve public policies. Nothing similar has occurred in education.

Experimentation and evaluation are legitimate federal roles. All states learn from these efforts, and no state takes into account the fact that evaluation results are useful to others. Without federal involvement there is likely to be too little investment in evaluation and knowledge production.

Let me emphasize, however, that federal information collection is not the same as federal control of the schools, and there is no reason to expect that more centralized decision making would result from the federal government taking on a leadership role.

The problem, of course, is that experimentation and educational evaluation are not policies with mass appeal.

Nonetheless, if we are to weed out bad policies and replace them with good policies, we need to accumulate evidence about performance.

CONCLUSIONS

Let me summarize.

1. Teacher quality is the key to improved schools.
2. Teacher quality cannot be readily linked to teacher characteristics; therefore, new and more extensive certification and training standards are unlikely to be effective.
3. Policies aimed at student performance instead of inputs offer the only real hope for improvement. Input policies, even though frequently popular, need to be resisted. At the same time, developing good accountability systems is central, and the federal government can provide leadership (without nationalizing the process).
4. The federal government should limit its role to concerns of equity and of knowledge and should not attempt to act like a local school board. At the same time, the federal government should require performance for funds it disperses, such as the Title 1 funds that aid the education of disadvantaged students.
5. Developing improved policy requires better information about what works, and the most effective way of accumulating this evidence is the design of systematic experiments and evaluation.

CHAPTER 6

INCENTIVIZED SCHOOL STANDARDS WORK

Herbert J. Walberg

Most economists, psychologists, and lay people think humans respond to significant incentives. Parents, managers, and others responsible for improving performance routinely use incentives to encourage desirable behavior. The lure of the top ranks in competitive sports attracts immense energies of youths and adults, whether players or spectators. Standards with incentives also work in universities: Because they expect later compensation in money and prestige, ambitious college students strive for admission to the top professional schools of business, law, and medicine. Faculty raises in most (nonunionized) universities depend on teaching, research, and service.

In the ideal world of Jean Jacques Rousseau and many romantic educators, "intrinsic motivation" would reign. Instead of responding to incentives, we would accomplish things when the mood strikes. We would only do things worth doing as ends in themselves—not to attain further ends such as money, prestige, or altruistic contributions.

The real world, though, usually provides standards and incentives for doing well. Good music, mathematics, and team playing require long, disciplined practice. Steady pursuit, however, can lead not only to noble accomplishments but also to deep satisfactions and financial and other

Talented Teachers: The Essential Force for Improving Student Achievement, pages 125–129
Copyright © 2004 by Information Age Publishing
All rights of reproduction in any form reserved.

As first appeared in *Education Week* [November 4, 1998]. Reprinted with permission from the author.

rewards. Top performance in many fields often appears to require a decade of 70-hour weeks.

Yet, schools—the very institutions that should academically prepare young people for doing well in adult life—make little use of effective incentives for accomplishments. School boards and administrators, for example, rarely measure and reward teachers' individual performance. Unions prevail in contracts that require paying public school teachers according to their degrees and years of experience, neither of which affects how much their students learn. After decades of declining union membership in other sectors, schools remain one of the few institutions that provide no merit incentives or even recognition for their workforce.

STUDENT INCENTIVES

As they themselves agree, moreover, students also lack standards and incentives. A 1996 Public Agenda national survey of high school students showed that three-fourths believe stiffer examinations and graduation requirements would make students pay more attention to their studies. Three-fourths also said students who have not mastered English should not graduate, and a similar percentage said schools should promote only students who master the material. Almost two-thirds reported they could do much better in school if they tried. Nearly 80 percent said students would learn more if schools made sure they were on time and did their homework. More than 70 percent said schools should require after-school classes for those earning D's and F's.

In these respects, many teacher-educators differ sharply from students and the public. A 1997 Public Agenda survey of education professors showed that 64 percent think schools should avoid competition. More favored giving grades for team efforts than did those who favored grading individual accomplishments.

Teacher-educators also differ from other employers and other professions on measuring standards or even employing them at all. Employers use standardized multiple-choice examinations for hiring. So do selective colleges, graduate schools, and professional schools for admission decisions. Such examinations are required in law, medicine, and other fields for licensing because they are objective and reliable. But 78 percent of teacher-educators wanted less reliance on them.

Though not all incentives are monetary, rational people require reasons to work hard.

Nearly two-thirds of teacher-educators admitted that education programs often fail to prepare candidates for teaching in the real world, and only 4 percent reported that their programs typically dismiss students found unsuitable for teaching. Thus, even starting with their undergraduate education, many prospective educators are laden with anti-competitive ideas against standards and incentives.

Seventy-nine percent of the teacher-educators agreed that "the general public has outmoded and mistaken beliefs about what good teaching means." They apparently forgot that citizens, who pay for schools, constitute their ultimate clients. Perhaps the public and students are right. It seems a good time to raise the question whether incentivized standards can work in schools as they do in much of the rest of society.

CAN INCENTIVES WORK IN SCHOOLS?

I recently carried out a follow-up study of what is to my knowledge the first clear-cut, large-scale trial of monetary incentives for public school students—the Advanced Placement Incentive Program, initiated by the O'Donnell Foundation of Dallas. The program made use of the Advanced Placement examinations, the only national tests that provide external, objective, and rigorous standards for high school students. Over half a million high school students take AP exams on the content of more than 25 college-level courses. Over 2,500 colleges grant course credit for passing grades, allowing students to graduate early or take more advanced college courses.

The foundation began the incentive program in response to widely voiced concerns about poor academic performance in Texas, a state becoming less dependent on agriculture and oil and competing with other states and nations in increasingly technical industries. Yet, of the typical 100 Texas students who entered kindergarten in 1981, only 72 graduated from high school in 1994. Only 36 of the original 100 entered higher education, and only 18 were expected to finish college in 1998. Test scores for students in the Dallas Independent School District, where the trial took place, were lower than elsewhere, and African-American and Hispanic students showed large disparities in academic performance.

Beginning with the 1990–91 school year, the incentive program paid students $100 for each passing score on the Advanced Placement examinations in English, calculus, statistics, computer science, biology, chemistry, and physics, plus a reimbursement for the cost of taking the exam. The program also provided a $2,500 stipend to each teacher undergoing training to teach advanced courses in those subjects. They also received $100 for each passing AP examination score of their students.

In the nine participating Dallas schools, sharply increasing numbers of boys and girls of all major ethnic groups took and passed the AP exams. The number rose more than 12-fold, from 41 the year before the program began to 521 when it ended in 1994–95. After terminating, the program continued to have carryover effects: In the 1996–97 school year, two years after the program ended, 442 students passed, about 11 times more than the number in the year before the program began.

Though these numbers speak for themselves, interviews with students, teachers, and college admission officers revealed high regard for the incentive program. They felt that even students who failed AP exams learned better study habits and the importance of hard work to meet high standards.

In addition, the program had other benefits: Students could take more advanced courses in college. Those who passed a sufficient number of AP courses could graduate from college early, which saves their families tuition and taxpayers subsidies. Those who passed AP courses also had a better chance for merit scholarships and entry into selective colleges.

The AP incentive program shows that standards and incentives work in schools as they do in many other spheres of life. The lack of incentives in school seems an important reason why students find academics so boring and sports so exciting. Social promotion and graduating students for mere attendance is insufficient. Nor can paying teachers for their years of experience bring out their best. Though not all incentives are monetary, rational people require reasons to work hard.

WHAT IS TO BE DONE?

This experiment and common sense suggest that we try further incentives and evaluate the results. Several possibilities are intriguing. The O'Donnell Foundation, for example, demonstrated that incentives work for English, mathematics, statistics, and science courses. Would incentives work for AP exams in history, foreign languages, and other subjects?

Business and factory managers often complain about the poor quality of high school graduates but rarely review the high school records of prospective employees. Would paying starting-wage premiums for those with superior grades and test scores encourage better workforce preparedness?

Citizens and state legislators are disappointed with the poor results of expensive educational reforms. Would incentives work better? Would, for example, merit scholarships and reduced college tuition for students who pass rigorous examinations improve the quality and productivity of state education systems? Would state funded incentives encourage students to take rigorous high school courses and graduate from college early, and thereby save tuition and tax funds?

Should school boards and administrators inform themselves of the achievement gains of each teacher's and each school's students in conducting performance reviews? Should students at poorly achieving schools be free to go elsewhere? Should state and local funds follow them to the public and private schools of their choice? Would such induced competition cause poorly achieving schools to improve or close?

Congress has spent more than $150 billion of citizens' monies on categorical education programs. Evaluations often show that students in these programs do no better and sometimes worse than comparable unserved students. Title I for poor children, for example, employs no incentives for educators or students to do well. Bilingual and special education programs employ perverse incentives, in essence paying districts to expand the numbers of students with poorly diagnosed English deficits and psychological pathologies while segregating them from others. What if good or improved performance was the standard for payment?

NOTE

Herbert J. Walberg is a research professor of education and psychology at the University of Illinois at Chicago.

Part III

DOES CERTIFIED OR ALTERNATIVELY CERTIFIED MEAN QUALIFIED?

CHAPTER 7

DOES CERTIFIED OR ALTERNATIVELY CERTIFIED MEAN QUALIFIED?

LEWIS C. SOLMON, MICHAEL PODGURSKY, AND ARTHUR E. WISE

Welcome to the session, "Does Certified or Alternatively Certified Mean Qualified?" This deals with a part of the No Child Left Behind Act that has always been confusing.

In education terms, "certified," "licensed," "credentialed," and even "qualified," are commonly used interchangeably. However, "licensed" actually means "official or legal permission to do something," and "certified" means "guaranteed to have met a standard." In education, all these terms are used basically to mean "to have permission to teach." Uncertified teachers are hired, usually out of desperation, but they generally have to become certified within a relatively short period of time.

Milton Friedman some time ago had a different categorization. He said there are three levels. One is registration, which means you just sign up to do something and that's basically to keep track of people. You'd have gun registration or taxi cab driver registration so you will know who's doing it, and maybe to prevent certain people from doing it. Then there is certification when a government agency certifies that a person has certain skills. According to Friedman's categorization, lack of certification does not preclude you from practicing, but you may have a Good Housekeeping seal of approval or not, and people could choose to go to you or not.

Talented Teachers: The Essential Force for Improving Student Achievement, pages 133–160
Copyright © 2004 by Information Age Publishing
All rights of reproduction in any form reserved.

Finally, licensing is when you need permission from some authority to engage in the occupation. But these three levels get confused in education. For teaching, obviously, every teacher has to get a license, either by traditional or alternative means, but she can start without a license. The debate here is whether or not traditional licensing, the preparation of which comes traditionally from education schools, generally leads to higher quality teachers, and is more likely to do so than a relatively unregulated system that probably would make licenses, or permission to teach, more available and less restrictive.

To argue this point about the value of certification and the congruence of certification with qualification, we have two of our nation's most distinguished policy analysts, both of whom have spent a great deal of time thinking about this question. Michael Podgursky is Middlebush Professor of Economics and Chairman of the Department of Economics at the University of Missouri, Columbia. He has published numerous articles and reports on education policy and teacher quality, and co-authored a book, *Teacher Pay and Teacher Quality*.

Mike has been supported by grants from almost every agency in Washington and many private foundations and state government agencies as well. He is a member of the Board of the National Center for Teacher Quality, and the American Board for Certification of Teacher Excellence. Before Missouri, he taught from 1980 to 1995 at the University of Massachusetts, Amherst. His degrees are from the University of Missouri and the University of Wisconsin, Madison.

Arthur Wise is president of the National Council for Accreditation of Teacher Education (NCATE) in Washington, D.C. Throughout his career, he has advanced education on a number of fronts, including teacher quality and professionalism, school finance, and educational research. He first came to prominence in 1968 with his book, *Rich Schools, Poor Schools, the Promise of Equal Educational Opportunity*.

Art has long been active in federal education policy and helped create the U.S. Department of Education in the late 1970s. He is the former director of the RAND Corporation's Center for the Study of the Teaching Profession. He has been central in proposing new policies and reforms in education, including teacher licensing and teacher evaluation. At NCATE, he has directed the design of performance-based accreditation and led efforts to develop a system of quality assurance for the teaching profession.

Michael Podgursky

I'm going to talk briefly about an economist's perspective on teacher licensing. I'd like to talk about three things here, starting with the research on this issue. However, before we talk about the research, I would like to try to convince you of a couple points that I think are pretty uncontroversial in the research community. If you are going to look at the effects of teachers on student achievement in terms of research methodology, your studies have to have random assignment or good control for prior student achievement. As an example of the former, you have teachers with a certain kind of teaching credential, and another group with a different kind of teaching credential, and you randomly assign students to one or the other type of teachers. This is the gold standard of research. There are no studies I am aware of on teacher licensing that meet this standard, although there are some under way. Mathematica, for example, is running a very interesting study on "Teach For America," and on alternate certification, and there are a few others in the works. Russ Whitehurst at the U.S. Department of Educations's Institute for Education Sciences is really pushing this model. I think in a few years, we are going to have some good random assignment studies in this area, but at this point we really do not have anything.

The second approach is nonexperimental research, in which you control for prior student achievement. If you are going to look at the contribution of a teacher in a particular year, since a lot of the kids are coming into class in the fall with varying levels of ability, you need to take account of where the kids are starting from, that is, look at value-added. This type of analysis is seen in some studies today. Now, if you ask how many studies that examine certification of some type or another, alternate certification versus full, meet this standard, the answer is you can count them on one hand, in fact on less than one hand. So there's very little research on certification that meets this standard for research. And the evidence here is very mixed.

Let me show you why it's very important to be able to control for prior achievement when looking at the effects of teachers. I didn't have individual-level student achievement data, so I took some aggregated data from California, and looked at fifth-grade math. The kids are tested every year in California, so I simply regressed grade five's scores on their Standardized Testing and Reporting (STAR) results, on the percent of teachers that didn't have clear certification, or preliminary certification. The result is on Chart 7.1. For every one percentage point increase in the proportion of uncertified teachers, it lowers the measure of student achievement by .21 percentage points. If you control for free and reduced-price lunch percent at the school, you get a dramatic reduction in this impact. We know a lot of these uncertified teachers are at high-poverty schools, so even with a crude measure of family background, like free and reduced-price lunch, the certification effects are dramatically reduced.

But free and reduced-price lunch is only a very crude measure of family income. When you go to a school that's 100% free and reduced-price lunch, there's a wide variation of family resources available. Some of the

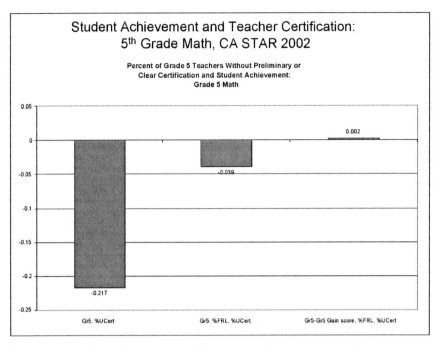

Chart 7.1.   Student achievement and teacher certification: 5th grade math, CA STAR 2002.

families are intact and supportive, but the father has recently been laid off and they're collecting food stamps; whereas in others, the parents may be absent or are homeless. By the same token, people who aren't free and reduced eligible, for example, your taxi driver from the airport and your radiologist, are lumped together. So it's a very inadequate measure, but even with that you get this dramatic reduction in the statistical association.

If you look at gain scores though, the relationship actually flips, and it goes to zero, and actually turns slightly positive, that is, a higher percentage of uncertified teachers is associated with slightly *higher* test scores. But the effect is practically zero, for all practical purposes. So the point is, the way you look at the effects of performance of schools and teachers is very sensitive to looking at gains. The story will frequently change when you shift from looking at absolute levels to achievement gains, but the latter is the more accurate way to estimate the effect of teachers on student learning.

If this research is ambiguous, does this mean teachers don't matter? No, it doesn't at all. Here we have to distinguish between *measured* and *unmeasured* teacher characteristics, and as many of you are aware, there's growing literature out there that points to the importance of teachers and teacher effects. Bill Sanders started this in Tennessee, but there are quite a few other studies now bubbling up out there, pointing to the fact that there's a lot of variation in classroom effects, and what we think are "teacher effects."

However, classroom and teacher effects are not correlated with measurable teacher characteristics. In a very impressive study of Chicago students and teachers that's making the rounds, over 95% of the variation in these teacher effects was unexplained by any measurable teacher characteristics—master's degrees, experience, college attended, and so on. Basically the best case you're going to make at this point, with the research we have, is that you've got a large dispersion in teacher effects and small differences associated with any measured teacher characteristic such as certification. This is illustrated in Chart 7.2. If we think of these as teacher effects on student performance, basically you've got small differences in the means, so the right distribution is certified, the left is uncertified. This is the best you're going to find with the current literature. But there's a tremendous dispersion within each of the groups.

Now this is what can help illustrate an economist's idea of the cost and benefit of teacher licensing. The mandatory certification requirement says you can never hire an uncertified teacher, if a certified teacher is available. So, what are the costs and benefits of that? The benefit might be you get

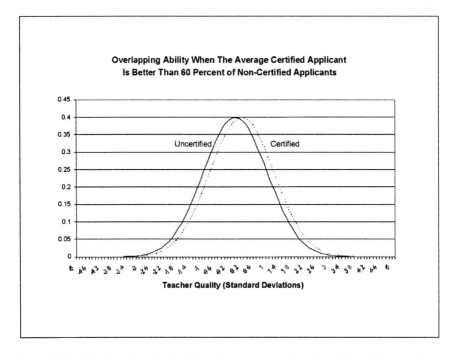

Chart 7.2.   Overlapping ability when the average certified applicant is better than 60 percent of non-certified applicants.

this small gain in the mean, but the cost is that you can only look at the uncertified people when there's no certified person available, however low their quality. And that's part of the cost here: in an applicant pool, it's not going to be uncommon for some of your best candidates to be the uncertified ones. What the law is saying is that an employer can't even look at them, forget hiring. Of course, depending on what No Child Left Behind does, you may never be able to hire them.

To make it a little more concrete, it's as if my dean (my boss is my dean) told me we know that grad students from the top 20 economics departments, are, on average, better quality than 21 and below. Then if my dean told me, "Podgursky, you can never hire anyone unless they're from a top 20 program," that's really a dumb policy; it has a cost. It may actually be that someone from the 23rd- or 24th-ranked program in my applicant pool is the best candidate. But I can't even look at them under this kind of a regime.

If the research evidence really is weak here, and I believe it is, then the second line of argument I run into in this area is the following. Would you send your child to an unlicensed doctor? This is the argument by analogy. I think there are a lot of problems with this argument. In fact, I think we could spend two hours talking about why teaching is not medicine. But the one thing I'll just zero in on here is that we don't see a lot of people practicing unlicensed neurosurgery. If you step back out of K–12 a moment, we see an awful lot of unlicensed teaching going on in our economy. These hotels, when we're not here, are filled with business conventions where training is going on. The business community makes hundreds of millions of dollars of investments in training our workforce. And most of that training is done by practitioners who aren't licensed. The military has, for a long time, been an important source of training in our economy, again, most of it conducted by unlicensed individuals.

Private K–12 education makes extensive use of unlicensed teachers, particularly at the secondary level and consider higher education. I'm not licensed as a professor in higher education (and many would say my students suffer as a result). But if you look at community colleges, which are basically doing what high schools should have been doing—there is an awful lot of remedial work going on—you will find unlicensed teachers.

Finally, the faculty at education schools aren't licensed. So we have a sense that the licensing regime and public K–12 is sort of like a little iceberg in this wide sea of unlicensed practice. The point here, in terms of thinking about school reform, is that this is a tremendous potential pool of (unlicensed) talent to draw upon for public K–12 education, and I think we're seeing evidence of that in many states.

The next line of criticism I've encountered concerns teacher turnover. Chart 7.3 shows a long quote from the latest report of the National Com-

If we know that high quality teaching makes a difference, why isn't every child in America getting it? The conventional wisdom is that we lack enough good teachers. But, the conventional wisdom is wrong. *The real school staffing problem is teacher retention.* Our inability to support high quality teaching in many of our schools is driven not by too few teachers entering the profession, but too many leaving it for other jobs. The ability to create and maintain a quality teaching and learning environment in a school is limited not by teacher supply, but by high turnover among teachers who are already there...

National Commission on Teaching and America's Future
No Dream Denied: A Pledge to America's Children. 2003

Chart 7.3.

mission on Teaching and America's Future. The whole thrust of the new report is that the real school staffing problem is teacher retention. We have a new crisis, teacher retention. There is some evidence that people coming in who are from nontraditional routes may have somewhat higher turnover. Actually, it's really quite mixed. Here in California, the evidence on the intern program suggests that their retention is about as high as traditional programs. Texas, which runs a big alternate certification program, seems to have very high retention too, but the commission reports some evidence suggesting folks who go through traditional programs have lower turnover.

However, in regards to this whole question of teacher turnover, we're reacting to a problem that's over. We're reacting to what I call the *Perfect Storm.* Basically the teacher turnover situation in the late 1990s had everything coming together to produce these giant waves, everything goes wrong at once, and you've got the perfect storm. Well I think the late 1990s, with regard to teacher turnover, were truly exceptional, and we're really not going to see a turnover situation like that in our professional lifetimes again in all likelihood.

If you look at Chart 7.4 you will see that three things were going on. First, we were in a period in the late 1990s that can only be described as a

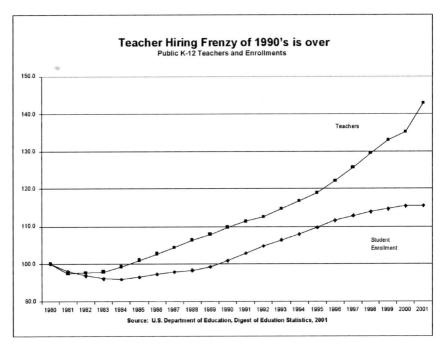

Chart 7.4.   Teacher hiring frenzy of 1990s is over.

teacher-hiring frenzy. Student enrollments from 1980 to the present grew by 16%, but teacher employment grew by 44%. There were more kids, and so you had to put teachers in front of them. The enrollments were growing, which are now leveling off, but more importantly, the student–teacher ratio was really dropping rapidly. And so, you had a whole lot of hiring going on. Now, there were two things that were set in motion. One is you hire a lot of new inexperienced teachers, and so you get more turnover. We know that the turnover of teachers is U-shaped; it's high in the initial years, drops, and then when you get to retirement it goes up again. So you're getting a lot of new teachers in there, some of whom decide teaching is not for them, and that's going to raise overall turnover. The second thing it set in motion was sort of musical chairs, and really a mass exit out of a lot of urban districts, including Los Angeles. Some of this was coming from class-size reduction initiatives. Many teachers in urban districts found that there were openings in the suburbs, and they were leaving what they saw as less attractive high poverty schools. Now again, my prediction is that that's dying down now. We were looking at an exceptional period.

The problem is that we don't yet have national data to demonstrate this. All of the data in this commission report is coming from the U.S. Department of Education's Schools and Staffing Survey, which is 1990–2000 data, the peak of this turbulence. But I can present some data from Missouri that demonstrates that turnover reached a peak in that period, and is coming down. If you look at Chart 7.5 you see that the upper graph is turnover and the lower graph is the Missouri unemployment rate, and this points to the third piece of the perfect storm. We were at unprecedentedly low unemployment rates in the late 1990s for the postwar period. You can see how teacher turnover tracks overall unemployment. During the 1990s teacher turnover, unemployment went down, and teacher turnover went up. But now the unemployment rate has gone up and teacher turnover has gone down. I would predict that when we get next year's data, we're going to see further declines in Missouri.

So what's the bottom line here? In my opinion, we're asking way too much of teacher licensing in terms of effects on student achievement. Basically the best we can expect out of teacher licensing is to screen out incompetent practitioners, and that's it. I think the important reform to make in teacher licensing is to make it simpler, and more transparent, and give schools the opportunity to audition more candidates, to open it up to more routes into teaching. These licensing systems are terribly complicated and as a result, almost no one is in compliance. Missouri Department of Elementary and Secondary Education issues 260 separate certificates

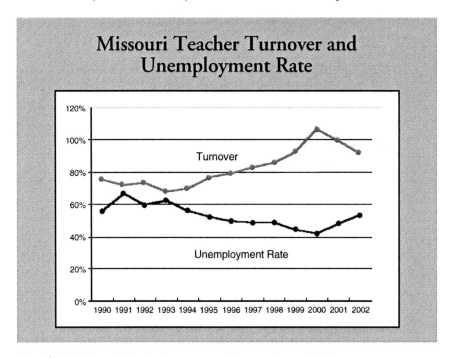

Chart 7.5. Missouri teacher turnover and unemployment rate.

and endorsements: 89 nonvocational and the rest vocational. Many education departments can't even name how many certificates and endorsements they have. And then when they get into the number that are "grandmothered," you're talking about the Human Genome Project—500, 600, 700 legitimate codes! It's terribly complicated, and think about this, your states are issuing *one* license in medicine, *one* license in law, *one* in veterinary medicine, *one* in dentistry, and 200 or more in K–12 education.

The result is predictable. No one is in compliance with this system. Even the highest-spending school districts are not in full compliance. This must be simplified and, in my opinion, I think we need to look toward opening up the doors for nontraditional candidates.

I found something on the Internet D3M: Data Driven Decision Making. It seems to me, that if we're serious about raising student achievement and closing testing gaps, we need to focus on drilling down into the data we're now accumulating. Many of you are testing every year, all of you will soon be doing so. School districts are moving forward, developing longitudinal data systems on students, and they can link these data to teachers and to classrooms and that's going to be an important basis for moving forward here.

In my view, we're not going to fix or even scratch the surface of our achievement gap problems by fiddling with teacher credentials or licenses. This is a quantative management problem. We've got to look at the data, and we've got to drill down and find out which classrooms are working, which investments are working, and which aren't. What's happening now? What is exciting is that districts are beginning to do this. Districts are building these databases, and that's an important way to move forward. Licensing has just a very minor role to play in this. I think the more important thing is to get incentives straight, and when we talk about teacher quality, addressing issues of rigid teacher salary schedules, the way we pay teachers, what we reward, and things like tenure and restrictive collective bargaining agreements. To a great extent, we already know the teachers who are performing and who aren't. It's an issue of acting on the information we have, or that we will be generating.

Arthur E. Wise

Let me begin by taking the time to raise the issue of the title of this panel, "Does Certified or Alternately Certified Mean Qualified?" because it demonstrates the point I'm trying to make. Policymakers have built a system of certification that they believe is tantamount to qualification. But first, everyone needs to take a look at the terminology being used and try to decipher it.

Over the last decade, policymakers have wrestled mightily with two phrases, often not clearly distinguishing between them: "alternate routes to certification" and "normal routes to certification." The "normal route to certification" means completion of a teacher preparation program in a College of Education; 80% of all people who go into teaching complete the normal route. There are also alternate routes to certification, meaning that ultimately individuals end up meeting the same requirements as those who have gone through the regular route.

Policymakers have also loosely tossed around the terms "alternatives to certification" or "noncertification" or "deregulation." For instance, "alternatives to certification" means taking people and more or less immediately putting them to work in the classroom. I would urge that we be very careful in distinguishing these terms because glib generalizations about whether people are in alternate or regular programs do not clearly distinguish between those who more or less have been through a regular preparation program and have been determined to have met state standards, versus those who have not. So as we move forward we need to clearly distinguish between these terms, and the people who are categorized in these terms.

Certification is a legal process. It's a curiosity that in our field we chose the word "certification" rather than the word "licensing." In fact, that is what states do. They determine whether an individual should be licensed to practice, and they issue certificates, which implies that the state has determined that this individual has met teacher qualifications set by the state.

Why does the state license teachers anyway? States license certain individuals; they don't license all individuals. They make careful choices about occupations that they will turn into professions. States generally decide to convert an occupation into a licensed profession when the professional is delivering the services, for example in the field of medicine. If a person has not been licensed by the state, we would be wary of obtaining services from that individual. The same can be said for lawyers, architects, CPAs, and so forth. At the point when these individuals are delivering services, it is not possible to closely supervise them.

The way schools are structured today, classrooms are run by one adult, in charge of around 25 children. That means we have to trust that professional behind closed doors with our children. Management literature says that one person can effectively supervise seven others. So if there was one administrator for every seven teachers, maybe teachers wouldn't have to be trained as much. But this is not a logical approach. We license people to ensure that they have what it takes to deliver their services. In the case of teaching, we want to know that teachers have the knowledge, skills, and dispositions to teach, and the ability to marshal those attributes and put them to the service of the children who are in their charge, and so to perform effectively as teachers. When we license individuals to teach, we want to be sure that the assessment process that we use gives us good evidence that they have the knowledge, skills, dispositions, and ability to teach.

Up until a decade ago, states used a process called "program approval." This was a wholesale approach to teacher certification. The idea was that if the state approved a teacher preparation program, then the graduates of that program, as determined by the university, would then be eligible for a license. But once this power was turned over to the schools of education, the state was making an assumption that the college would be providing a candidate with the content knowledge, pedagogical knowledge, and teaching skills. The colleges were supposed to be making sure that individuals had the relevant dispositions and the skills necessary so that all children learned. If a person prepared to become a teacher for four years, a lot of people would opt out along the way, and a lot of people would be encouraged not to continue with their plans to be a teacher. In a way, that process worked, but not well. We have begun to make changes in the system in order to perfect that process.

Evidence is overwhelmingly supportive of the idea that teacher preparation and the teacher certification process matters, in spite of the fact that the research does not meet the "gold standard." Today there are a few studies in K–12 education that support teacher preparation; but educational research has been an impoverished enterprise for many years.

Without merely relying on research, we can still be fairly certain that a person who does not have content knowledge cannot teach that content knowledge and we can be fairly certain that if a person does not have the ability to convey that knowledge to others, particularly children, then they're not likely to be able to teach effectively. The work on credentialing is important. I encourage work in this direction, even though there is no sound evidence that uncredentialed people will succeed in large numbers. Based on a SAS study from the National Commission on Teaching and America's Future using the Schools and Staffing Survey Database, which took a national sample of teachers in America, the evidence suggests that 25% of uncredentialed individuals who start teaching are gone by the end of the first year. The more we rely on unprepared individuals, the steeper and steeper the curve will have to be in order to compensate using that method.

At least the frenzied hiring has slowed down due to the economy. Teachers are not leaving teaching for greener pastures; there are no greener pastures. States and localities are starting to figure out that they can afford the small class size, which research supports, especially for certain kinds of children. There is not a lot of evidence that large numbers of people are frantically trying to get into the field of teaching. There is some anecdotal evidence of individuals who would seem to make good teachers trying to get into the system but not in terms of very large numbers. Whether or not these individuals will be superior on average to those who are already in the teaching force is unclear.

Contrary to what most people believe, high school teachers come from the upper half of college students—and they are students from mainstream colleges. If high schools can draw from the top half, that's not bad, especially given the kind of pay offered to teachers. One study compared the content qualifications of individuals who had prepared to teach versus those who had not prepared to teach. The study found that one-third of the individuals who were graduates of liberal arts colleges could not pass state licensing exams.

The perception that there are large numbers of individuals who can fill the vacant positions is beginning to dwindle. Now there is the realization that we need to take account of consumer behavior in our schools. Teachers are employed by school boards who are, in turn, hiring according to the labor market of teachers. Overwhelmingly, school districts with higher salaries will only hire fully qualified personnel. In fact, 80–85% of the school districts in the United States only hire certified personnel. Even when presented with individuals who might not have been prepared, districts prefer to hire those individuals who are prepared and certified as teachers.

The biggest flaw of the American education system is its effect on urban areas. We need to strengthen our existing teacher certification laws. They provide a strategy for uplifting the quality of teaching in these urban areas. Rather than subjecting individuals in cities who mostly need what competent teachers have to offer, if we created a floor, we would raise the level of teaching that goes on in our urban areas. If you look across the spectrum of human services, whether it be medical services or legal services, and so on, you will find that the residents of cities, including the poor residents, will be served by people who have been prepared and qualified for the work that they do. I believe teacher certification continues to make sense as long as we improve upon it.

Many of our states now test teacher candidates for basic skills. I think that the system for teachers needs to raise the bar. Teacher candidates should also be required to demonstrate high levels of literacy and numeracy as well as writing and speaking skills as a condition for teaching. Certainly, we want teachers to have content knowledge. In 38 states, a content major is required of teachers. In colleges of education that have high standards, that expectation is already built in. But we still need more rigorous content examinations for teachers. We need to raise our expectations of performance on the current licensing exams. We also need tests of teaching knowledge that are different from the current tests.

It is critical that all teachers be prepared to understand and critique education research. It is imperative that they be prepared to understand and critique the various schools of thought that affect schooling in America. Teachers must have the basic tools to understand educational research, to be able to interpret it for its meaning in their work. But most importantly of course, we should expect as a condition of teacher certification that a teacher provide evidence that he or she can teach so that children learn. This means that we should not license teachers right out of college. We must expect a year or more of teaching on the job and a serious assessment of that experience as a condition for a regular teaching license.

Michael Podgursky

I think the important piece of the story that's changed, of course, is the standards revolution. Education leaders are doing the heavy lifting of going out and testing the kids and highlighting these major gaps that we're seeing in achievement. And that's the big change. We lived in a world in which essentially inputs were regulated. And now we're going to one in which we're focusing on the performance of schools, that is, outputs. I think that's very important. The simple economics of regulation is you can't regulate something unless you can measure it or monitor it. We can measure achievement; we can see if the kids are learning. We can see if they know math. But the simple fact is it's very hard to measure teacher quality at all well in spite of what some of these commissions claim. And we need to focus on what can be measured and what can be regulated. We need to determine whether learning is occurring and I think we're just asking way too much of licensing. We can make sure the teachers have basic content knowledge and do a criminal background check. But once you go beyond that, it's hard to demonstrate that you're going to get big, or even small achievement gains.

When Art says research in education schools is an impoverished enterprise, I have to smile. As an economist coming into this field, my mouth drops at the huge amount of money that comes from the U.S. Department of Education and foundations to fund education research. Compare the income in an education school with that in a psychology department (or an economics department!). But the problem here, in my opinion, is that too often the research that's emanating from schools of education is not meeting the research standards I described. You can give a psychologist a $20,000 grant and he's going to go out and do a random assignment study. The psychologist has a basic commitment to these principles of scientific research design. That's not true with much education research. It isn't a matter of resources, it's a matter of putting in place high-quality research designs. I can't tell you the number of studies I've seen where hundreds of thousands of dollars and even million-dollar studies haven't put research designs in place so that we really know if something works. I think that's changing with Dr. Whitehurst at the Institute for Education Sciences at the U.S. Department of Education. The bar has clearly been raised on research that the U.S. Department of Education will fund. I think that's an important change that we're seeing and should be applauded. Had that been done 20 years ago, we'd have a body of research now and that could really give us these answers. And again, if you don't have those kinds of scientific protocols in place, there may be 5,000 of the studies, but they're really not telling you anything.

Arthur E. Wise

We have to act. We all make decisions. If we all had to wait until we had research evidence before we acted, I don't think we'd be doing very much in this life. Let me ask you, how many non-Ph.D. economists are there in your department or in the economics departments of this country, and who did the study that suggests that a Ph.D. in economics was required for participation in a department of economics?

Michael Podgursky

You walked right into this one, Art. I have a faculty of about 14 at present. We keep downsizing; we've been shrinking in the 1990s. But one of my economics faculty has a Ph.D. in sociology. He has an undergraduate degree in applied math from Harvard. He went to the University of Chicago and got a Ph.D. in sociology. But he worked with Gary Becker—a Nobel Laureate in Economics who has a joint appointment in sociology, economist Sherwin Rosen and the famous sociologist James Coleman. But I think the interesting point here is in higher education, we encourage this sort of interdisciplinary activity. The NSF and other organizations encourage interdisciplinary teaching and research. We've now got ourselves in a situation where we're generating all these numbers about "teaching out-of-field" in K–12, and much of what we do in higher ed is teach "out-of-field." If we measured it elsewhere we'd be lawyering out-of-field and doing medicine out-of-field, and so on.

Lewis C. Solmon

Assuming that there is a set of teacher skills and knowledge of behavior that need to be credentialed, what is the necessary role of education schools? In other words, could it be that a Teach for America experience in a summer and an undergraduate degree in physics and a minor in adolescent psychology would be enough? Does credentialing mean education schools or are there other ways of doing credentialing without education schools?

Arthur E. Wise

I think we inextricably confuse preparation and certification.

Lewis C. Solmon

But does certification require a certain kind of preparation?

Arthur E. Wise

Let's take a step back and look at some other fields. I find it illuminating to look at other fields that have advanced themselves and that are highly respected in our society for doing reasonably good work. They all have decided that preparation is important and not always for the reasons that we think. Maybe the most outstanding example is the case of the legal profession, which until not that long ago you could get into in a variety of ways. But the leaders of that field gathered together one day in 1950 or somewhere around there, and they said there are a lot of awfully young people coming into law today and they're so young that they really cast a negative image of our field. They decided to make as a prerequisite to law school, four years of college. They didn't go there right away. They started with two years of college, then they moved it to four years of college. You can find no empirical study for that other than a belief that college was a maturing experience, at least it aged the people for four years and maybe taught them a few things along the way.

Knowledge is imparted and knowledge is assessed in a field like teaching where interpersonal behavior and interpersonal skills are essential. One of the things that does happen in the course of the preparation experience is that people try it out a little bit and sometimes find it's not to their liking. Then they go somewhere else. Or they have such a human relations disaster of a personality that advisors in the program sit them down and say really, you'll have to take your knowledge of history and go somewhere else with it.

If you short-circuit that process completely, for example, if you create an organization such as the American Board for the Certification of Teacher Excellence, which essentially creates a one-day opportunity to demonstrate that you have what it takes to be a teacher by virtue of taking a content test, perhaps a pedagogical test and have a criminal background check, you run the risk of putting into the classroom individuals who are temperamentally unsuited for that work. I think preparation does a number of things. It allows the teacher to learn content knowledge and it also performs or begins to play a selection role that is quite important.

Michael Podgursky

This whole question of comparing teacher turnover in various routes into teaching depends on where you put the meter. The National Commission on Teaching and America's Future sets the meter at when you start the job and makes comparisons. But why don't we back it up one year and say let's look at all the students that passed through teacher training programs who never become a teacher. Why don't we count that as turnover? One attractive feature of these alternate certification programs is they're targeted toward individuals who are already working. They're efficient in the sense that they're focusing on shortage fields—science and math—and they are targeting people that are on the job. What's happening in many education schools is that we're training lots and lots of elementary education majors who never become teachers and there's just a glut. Of course in any higher education institution, an education school dean wants to get his numbers up, and so, instead of doing the heavy lifting of training math and science teachers, they just produce lots of elementary education majors.

But on this question of certification, clearly you could produce other certificates that may not involve certified schools. I think states already do this to a certain extent. Many states already have the option of a certificate indicating if people are coming from another state, or have demonstrated extensive prior experience in private schools. They can get credits toward certification and even full certification. So, no one is arguing here to let anyone walk into the classroom, the question is to make it more flexible so that you can open the door to people who've demonstrated, through all of the many areas where training is going on, at least the potential for teaching. And of course they will need to be monitored in the classroom to make sure that they're not causing harm, and that's what we see in a lot of these programs. The intern program here in California, alternate certification in Texas, at least they're supposed to be monitoring.

Lewis C. Solmon

For those of you who don't know, I used to be the dean of an education school. I liked when you talk about law and medicine having certification.

If you go to medical school in Chicago, or if you go to medical school in California, or anywhere in the country, you're probably going to take the same courses and the content is going to be relatively the same. The same thing in law school, everybody takes constitutional law, everybody takes civil procedure, and they often even use the same books across the country.

But my experience, when I looked at various teacher education programs, not only were the courses different but the content of course was incredibly different. I remember at UCLA, for example, technology was the vogue when I was there. So, we had a course on using technology in the classroom. We got somebody who sort of knew something about technology and they showed them how to work a computer. My question is, has this changed? Is there a commonality of knowledge being developed in education that makes it more similar to law and education? Is there a common core of knowledge that all schools of education teach and all teachers must know?

Arthur E. Wise

I think it is certainly changing in the face of the standards that NCATE has developed and most of the states are now following. We are specifying the kinds of knowledge and skill that we expect to see colleges of education develop. We are not specifying what the curriculum should look like. We've gone to a performance emphasis, which means that we are specifying very clearly the kinds of knowledge and skill that we expect to see new elementary teachers, new social studies teachers, new science teachers, and new math teachers display. We have very highly developed expectations for knowledge and skill, and I think that is leading to a greater degree of good uniformity.

On the other hand, one of the characteristics of schools of education when you were a dean was "anarchy," if I might use it that way. Every professor did his or her own thing and every student did his or her thing and when 120 credits mounted up, then you had a teacher.

Audience Question

As I understood, Dr. Podgursky was saying that we have a fairly clear idea that teaching and learning goes on without licensure if you like, because we look around at the military, at private schools, at business, and there are all kinds of people who are successfully teaching other people to do things. And they're doing it quite well and they go along in the marketplace quite happily having taught whatever they're going to teach and learned whatever they're going to learn. But in a public school situation the circumstances are slightly different. It seems to me one of the big ways that they're different is that we compel children to go to them, you don't have a choice. You must go and you must be with these people here. And so we must be able to turn to those children's parents and to the children themselves and say we are going to promise you that the person standing in front of you is of some quality, can do something. How do we promise them that? And I would say that we're not doing a very good job of that right now with our current licensing system if the NAEP scores are any indication of success. But how do we do that efficiently and effectively and bring as many people as we can into it but still promise them high-quality teachers because they can't walk away from us.

Michael Podgursky

I guess my first response is there used to be a draft and there was a lot of training that went on in the military of kids who dropped out of high school and shaped up. But again, I wish I had a simple answer to tell you but I think you're doing the right thing. You're focusing on the outcomes. Are the kids learning? That's your protection. You're saying if kids aren't learning in this school we're going to shut it down or we're going to reorganize it or we're going to let the kids go somewhere else, rather than trying to regulate something that you really can't regulate very well, because sitting as a regulator in your state capital, you don't know who's a good teacher. Finally, in my opinion, the best way to protect parents against an incompetent teacher is to give them more school choice options.

Audience Question

Is the follow-up to that, then, that it isn't just that certification needs to be modified, but we need to be able to pretty quickly and without a lot of fuss or muss, fire people who aren't doing the job? And isn't that really the big problem? Not that we have to certify them, but we can't get rid of them once we have to?

Michael Podgursky

Absolutely. Why are we having this discussion about something that doesn't matter that much—licensing—and we're *not* having the discussion about something that does, which is tenure?

Audience Question

I was at a meeting at Michigan State and the discussion was, is the research in education sufficiently rigorous to answer significant questions in education? And the conclusion among those sitting at the table was that it's not. Now that may or may not be true, but that was the conclusion. It seems to me that if the presumption is that there is a knowledge base, there is a set of skills, and there is a set of attitudes that can to some extent be more or less correlated with improved student learning outcomes, then it behooves us to identify those things and to make them the basis of how we go about bringing people into the profession. So it seems to be that instead of arguing at the margins, it's more along the lines of necessary and sufficient that we can identify some things that are necessary, what is sufficient to be an effective instructor, an effective teacher. So, I'd be interested in exploring what is that array of behaviors, of the knowledge base, of attitudes that go toward making a significant contribution to improve student learning outcomes.

Arthur E. Wise

I would agree.

Michael Podgursky

Well, certainly there's a lot that's been learned. Here we have Herb Walberg and he's done meta-analyses in this area. And his studies would be on any of these reading lists. But the question is, as a regulator, how are you going to make sure that these things are in these programs? What's being taught in certified schools often isn't grounded in this scientific research base.

Audience Question

It seems to me that, since we don't know exactly what makes a good teacher and we don't have measurements of that, why don't we let the consumer decide? Why don't we let the parents decide whether, just like when you go to a lawyer or a doctor, you know whether you're going to get your money's worth because you have a whole bunch of ways of finding out. And if they don't perform the way you want them to, you don't use them anymore? Well we don't have that choice in public education, but we ought to. Could you speak to that please?

Michael Podgursky

Given my audience today, I can only take small steps here. But we do need more choice for parents, no question about it. More competition for education schools as well. I'd argue that competition can not only produce better outcomes and more choice for parents in terms of picking schools and so on, it's also good in terms of training the teachers. I worry when people say we need to just standardize teacher training all across the country. I think that competition can bring out better teacher training programs. And more training programs aligned with what parents want. Obviously a lot of consumers like Core Knowledge but the typical school of education hates Core Knowledge. So, maybe we should have some opportunities for education schools to do things like that.

Lewis C. Solmon

So you get criticized when you standardize the curriculum. And you get criticized when you don't standardize the curriculum.

Arthur E. Wise

But of course in a way, this lady actually answered her own question. She said that she could choose among doctors and lawyers but not among teachers. You see, you have a tremendous amount of information when somebody is called a doctor or a lawyer. You know a whole lot about them and you can choose A, B, or C, but before you even get around to making that choice, you know a tremendous amount about them. And all we're saying is that you should know something about the abilities of people who are going to be found in the nation's classrooms.

Audience Question

I want to challenge the assertions about the degree to which we have a lot of information about outputs and therefore we ought to turn from too much of a reliance on inputs. That is probably true, it seems to me, where the building is concerned or where the system is concerned. But I don't think we've gotten very sophisticated about outputs at the individual teacher level. And there are all kinds of things that factor in there. Bill Sanders has done probably the most sophisticated work around, and you don't see his work replicated too many places, at least at that level of sophistication, so you can really start thinking about the value that's added teacher by teacher. And in the absence of that kind of information, it seems to me that you run a risk by focusing too much on the output side because we don't have very good systems for measuring the outputs just yet, at least on the individual teacher level. The credentialing process that's fairly traditional is a "safe to teach" sort of standard. It doesn't presume that the person is at all at the level they need to be ultimately, but it is a safe to teach standard. If they come via a nontraditional route and if you're going to rely on outputs, they're in the presence of kids for a year before you know what you've got. You may have a problem. You run the risk of wasting that full year in the presence of a teacher whose prospects for success are low and you have very little indication of that. Especially while you're waiting for the output measures to become available.

Michael Podgursky

You're right, drilling down to the teacher level is new, but we're starting to do that. Certainly at the school level you're protecting the public by saying here's a failing school, or at least the principle is there of identifying the whole school. Now what part of the school that's failed is another question. Is it the principal or particular teachers? The current system is sort of a "safe to learn" and I think that you can get that a lot of ways, and that's the best that you're going to get out of this sort of minimum, "safe to learn" standard. But since you've all seen Bill Sanders's work, remember that variation in teacher effectiveness overwhelmingly involved certified teachers. The output of this system that's supposed to be doing quality control had this tremendous dispersion of performance.

Arthur E. Wise

I believe it's very important that we have standards and assessments. Almost certainly under any system I can imagine, the assessments will never be adequate to assess the standards in their richness. If you look at the standards themselves, they are generally wonderful and unexceptionable and robust. And when you look at them you say, well, if every child could do this, it would be a great place. But as a practical matter, to test that on a universal basis, that level of richness of outcome on a universal basis, we'll never get there, or we'll be spending as much money on assessment as we do on teaching. So yes, we do need assessment of the kind that the states are undertaking at the present time. But we also need highly competent and well prepared teachers who will teach the rest in ways that we may never get around to being able to assess in the ways that we find so satisfying today, namely standardized, multiple-choice tests.

Audience Question

I looked on the Title II website where they're grading the universities in terms of how many teachers at each university who take the Praxis II test, which is the content test, pass it. I thought this would be interesting, we'd get to see how the schools of education are doing. And basically if you look down that list, no matter which school you picked from which state, the pass rates were all above 95%. That was the only information that you could get in terms of knowing a lot. So it just seems a little odd that the schools of education are either doing that well or that, as you mentioned earlier in your talk, that the standards for passing are so abysmally low by each state that you're sort of not really certifying anything. You're certifying that you can lower the pass rate down to a rate where 95% of the people can pass. So what kinds of plans are in place so that parents and concerned people can know more about these teachers that their kids have?

Arthur E. Wise

Those high percentages are a product of two developments, one being that the test score levels are too low, but the other is a good development. What has happened is that schools of education have raised their admission standards and their exit standards to reflect that percentage pass rate, which means that the colleges are doing more or less what the Congress was asking. They do not recommend for certification in the state a person who cannot pass the state licensing test. And so having said that, we do need to do some work to ratchet up expectations. Some people have looked at that data and found it appalling, but they might be surprised to discover that as they look at medical schools they will find exactly the same picture. And that has gone on of course for decades and we tend to think of medical education as a very rigorous experience and it is. I'm not here to dispute that. But they do something very interesting in medicine, they have a three-part credentialing exam. The first part they give after two years of medical school. Most medical schools will not let you into the third year until you pass that first test. They then have another test at the end of the fourth year, and they don't let you out of that fourth year until you pass that second part of the test. So we shouldn't be appalled at schools of education that end up with very high pass rates, but we do need to look beneath the surface at what is being measured at the level at which it is being measured. And I would want to go much further than what is now being measured at that level. I think we need a much more comprehensive set of measures if we are to develop high confidence in the nation's teachers.

Audience Question

To continue the discussion on education schools, if you go to USA Today.com and type in the keyword *mediocrity*, you'll pull up a scathing editorial on education schools. It talks about how many education school professors are anti-standards, anti-testing, and that they work against state accountability programs. And Michael, you made the point that a typical education school hates Core Knowledge and we have many parents who love Core Knowledge. So I think that there needs to be a change of culture in many of the ed schools. How can that be brought about?

Michael Podgursky

Well, I like competition. I think that if they won't produce the teachers that schools need, then I think you open the doors to alternate routes. And I think an even stronger case can be made for administration. We have to have principals and school administrators who can drill down and look at these data if we're serious about raising these targets and closing these gaps. While it isn't true of all education schools, most are just not training students to do this kind of quantitative research. There's "qualitative research" and all kinds of other stuff. But I see no reason why teachers shouldn't be able to take statistics courses and economics courses to help them prepare to do the heavy lifting of moving forward and understanding and analyzing these test data that are being generated. I think that if you open the doors and let others compete, you'll get better-quality products. Look at the companies that are entering this market to help districts analyze these data, Standard and Poor, SAS In Schools. It's not coming out of the certified schools or the traditional education research community. And I think that's healthy competition.

Arthur E. Wise

I would say that practice is changing in schools of education. We have come out of a period described earlier as anarchy, which was when people did their own thing. We now have Colleges of Education developing coherent programs of study that are informed by what's going on in the real world of schooling. The real world of schooling is undergoing profound changes and colleges could not prepare candidates to work in a world that did not exist. So the world of teaching and learning and schooling almost has to change first, before Colleges of Education can produce people who can work in that environment. That is true across all professions: practice changes first and the preparation programs then build themselves to prepare people to work in that new environment.

Lowell Milken

The standard today in passing most of the teacher licensure exams is obviously quite low. I think one of the key difficulties is that many of the people who barely score a passing grade on those tests end up teaching in the hard-to-staff schools. The experience we've seen through all of our focus groups, and a lot of our work, is that a lot of the other teachers unfortunately leave and they'll teach in a different type of environment for a whole slew of reasons. We're having a discussion today about raising the standards, and so on. But in our schools for 15 years, 20 years, we've had an incredible number of teachers who have neither a major nor a minor in a subject and they're teaching various kinds of disciplines and they're totally unqualified to do so. And we've had all kinds of problems in trying to attract quality teachers at least any kind of high standard for our lower-achieving schools. So what I'm confused about is what is going to really change this dynamic? I don't see how anything's going to change the dynamic other than perhaps just the sheer numbers. If it was really an aberrational situation where we had a high demand for teachers and that's going to scale itself. Michael, maybe you could speak on that issue, whether you think the sheer numbers itself may end up having an impact on the matter.

But when I look at the reality of the situation, I think we could be sitting here having this discussion in three to five years, and we'll still have all these kids passing through a system with nonquality teachers.

Arthur E. Wise

There aren't simple answers to any of these things. But in fact, we need to prepare people to work in hard-to-staff schools first. We need to restructure hard-to-staff schools so that they become places where reasonable people can work. We also need to adjust compensation in those schools to reflect the fact that they are places where it is challenging to work.

We're going to announce a project shortly where we're going to work in four cities, picking up on some schools like that, creating a strategy that we call professional development schools as a means by which to recruit and prepare people specifically to work in urban environments. We won't be able to tackle the compensation piece but we will be tackling some of the other pieces about really teaching people how to work effectively in that environment. One of the great challenges that we have is that because people leave those environments, we don't have any senior people left to train new people to come into them. So we have to do something different in those places and we have one strategy that we're going to propose. I'm sure there are countless others that others could propose, but simply going on the way we have is not adequate.

Michael Podgursky

If you look at the time series data, there has been a relentless decline in the student–teacher ratio in the United States. And if you go back to the late 1960s it was over 25 students per teacher, now it's down to around 15. In Massachusetts it's 12.5 students per teacher in the latest data. There's some simple arithmetic here. If the medical model is your point of reference, consider this: a radiologist doesn't raise his salary by seeing fewer patients. The student–teacher ratio is really a measure of productivity and so it's going to be very hard to meet all these goals and say, well we're going to have everyone fully credentialed and they're going to have majors in the field, *and* we're going to have student–teacher ratios of 13 and 14. It's just not going to work.

Audience Question

In terms of teacher preparation, you didn't take the analogy with the medical schools far enough. After you do medical school, you go to residency. And residency is three years of intimate acquaintance with the trade. The BTSA program in California did some of that, but didn't go far enough. And I think if you want to have teachers remain in the program, remain teaching, you've got to put a lot more time and attention into mentoring those teachers in the classroom with master teachers, such as you do in a residency program in medicine. So that they can make mistakes but they're not fatal mistakes and they can learn from their mistakes and they can go on and become good teachers. But right now you toss them into the classroom and it's sink or swim. That's going to result in sinking most of the time. So you've got to change what happens after they get out of the schools of education, when they're trying to practice their trade, that's fundamental.

Someone raised the point about this body of knowledge that teachers should have. And, you know, one of the things we're debating here is whether it's preservice or post-service. I mean, there's nothing that would preclude continuing while they're on the job, with this coursework, and that's how most of these alternate certification programs work. There's mentoring and they continue to take classes during a probationary period here in California. It's a two-year internship program. So it doesn't preclude doing the coursework, it's whether it's front-loaded or while you're on the job.

Arthur E. Wise

There's a tremendous amount of evidence to suggest that high-quality mentoring experiences reduce teacher attrition, increase student achievement, and do what you would expect and want it to do. But a high-quality mentoring experience is very expensive.

Audience Comment

It's not as expensive as reduced class size, certainly in terms of the outcomes per dollar spent.

Arthur E. Wise

And speaking about teacher education in general, no four-year program of undergraduate study that results in a college major can by itself fully prepare a person to teach, especially in urban settings. And so we need to extend the process through paid internships, through professional development schools, and through other strategies that will allow people to learn effectively on the job.

Audience Question

Several people have brought up this whole issue of the test. You talk about medical boards and law boards and the extent to which people have to go to pass those is pretty rigorous. Can you give me an opinion about Praxis and NTE and the levels of those tests, because a lot of the data suggests those are really low. When you compare those to the other professions we're talking about and depending on your impression of those, would you still continue to compare taking more of those tests to becoming a lawyer or a doctor? I mean, do you see a parity of levels there?

Arthur E. Wise

Well, let me just say tantalizingly, stay tuned in the next few weeks, you will see some new information on this topic, some possible changes in store. I certainly think that the tests themselves are okay, the cut scores are not okay.

Lewis C. Solmon

Just a couple of comments. First of all, I'd like to thank our two panelists. And second, I would say that for those of you who haven't read Lowell's book on the Teacher Advancement Program, a lot of the discussion here implied that maybe what we're doing is okay. So that's very encouraging. I encourage you to read that.

PANEL CONTRIBUTIONS

CHAPTER 8

MEETING THE HIGHLY QUALIFIED TEACHERS CHALLENEGE

Statement of Arthur E. Wise

President, National Council for Accreditation of Teacher Education on the U.S. Department of Education Report on Teacher Quality "Meeting the Highly Qualified Teachers Challenge," Released June 13, 2002

TITLE II DATA

A new U.S. Department of Education report asks states to revamp licensing requirements to reduce the number of teacher preparation courses required for licensure. The report says "teacher preparation programs are failing" (p. viii, *Meeting the Highly Qualified Teachers Challenge*) at producing the kinds of teachers the nation requires.

Our view is that Title II data support a different conclusion. Title II data show that most programs graduate teachers who meet today's state licensing requirements. These requirements include a content major for prospective teachers in 38 states. In the structure of government in America,

Talented Teachers: The Essential Force for Improving Student Achievement, pages 161–164

the States have the right and responsibility to set standards for teacher preparation. Against these standards, teacher candidates, especially those at *professionally accredited* institutions, are doing a commendable job. Teacher preparation programs today have met the challenge set when Congress passed Title II of the Higher Education Act in 1998.

The Department gives low marks to traditional teacher preparation programs, yet their graduates do remarkably well on the largest accountability study ever done in teacher preparation—Title II. Institutions report to states; states compile the information on institutions and send it to the U.S. Department of Education in order to determine which institutions are producing teacher candidates who meet today's standards. Data show weakness at a few institutions, but the vast majority of candidates have passed with flying colors.

Since Title II has been implemented, institutions have changed entry and exit requirements for teacher preparation, and have tightened requirements for those being recommended for licensure. Title II data show that if states and the profession raise the level of expectation, institutions will rise to the challenge of those increased expectations.

While the Department says that teacher preparation programs are failing, it recognizes programs such as Teach for America. Whatever the merits of Teach for America, it is not an answer to staffing the nation's schools. America must add 200,000 teachers a year to a teaching force of 3 million. In its entire history, Teach for America has placed 8,000 teachers in schools; approximately 2,000 of them are still teaching.

Revamping teacher preparation courses to vastly reduce the program to a Teach for America format is not the answer. Just because one is an Albert Einstein does not mean that he or she can successfully teach seventh grade algebra to middle schoolers.

TEACHING SKILL AND CONTENT KNOWLEDGE

Teaching Skill

In terms of teaching skill, *graduates of teacher preparation programs outperform those who have not been prepared.* The Charles A. Dana Center at the University of Texas found that students of all ethnic backgrounds scored significantly higher on the Texas student assessment when the great majority of their teachers were fully prepared and licensed [1]. Other studies support this data.

Many eminent experts believe that the balance of existing studies supports the proposition that teaching is a skill that can and should be taught. Most if not all other professions prepare their entrants with skills courses and practice in an academic setting. Common sense and experience indicate that there is nothing unique about teaching that its practitioners should be prepared differently from such other licensed professionals as doctors, engineers, accountants, and pilots. These professionals require grounding in the profession's knowledge base and in how to apply it as required through extended supervised practice. The pilot doesn't learn to fly the plane while it's in the air; neither does the doctor operate for the first time alone. The public understands these analogies.

Content Knowledge

A landmark ETS study in 1999, the largest study of teacher qualifications completed to date, studied 270,000 teacher candidates who took Praxis II, a content knowledge exam used by 23 states as the state licensing examination for teachers. The study found that 91 percent of the graduates of institutions accredited through the National Council for Accreditation of Teacher Education passed this exam of content knowledge. Only 73 percent of those who did not study teacher preparation passed the exam of content knowledge—a difference of 18 percentile points. The study was conducted before Title II changed policies to ensure that most candidates passed the examination, and thus is a valid measure of the effectiveness of schools of education.

The misconception that those in teacher preparation do not know the subject matter they plan to teach or are otherwise poor students, is just that—a myth. Indeed, the Department's report reveals that 38 states already require a degree in content knowledge for teacher preparation graduates. The majority of teachers are specialists in the subject they are teaching. Unfortunately, *districts have routinely assigned teachers to teach out-of-field* in some areas when they cannot find qualified teachers for specific subject areas.

America must address the fundamental issues of teacher retention and turnover through significant salary increases and changes in working conditions. If these are not addressed in a meaningful way, we cannot and will not have a *uniformly* high quality teaching force, and we will have to run faster and faster to stay in place.

STATE LICENSING REFORMS

The U.S. Department of Education also calls for state licensing standards to increase in rigor. We agree that the licensing process is not all it needs to be, and reforms are necessary. But those *reforms should include strong teacher preparation programs as an important part of licensure requirements.* There must be increased rigor in the evaluation of new teachers as well as comprehensive assessment and a well thought out induction period for all new teachers—in other words, a reformed licensing system.

The U.S. Department of Education calls for increasing rigor in the assessment by states of teachers' content knowledge. That step is important but states need to go further. The general public, parents, and students want and deserve to know that teachers can convey that content so that students learn. While many states are working on plans to assess teaching skills, few have implemented those plans. While many states have taken steps toward properly supervising—and assessing—beginning teachers, few have well-structured systems in place. States must implement licensing assessment systems that assure the public of the integrity of the license to teach—the title "teacher" must convey that the person who receives it has the knowledge and skill to help all students learn.

REFERENCE

Fuller, E. (1999). *Does teacher certification matter? A comparison of elementary TAAS performance in 1997 between schools with high and low percentages of certified teachers.* Charles A. Dana Center, Austin: University of Texas.

CHAPTER 9

WHAT'S WRONG WITH TEACHER CERTIFICATION?

Arthur E. Wise

Current teacher licensing, or teacher certification, as it is commonly called, does not do what it is intended to do. It does not differentiate clearly between those who are qualified to teach and those who are not. The victims are the children. With many children being left behind, especially in our largest urban districts, it is no wonder that there are many end runs around the system.

"Certification" is literally the grant by the state of a "certificate" that attests to the fact that the state has determined that an individual is qualified and thus authorized to teach. This process is similar to the process states employ to determine that doctors, lawyers, psychologists, and physical therapists should be licensed to practice their respective professions. (For reasons now obscure, the term "certification" entered the lexicon of teaching rather than the conventional term "licensing.")

Before a state licenses a person to practice a profession, it establishes the requirements for that license. These requirements typically include educational prerequisites and assessments of the knowledge and skill expected of a beginning professional. Then, if a candidate satisfies the educational prerequisites and demonstrates adequate knowledge and skill through tests and performance assessments, a state grants the candidate a license.

Talented Teachers: The Essential Force for Improving Student Achievement, pages 165–170
Copyright © 2004 by Information Age Publishing
All rights of reproduction in any form reserved.

This article as first appeared in *Education Week* April 9, 2003. Reprinted with permission from the author.

In most professions, the process works well enough that policymakers and the public generally accept the fact that an individual who is granted a license is fit to practice as a beginning professional.

In most professions, candidates complete a course of study that typically includes four years of liberal arts education, two to four years in a professional school, and substantial internship experience. Professional study must be in a school that has been accredited by a national professional accrediting agency. In some professions, internships must also be professionally accredited. These educational and internship requirements, carried out according to rigorous standards, begin to build the foundation for public confidence in the quality of beginning professionals.

A visitor to a university can be confident that every professional school on campus is professionally accredited, with one notable exception. Coincidence or not, that professional school spends less per student than any other professional school on campus, yet its students generally pay the same tuition as other students.

Though candidates in the established professions have high-quality educational and internship experiences, the states properly insist upon external validation that candidates are, in fact, ready to begin to practice. That external validation is the licensing process. The process assesses candidate knowledge, skills, dispositions, and performance. Assessment is not limited to fixed-response, multiple-choice tests; it includes multiple measures of the above-named attributes. A record is built, with evidence accumulated from the beginning of professional study to the final assessment required by the state. It is this aggregation of information that assures the public that a beginning professional is fit to practice, and that provides the basis for public confidence in the quality of beginning professionals.

Teacher preparation and teacher certification clearly do not conform to the mainstream model of professional preparation and certification. In some cases, less is required for teacher certification than for occupational licensing. How is it, for example, that a substantial period of apprenticeship is required for those who trim our nails, our curls, or even the limbs of our trees, but is not required for those who are to help shape the minds of the next generation?

Even today, the vast majority of new teacher graduates begin to teach with only four years of preparation. "New teacher graduates" are candidates who major in education (elementary teachers) and those who major in a discipline and minor in teacher preparation (secondary teachers). In these four years, education candidates (elementary and secondary) must acquire a liberal arts education, content knowledge, teaching knowledge and skill, and clinical experience. Thus, new teacher graduates begin with less overall preparation than do peers entering other professions. They have had to accomplish in four years what other professionals accomplish in six to nine years. In addition, professional accreditation of education schools is voluntary. Thus, teacher preparation may be delivered according to rigorous standards ... or not. Because of the unevenness of teacher preparation, the preparation experience provides an uncertain basis for public confidence in the quality of beginning teachers.

The certification process is weak in comparison to the licensing process in most professions. The public should expect the certification process to provide independent validation of teaching candidates' liberal arts education, content knowledge, teaching knowledge and skill, and teaching performance. Most state certification processes fall short of that expectation. The public should expect new teacher graduates to have a foundation in general and liberal arts studies. Yet no state assesses more than basic skills and only 40 states do that. Despite the outcry that new teachers should have content knowledge, only 34 states require a content test, and many of those states do not test in all content areas. Moreover, there is widespread agreement that state cutoff scores are too low. Only 23 states check to see whether new teachers have mastered subject-specific pedagogy, despite research that such knowledge is essential.

What the public wants to know—and what the certification process should reveal—is whether new teachers can put to work what they have learned, so that their students will learn. Unbelievably, only seven states assess teaching performance. Today's certification processes are very uneven and collectively do not provide a basis for public confidence in the quality of new teachers. In the face of this reality, what is being done?

What are education schools doing? Long maligned, many of these schools now deserve kudos. Accredited education schools and those seeking accreditation are engaged in strengthening their programs and providing more information about the performance of their candidates and graduates. First, they are becoming explicit about the knowledge, skills, dispositions, and teaching performance that they expect candidates to develop. Second, they are designing and implementing systems to assess whether their candidates are developing consistently with these expectations.

The real challenge for them is to determine how to assess the impact of their candidates on student achievement. Education schools know that they must gather evidence on candidates while they are still candidates, but they also know that the most persuasive evidence will come from studies of recent graduates.

Instead of relying on current systems, we should devise and implement a "professional beginning-teacher licensing process."

Accredited education schools are developing strong partnerships with schools that enable candidates to have high-quality practical experiences. They are figuring out ways to prepare teachers to work with today's diverse student population. University faculty members are changing the ways they teach, including integrating technology into their instruction. Universities are investing in the preparation of teachers at accredited education schools. Six hundred and sixty education schools are on the move. We do not know about the half (about 600) which operate without the benefit of professional scrutiny. Not only would this situation not be tolerated in other professions, it would be illegal.

Nowhere is change more evident than in the approach of accredited education schools to teaching content. These institutions have placed content front and center for teacher-candidates. The largest and most comprehensive study to date of new teachers reveals that accredited education schools are very effective in preparing candidates to meet today's teaching-content testing requirements. Graduates of accredited schools passed state licensing tests at a much higher rate than liberal arts graduates and graduates of unaccredited schools.

In 1998, Congress, through Title II of the Higher Education Act, effectively challenged education schools not to graduate candidates who could not pass state licensing tests. These schools rose to the challenge and immediately imposed more-rigorous entrance and exit requirements, producing very high pass rates on today's licensing tests. Critics incorrectly alleged that colleges have manipulated the data. Instead, they have responded to the mandate of Congress and to today's state requirements. That is the good news.

The bad news is that today's teacher-certification procedures provide far too little information about whether new teachers are ready to teach.

Most accredited education schools have also opened alternate routes to teaching for nontraditional candidates. Indeed, most accredited education schools provide options like five-year programs, fifth-year programs, and internship programs to meet the variety of needs presented by traditional students, recent college graduates, and more mature candidates. Partnerships between education schools and school districts are also resulting in a variety of high-quality alternate routes to certification.

Some responses to the teacher shortage, however, contradict the mounting evidence that teacher preparation matters. Administrators, especially those in the largest urban areas, routinely hire individuals with no preparation. They do not want to do this, but the conditions in some schools make it difficult to attract and retain qualified teachers.

Meanwhile, recent research suggests that one-fourth of those who enter the teaching field without preparation quit by the end of their first year. Yet, those who have the knowledge and skill provided by teacher preparation have a first-year attrition rate that is half that of those who have no preparation.

Alternative certification (including temporary and emergency certification) and alternatives to certification (let anyone teach) will not do the job.

In a misleading use of language, these certificates literally mean that the state is certifying that these certificate holders are not yet certifiable under the state's own laws and regulations. Dissembling is not a strategy for enhancing public confidence.

Instead, we should revolutionize teacher-certification procedures so that they achieve the purpose for which they are intended. We should devise and implement a "professional beginning-teacher licensing process." These would be its requirements:

- **General Knowledge**. Basic-skills testing should be replaced with tests that measure the outcomes of liberal arts and general studies, including high-level literacy and numeracy and writing and speaking skills. Teachers need to be—and be seen as—well educated.
- **Subject Matter**. Rigorous content tests, aligned with professional standards for teachers and students, should be required of all, and professional cut scores should be set.
- **Teaching Knowledge**. New teaching-knowledge tests should be developed. These should be based on the idea that teachers should be able to understand and critique educational research and various schools of thought about teaching and learning. Educational knowledge and practice, like medical knowledge and practice, undergo continuous development. Teachers need to be given the intellectual tools for evaluating new information and using it to guide their practice.
- **Assessments of Performance**. Assessments of teaching performance, including the impact of a teacher on student achievement, must be a prerequisite for a professional teaching license. Assessments should begin during preservice teacher preparation and continue at least until the end of the first year of teaching. Every first year teacher must have a real mentor, not just another teacher with full-time responsibilities who drops by when time permits. Every first-year teacher must be mentored as part of a systematic induction program which provides instruction and support.

No one should receive a professional teaching license until he or she meets all of these requirements. Some states have already created a tiered licensing system, with the first-year teacher on a provisional license.

If a school cannot hire enough prepared and licensed teachers, then it should be restructured so that master teachers are responsible for all children and supervise the work of all unlicensed personnel ("The 10-Step Solution," *Commentary*, Feb. 27, 2002).

If the licensing process were as rigorous as what is outlined here, it would end the call for end runs. If the process had sufficient integrity, it would reveal those few unusual individuals who do not need much preparation to teach. However, most who enter teaching need and want high-quality preparation. We must devise and implement a professional beginning-teacher licensing process so that schools, including those in our largest urban districts, will leave no child behind.

NOTE

Arthur E. Wise is the president of the National Council for Accreditation of Teacher Education, based in Washington.

CHAPTER 10

REGULATION VERSUS MARKETS

The Case for Greater Flexibility in the Market for Public School Teachers

Michael Podgurksy

INTRODUCTION: CENTRALIZED REGULATION OF A DECENTRALIZED INDUSTRY

Public K–12 education is a decentralized industry with many small employers and a handful of very large ones. There are roughly 85,000 establishments (schools) organized into 15,000 firms (school districts) that employ approximately 2.7 million teachers. There is considerable variation in the size of these school district "firms," with a good deal of concentration in the largest of them. In 1995–1996, the largest 216 districts enrolled 25,000 or more students. This accounted for 1.5 percent of all districts, but enrolled 30.5 percent of students. At the same time, 70.9 percent of districts enrolled fewer than 1,000 students. These small firms accounted for 13.1 percent of enrollments (U.S. Department of Education, 1998, Table 90).

Fifty state education agencies regulate entry into this diverse labor market by licensing practitioners and promulgating extensive rules governing renewal of teacher certificates, specifying which certified personnel can teach which courses, and a range of other personnel policies. They also regulate the training of teachers by institutions of higher education, specifying what must be taught and who may enter the training market. On top of extensive state regulation, employment relations and personnel policies in public schools are also regulated by the collective bargaining process and the complex web of administrative law surrounding that process. While nominally professionals, a larger share of teachers are covered by collective bargaining agreements that include virtually any blue-collar or manual trade. In 1988, 19 percent of the work force was unionized. Among public sector workers the share was 43 percent, whereas among public school teachers the rate was 75 percent (Corme, Hirsch, & MacPherson, 1990).

Proposals for reforming this regulatory system vary widely. Some advocate adopting the medical model and letting teachers regulate themselves (using state power to enforce their regulations). This is a position taken by the National Commission on Teacher and America's Future (NCTAF), a private organization representing teacher union and various education organizations, which calls for tighter regulation of the market (NCTAF, 1996, 1997). The elements of the model they would implement include practitioner-dominated professional boards in states, national "performance-based" standards for initial licensure, and national standards for certification and accreditation. NCTAF has also been highly critical of the use of emergency or provisionally licensed teachers in many states. The Clinton administration, along with many states, embraced a number of elements of this agenda.

On the other hand, some states, including those that embraced elements of the NCTAF agenda, have simultaneously introduced policies that tend to lower entry barriers into teaching and deregulate other areas of personnel policy.[1] Examples include alternative certification programs and programs such as Teach for America and Troops to Teachers, which seek to streamline entry of promising nontraditional recruits into the classroom. The deregulation approach is most explicit in the case of charter schools. Currently, 13 states with charter school laws allow charter schools to hire uncertified teachers (some set limits on the uncertified share, others do not). Vouchers would take deregulation much further, since private schools for the most part operate outside the teacher regulatory framework.[2]

To a great extent, these policy debates center on the costs and benefits of relaxing or tightening the regulation of the teacher labor market. In this chapter, I focus on two features of the public sector labor market—mandatory certification and the single-salary schedule. Both of these features restrict the operation of the market and suppress competition—the first by limiting market entry, and the second by standardizing pay over large groups of teachers. Both of these features of the labor market play an important role in determining the quality of the teacher work force. In each case, I discuss some of the costs and benefits of the restriction and then contrast the policies of public and private schools. I argue that there are two important factors that influence private school behavior. First, private schools operate in a fairly competitive market and thus are forced to seek cost-effective strategies for delivering educational services. Second, the size of the wage-setting unit is much smaller in the private sector. The small size of these units tends to ameliorate information problems concerning teacher quality and performance, and helps make pay more market-sensitive and performance-driven.

MANDATORY TEACHER CERTIFICATION

All 50 states require teachers to hold a license to teach in a public school classroom. This represents what economists term a "barrier to entry" into the labor market. In order to enter the market, a prospective teacher must invest time and money to acquire a license to teach. In practice, this investment takes the form of one or two years of coursework in an approved training program, typically followed by an examination.

Teacher licensing is often justified by comparison to professions such as law and medicine. However, there are important differences between these two markets that are often overlooked.[3] First, in most other professional, licensed practitioners sell their services directly to the public. In this circumstance, licensing is justified by the argument that the consuming public lacks the technical training to make informed decisions and needs protection against incompetent practitioners. (Economists have long pointed out that licensing also protects the incomes of incumbent practitioners against competition; e.g., Friedman, 1962; Rottenberg, 1962.) However, the market in education is very different from these traditional professional markets. Parents do not purchase the services of teachers directly; rather, these services are purchased for them by principals and superintendents—experienced professionals who are also licensed by the state. The argument, therefore, is that teacher licensing is necessary to protect the public from the malfeasance by another group of licensed practitioners.

A second notable difference between licensing in teaching versus licensing in other professions is the much greater bureaucratic complexity in teaching. In other professions, regulatory boards typically issue a single license that allows practitioners to enter the market and practice whatever specialty they choose (e.g., law, medicine). In education, by contrast, licenses are very narrowly defined. States typically have a lengthy and complex set of certifications and endorsements. All of the hundreds of courses taught in Missouri schools are similarly coded, with a complex crosswalk defining which certificates and endorsements match which courses. Missouri is hardly unique. In Georgia, there are 178 certifications and endorsements; in New York there are nearly 100.[4] As a consequence of these certification labyrinths, each term school administrators confront a daunting assignment problem of matching the supply of certified staff hours—with each teacher being certified in only a small number of areas—to demand for a large range of courses. Not surprisingly, administrators often fail and assign teachers "out of field" or use emergency or provisionally certified staff.

Like any regulation, teacher licensing has costs and benefits. Some of the costs are obvious. For potential teachers, there are out-of-pocket costs associated with enrolling in teacher-training programs. These include tuition and fees for education courses, books, fees for licensing, and licensing exams. Of course, since higher education is heavily subsidized, the private costs are less than the total or social cost of the mandatory pedagogical training. However, in addition to these direct training costs, these is another important cost of training—the opportunity cost of time for the students. Economists who have analyzed education and training decisions have long recognized that the opportunity cost of time is one of the most important costs of any education investment (Mincer, 1974). Students who are attending school on a full-time basis, for example, are usually giving up significant earning opportunities. The popular saying sums it up—"time is money."

Licensing requirements that take the form of required coursework thus impose a higher cost on students whose alternative time is more valuable. This group of candidates includes more academically talented students who might have pursued other academic disciplines, as well as maturer "second career" entrants, including second-career women with young children. In other words, a licensing system that screens out candidates primarily on the basis of seat time in education courses is imposing a larger cost on, and thus discouraging entry by, precisely the type of individuals many would seek to recruit to teaching. If this hypothesis is correct, then relaxing transcript-based entry requirements should elicit a more elastic response from these same groups. In fact, the experience of states such as New Jersey and Texas, which have relaxed entry barriers by enacting ambitious alternative certification programs, provides evidence for this hypothesis. The academic quality of new alternative route candidates is generally superior to that of traditional candidates (Feistritzer & Chester, 1998; Dill, 1996, p. 951).

Of course, these costs must be balanced against the benefits of the licensing requirements and, specifically, the value of required pedagogy courses. I will not attempt an exhaustive survey of this literature, but rather will give some summary observations. There are several strands of research that have been cited in defense of mandatory pedagogical training. The most studied measure of teacher pedagogical investments is whether the teachers have a master's degree or further graduate training in education. If pedagogical training raises teacher performance, one would expect teachers with graduate training to outperform those who do not. Since teacher salary schedules universally reward graduate degrees, one would also hope for commensurate increases in productivity. In fact, there is little evidence in the literature indicating that teachers holding a master's are better teachers, at least when productivity is measured by student performance. Hanushek's surveys find no consistent support (Hanushek, 1986, 1996). A meta-analysis of this literature by Greenwald and colleagues (1996) finds some support for a positive effect of graduate training; the magnitude of the master's effect, however, is highly sensitive to the inclusion or exclusion of studies. In fact, in the full sample of the 46 studies of the meta-analysis that examine the effect of graduate teacher education, seven found a significant positive effect, six showed a significant negative effect, and 33 showed no significant effect, with approximately equal numbers of positive and negative point estimates (Ballou & Podgursky, 2000).[5]

Another body of research compares emergency- or provisionally certified teachers to traditionally trained teachers (for a survey, see Evertson, Hawley, & Zlotnik, 1985). If certification were a good indicator of quality, one would expect to see fully certified teachers outperform uncertified or emergency-certified teachers. Unfortunately, relatively few of these studies actually compare the scores of students of the two types of teachers. Even among those that do, the studies often do not control for the experience, the general academic achievement, or even the content knowledge of the teachers. One frequently cited study by Hawk, Coble, and Swanson (1985) illustrates this problem. These authors analyze the math test scores of the students of 36 North Carolina mathematics teachers, 18 of whom were math certified and 18 of whom were not (i.e., "out of field"). Roughly 300 students of these teachers were given a pretest and a posttest in mathematics.[6] The study found that the general mathematics and algebra gain scores were lower for the students of the uncertified teachers. However, the same study reported general mathematics and algebra test scores for the teachers themselves. For both tests, the scores for the uncertified teachers were lower, particularly in elementary algebra, suggesting that the uncertified teachers had less content knowledge of the material they were teaching. Thus, it is not clear whether lower content knowledge or less pedagogical training produced the weaker student performance.

In order to get reliable and more nationally representative results, we need studies that estimate the effect of teachers (teacher effects) and teacher characteristics using large, longitudinal files that track student achievement and compile data on the students' teachers. Ideally, we would like repeated observations of the teachers as well as the students to more accurately estimate teacher effects. Unfortunately, large longitudinal data sets on students that permit us to estimate teacher effects and correlate these effects with measurable teacher characteristics are scarce. Two studies that allow us to estimate the value of teacher coursework and academic majors are those by Goldhaber and Brewer (1997; 1999) and by Monk (1994).[7] Both of these studies focus on math and science test scores and are based on nationally representative longitudinal student-level data files. Monk analyzes a sample of students from the 1997 Longitudinal Study of American Youth. He finds some evidence that both academic and pedagogical coursework by teachers influence student test scores. Goldhaber and Brewer (1997, 1999) analyze a sample of tenth-grade students in mathematics courses drawn from the National Educational Longitudinal Survey of 1988. They do not analyze coursework per se, but rather the teacher's major and minor and type of certification. They find that math certification is associated with higher student test scores, as is an undergraduate or graduate degree in mathematics.[8] The results are much weaker for science, however.

Both of these studies suggest that, at least in mathematics instruction, both content knowledge and pedagogical training improve student performance. In addition, a consistent finding in the education-production function literature is that teachers' general academic skills, as measured by tests such as the ACT or SAT, are associated with higher student test scores.[9] Consider a simple regression equation (controlling for other student and school attributes):

$$Q = a \text{ Pedagogy} + b \text{ Content} + c \text{ } G, \text{ } a, \text{ } b, \text{ } c > 0$$

In this equation, Pedagogy represents a teacher's formal coursework in pedagogy, Content is a measure of the teacher's content knowledge, and G is a measure of the teacher's general level of academic skills (e.g., SAT score). There is evidence in the literature that all three of these coefficients—a, b, and c—may be positive. Proponents of conventional teacher licensing emphasize the positive effect of pedagogy. However, this same type of education-production function evidence points to the potential for substituting one input for another. The same regression coefficients suggest that an uncertified teacher's deficiency in pedagogical training can be compensated for by increased content knowledge or general ability with no loss in student performance. In other words, the regression studies that demonstrate the value of pedagogical training also demonstrate the possibility that schools can trade off such training for other productive teacher attributes.

COSTS OF EXCLUSION

The literature on the benefits of teacher certification is rather mixed. Within the area of math and science, it suggests that certification and content knowledge matter. Outside of math and science, the evidence is thin. However, even if it were the case that certified teachers in all fields were, on average, superior teachers, that would not necessarily mean that uncertified teachers should be excluded from the market. This is a point often overlooked by proponents of traditional licensing, who justify mandatory certification by pointing to evidence showing that, on average, certified teachers are superior.

The case for *mandatory* teacher licensing, however, requires more than a simple demonstration of a difference in average quality. It is almost certainly true that the dispersion of teacher quality within the certified and uncertified populations is large relative to the mean. We know, for example, that the dispersion of test scores within the population taking teacher-licensing exams is very large and that many of these test-takers have not completed teacher-training programs (Educational Testing Service, 1999). In addition, while a growing literature points to the importance of "teacher effects" on student performance, measured teacher characteristics, including teacher certification and coursework, explain relatively little of the variation in these teachers effects (Goldhaber & Brewer, 1997). In other words, while the literature points to some statistically significant teacher characteristics, the majority of the variation in teacher quality remains unexplained.

When the dispersion of quality is large in both the certified and uncertified populations and the effect of certification is small relative to the variance, then many uncertified candidates will be superior to certified candidates. Mandatory certification, when strictly enforced, prevents a school official from *ever* hiring an uncertified candidate if a certified candidate is available. An implicit cost of licensing therefore arises when a school is prevented from hiring a superior unlicensed candidate.

Figure 1 represents a hypothetical scenario in which teacher certification is a good signal of teacher quality. In this graph we plot the distribution of teacher quality for two populations of teaching applicants—certified and uncertified. In this case, the average certified applicant is superior to 90 percent of the uncertified applicants. This is a very large difference in mean quality. However, even with this sizable difference in the means between the

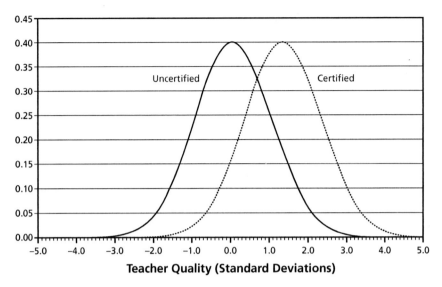

Teacher Quality (Standard Deviations)

Figure 1.   Average certified applicant is better than 90 percent of noncertified applicants.

two populations, there remains a great deal of overlap, which means that many uncertified teachers are superior to many certified teachers.

A few calculations illustrate this point. Suppose we randomly select one teacher from each distribution in Figure 1. It turns out that 18 percent of the time the certified teacher will be superior. Suppose that there are four applicants for a single teaching job—two uncertified and two certified—randomly drawn from the two distributions. In this case, the highest quality applicant will be an uncertified teacher 13 percent of the time. Since there are far more noneducation than education majors in the population, it is possible that in some circumstances there would be more uncertified than certified applicants. If there are two uncertified and one certified applicants, randomly chosen, for this position, an uncertified applicant is the best candidate 29 percent of the time.[10]

Thus, even in a best-case scenario in which certification is a very strong signal of quality, the best candidate for a teaching job will often be uncertified as long as there is substantial dispersion in quality within the certified and uncertified populations. In fact, judging from the relatively modest coefficients one finds in the education-production function literature, the information conveyed by certification is likely much closer to that depicted in Figure 2. In this case, the average certified teacher is better than 60 percent of uncertified applicants. If we randomly choose a certified and an uncertified candidate, the uncertified candidate will now be superior just 43 percent of the time. With four applicants (two certified, two uncerti-

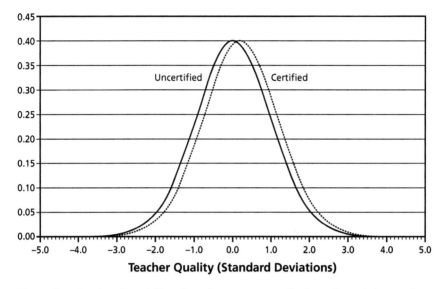

Teacher Quality (Standard Deviations)

Figure 2.   Overlapping ability when the average certified applicant is better than 60 percent of noncertified applicants.

fied), the uncertified candidate will be the best 41 percent of the time. Finally, if there are two uncertified and one certified candidates, an uncertified candidate will be the best candidate 59 percent of the time. These probability calculations are summarized in Table 1.

Table 1.   Probability that an Uncertified Candidate Is the Best Applicant

Sample	Average Certified Applicant is Superior to 90 Percent of Uncertified Applicants (Figure 1)	Average Certified Applicant is Superior to 60 Percent of Uncertified Applicants (Figure 2)
1 Certified & 1 Noncertified	.18	.43
2 Certified & 2 Noncertified	.14	.51
1 Certified & 2 Noncertified	.29	.59

These calculations illustrate a cost of licensing entry barriers. When employers are prevented from hiring the best candidate, productivity falls. Of course, if no other information on teacher quality were available, it might be worthwhile to exclude all of the uncertified teachers from the market even if certification were a relatively poor signal of quality. However, other information is available. Local supervisors are in a good position to assess the quality of teaching applicants directly through interviews, student teaching, and practice classes. A number of education-production function studies find that principal evaluations of teaching performance are valid predictors of student performance (Armor et al., 1976; Murnane, 1975; Sanders & Horn, 1994).[11] The important question, then, is whether the educational firms in this market are structured to take advantage of this information, and whether they have an incentive to do so.

SIZE OF WAGE-SETTING UNITS

Economists have long recognized that size plays an important role in a firm's level and structure of compensation, as well as in its choice of wage-payment mechanisms. The reason for these differences centers on the cost of monitoring employee performance and quality in large and small firms (Brown, 1990; Garen, 1985). An important advantage enjoyed by private schools in this regard is that the wage-setting unit is typically the school, while in the public sector pay is set at the district level.[12] This means that the difference between the average sizes of the typical wageset-ting units in the two sectors is very large. The data in Figure 3 illustrate this point. Here we plot the average number of full-time (FTE) teachers in schools and school districts in the public and private sectors. The average public school district employs 168 FTE teachers. The average school district, however, does not represent the situation of an average teacher. As noted in the introduction, the distribution of enrollments in public school districts is highly skewed, with the largest districts accounting for the bulk of enrollments. In 1993–1994, the 731 school districts with enrollments of 10,000 or more students employed on average 1,486 FTE teachers and accounted for 46 percent of FTE teacher employment. In other words, most public school teachers are employed in large wage-setting units with well over 1,000 teachers.

At the other end of the size distribution are private and charter schools. The average private elementary and secondary school enrolls less than half as many students as a comparable public school. While the student-teacher ratio is somewhat lower in the private sector, this does not offset the much smaller average size of the school. The result is that the average FTE employment of teachers in private schools is remarkably low. The average private high school employs just 27 FTE teachers, and the average private elementary school employs 11 FTE teachers. The best available evidence to date suggests that charter schools are also smaller than traditional public schools. The average charter school in 1997–1998 enrolled 238 students. Assuming the public-sector average of 17 students per FTE teacher, this implies an FTE employment of just 14 teachers.

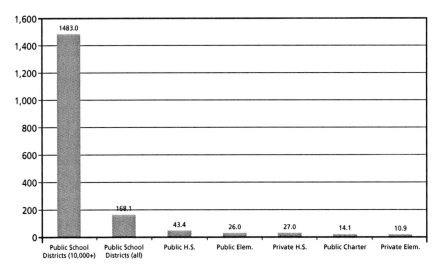

Figure 3.   Average FTE teachers employed in public and private districts and schools.

In rough terms, then, the typical wage-setting unit in the public sector is 100 times larger than it is in the private sector. This has important implications for personnel and compensation policy in the two sectors.[13]

EMPLOYMENT OF CERTIFIED TEACHERS IN PRIVATE AND CHARTER SCHOOLS

The private school sector provides a useful test of the value of certification. Private schools operate in a competitive market and are under strong pressures to deliver quality educational services in a cost-efficient way. Private school parents—particularly those in the most expensive nonsectarian school sector are likely to be well informed consumers, given their education levels and the substantial sums they spend for tuition. Private schools are also much smaller "firms" and thus in a better position to directly monitor quality. As a consequence, they may attach less value to readily observed credentials such as certification in making staffing decisions.

Table 2 provides data on certification rates of private school teachers. The analysis variable is whether the teacher holds state certification in his or her primary teaching area. The rate for the public sector is 95.6 percent, whereas the rate for private schools is much lower, particularly in nonreligious schools, where just 55.9 percent of teachers are certified. The rates are lower still at the secondary level. In nonreligious secondary schools, the certification rate is just 35.1 percent. Thus, while private schools do hire certified teachers, they also hire substantial numbers of uncertified teachers.[14]

**Table 2.   Teachers Certified in Primary Teaching Field
(As a Percentage of All Teachers)**

	Public School Teachers	Private School Teachers		
		Catholic	Other Religious	Nonreligious
All Teachers	95.9%	73.6%	50.2%	55.9%
Elementary	96.7%	77.1%	51.9%	49.2%
Secondary	94.8%	67.7%	46.4%	35.1%
Combined	96.0%	72.2%	49.6%	62.8%

Source: 1997–98 Schools and Staffing Surveys, reported in Ballou & Podgursky, 1997.

How does the academic quality of uncertified teachers compare to that of certified teachers? One measure of teacher quality is the selectivity of the college from which the teacher graduated. Several production-function studies find that the selectivity of a teacher's undergraduate college is correlated with student academic achievement (Winkler, 1975; Summers & Wolfe, 1977; Ehrenberg & Brewer, 1993, 1994). The data in Table 3 suggest that private schools use this flexibility to trade off teacher certification to get higher academic quality for teachers. The share of teachers graduating from selective institutions is consistently higher in the uncertified population.

Table 3.   Measures of Teacher Quality in Public and Private Schools

	Public All	Private Religious		Private Nonreligious	
		Certified	Not Certified	Certified	Not Certified
College Selectivity: Most Competitive	1.0	.9	2.4	3.4	14.6
Other Selective	5.4	4.1	5.7	9.8	15.0
Total Selective	6.4	5.0	8.1	13.2	29.6
Math and Science Majors	5.4	5.3	5.8	6.7	10.0
Academic Majors	21.5	24.5	30.9	30.6	50.2

Source: College selectivity from Ballou & Podgursky, 1997. Math, science, and academic majors are tabulated from 1993–94 Schools and Staffing Surveys.

Several studies have called attention to the number of secondary teachers who did not major or minor in their primary teaching field (Ingersoll, 1998; U.S. Department of Education, National Center for Education Statistics, 1999). Table 3 reports the share of teachers in private schools who majored in math or science, or who had an academic major. Unlike the Ingersoll or

National Center for Education Statistics studies, however, undergraduate education majors are not included in the math and science count, nor are they included in the academic count. Overall, the private sector employs more math, science, and academic majors. The important thing to note, however, is that the private sector mean is raised primarily by uncertified hires. The certified-uncertified quality gap is particularly striking in the private, nonreligious schools. The data in Table 3 are consistent with the substitution hypothesis discussed above—the evidence suggests that private schools compensate for the lack of certification by substituting other academic skills.

Like private schools, charter schools are held accountable through market pressures. Since education dollars follow students, if parents do not enroll their children, charter schools will close. In fact, while little evidence is available to date on students' academic performance, charter schools have proven very popular with parents. The majority of charter schools have waiting lists, which are often very long (Center for Education Reform, 1999). Moreover, charter schools are also held accountable through the charter renewal process.

As noted earlier, charter schools in a number of states are allowed to bypass licensing requirements and hire uncertified teachers. When given the opportunity, do charters avail themselves of this option? The evidence in Table 4 suggests that they do. Here we present data from the third-year report of the major U.S. Department of Education study of charter schools. We present data from states that: (a) permit charter schools to hire uncertified teachers and (b) had at least 20 schools answer the survey. In these charter schools, roughly one quarter of the teachers is not certified. (Unfortunately, these data do not permit us to compare elementary and secondary schools.)

Table 4. Percentage of Instructional Staff in Charter Schools Who Are State-Certified

State	Percentage of Instructional Staff Who Are Certified	Number of Responding Schools	Number of Charter Schools (1997–98)
Arizona	72.7	127	135
California	79.5	120	135
Florida	71.0	31	34
Massachusetts	73.4	21	24
North Carolina	64.7	27	34
Tennessee	70.2	29	41

Source: U.S. Department of Education, Office of Educational Research and Improvement, 1999. Data for 1997–98 school year. States that permit charter schools to hire uncertified teachers and in which at least 20 charter schools responded to the survey.

In sum, private and charter schools are held accountable through market pressures and, in the case of charter schools, through the potential of having one's contract or charter revoked. Since the wage-setting unit in these two sectors is small, and since they are unencumbered with licensing regulations, many of these schools have chosen to hire uncertified instructional personnel. In effect, these schools are exploiting the fact that their small size permits them to efficiently monitor the quality of new staff.

One might argue that the tight budgets of private and charter schools do not permit them to hire certified teachers (and that these schools in effect "cut corners" by hiring uncertified teachers to the detriment of their students). This type of argument implicitly assumes that the parent "customers" are not well informed in choosing to send their children to such schools. To determine the merit of this logic, it is useful to examine the behavior of very wealthy school districts. Do the wealthiest school districts attach high value to teacher certification? In Figure 4, we present data on the percentage of district teachers who are uncertified by the average level of school-district spending for Westchester county, a suburb of New York City that is well known for its expensive homes and fine schools. These small districts have among the highest levels of spending per student in the nation. The average teacher salary in these districts in 1997–1998 was $68,400, and many districts had maximum scheduled salaries in excess of $80,000. However, in spite of their high levels of teacher salaries and per-

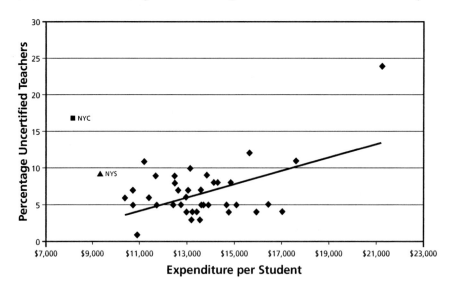

Figure 4.   Expenditure per student and percentage of uncertified teachers: Westchester County, 1997–98.
Source: New York State Education Department, *New York, The State of Learning* April, 1999, Part II, Table 3; NYC= New York City average, NYS = New York state average

student spending, a non-negligible share of these teachers are not certified. Indeed, several of these districts have noncertification rates that exceed the state average, and the uncertified share of teachers tends to rise with the level of per-student spending. These are not districts that "cut corners"—they have chosen to devote the majority of their additional operating spending to higher teacher salaries and smaller class sizes, but not to a fully certified teaching workforce.

RIGID PAY STRUCTURES

The single-salary schedule, which bases pay entirely on the experience and academic credentials of teachers, is a nearly universal feature of public sector teacher labor markets. Under a single-salary schedule, all of the certified teaching personnel—kindergarten as well as secondary chemistry and mathematics teachers, along with a variety of special education teachers—are paid according to the same schedule with no differentials reflecting field, individual effort, talent, or merit. By the same token, all teachers in a school district, regardless of the character of the school's working conditions, are paid identical salaries.

In a 1962 RAND study on teacher pay, Kershaw and McKean (1962) wrote:

> The distinguishing characteristic of the single-salary schedule is that the salary class to which a classroom teacher is assigned depends on the professional qualifications of the teacher rather than the school level or assignment. This is the definition of the National Education Association, which has been the most active proponent of the single-salary schedule. There are two (and only two) ingredients to "professional qualifications"; these are the amount of training a teacher has had, measured by counting courses, and the number of years the teacher has taught. The length of time taught is sometimes restricted to years in the district paying the salary, though often credit for teaching elsewhere is allowed up to a certain maximum number of years. The points to note are the particular steps or differentials that are allowed and their completely automatic nature. It is the number of years at college that counts, not whether the college was the best or the worst; it is the number of graduate courses taken, not their excellence or usefulness or (usually) their relevance. Finally, the pertinent factor is how long the teacher has taught, not how well. And the difficulties of recruiting or retaining particular teaching skills are completely irrelevant in such a schedule. For any given set of "professional qualifications" so defined, a teacher's salary is uniquely determined by reference to the schedule. (Kershaw and McKean, 1962, p. 23)

Nearly three decades later, this is still a fairly accurate description of the wage-setting process for public school teachers.

There are many features that differentiate teacher labor markets from those of other professionals, but certainly the single-salary schedule is one of the most notable. Differential pay by field within professions is pervasive. Cardiologists on average earn much more than general practitioners; corporate lawyers earn more than public-interest lawyers; and intensive-care nurses earn more than school nurses. Of course, there are also large differences in academic salaries by field in higher education. Even community colleges differentiate pay by field.

Economists see these types of pay differentials as central to the efficient operation of markets. Professional fields that require greater training or draw on relatively specialized skills typically command higher earnings. Alternately, some tasks involve greater stress and less pleasant working conditions. Other things being equal, these too will command higher earnings. Even the U.S. military recognizes the principle of compensating differentials with overseas and hazardous-duty pay.

The single-salary schedule suppresses these differentials and its rigidity yields perverse, unintended consequences. Rather than allowing wages to adjust to compensate for differing working conditions, teachers must adjust instead. Special education teachers "burn out" and leave the profession, or transfer over to assignments outside of special education. Troubled schools in urban districts end up with the least experienced teachers as more experienced teachers use their seniority to transfer to favored schools. Teachers move but pay doesn't.

If schools differ in terms of nonpecuniary conditions (e.g., safety, student rowdiness), then equalizing teacher pay will disequalize teacher quality. On the other hand, if districts wish to equalize quality, they will need to disequalize pay. Collective bargaining agreements in large, urban school districts, which impose the same salary schedule over hundreds of schools, suppress pay differentials and induce teachers to leave the most troubled schools. The recent proposal by New York City's Chancellor Crew to pay bonuses to teachers to move to failing schools recognizes this problem (Hartocolis, 1999). Unfortunately, this type of flexibility is very unusual in urban contracts.

PUBLIC–PRIVATE COMPARISONS

As noted earlier, the wage-setting unit is far smaller in the private sector. This allows private sector pay to float to the market level much more readily than it can in public schools. Even if everyone in the school earns identical pay, the pay at the school can more readily reflect the skills of the workforce, as well as the amenities or disamenities of the school. For example, with smaller wage-setting units, one important rigidity in the single-salary schedule would be relaxed as elementary and secondary pay are allowed to float to their respective market levels. Evidence suggests that when this occurs, elementary pay slips below that of secondary. Indeed, this was typically the case in the public sector prior to World War II and the spread of the single-salary schedule (Kershaw & McKean, 1962).

Data from the 1993–1994 Schools and Staffing Surveys allow us to examine whether elementary school pay is below that of secondary schools in the private sector. Table 5 reports regression coefficients from a simple model of private school pay. In the survey, private school administrators who reported using a salary schedule were asked about pay at different points on the schedule. For this regression, two of these are used as dependent variables: starting base pay (bachelor's degree and no experience) and base pay for a teacher with a master's degree and 20 years of experience (MA-20). Controls are included for region, religious affiliation, and a

Table 5. Teacher Salaries in Elementary and Secondary Private Schools: Estimated Regression Coefficients

Independent Variable	Dependent Variable BA Starting Pay, Exp = 0	Dependent Variable MA Pay, Exp = 20
Region		
Northeast	−1076.7***	−506.8
Midwest	−1708.2***	−1574.9***
South	−2281.2***	−3889.1***
West	—	—
School Type		
Catholic	−2372.5***	−4453.9***
Other Religious	−2041.9***	−5049.3***
Nonreligious	—	—
Rural Location	−1500.8***	−3493.4***
School Level		
Secondary	2170.7***	4815.7***
Combined	561.8**	873.6*
Elementary	—	—
Adj. R^2	.128	.164
Sample size	1746	1746

Level of significance: 10% (*), 5% (**), 1% (***). Average base salary for a teacher with a BA and no experience was $17,531. Average base salary for a teacher with a MA and 20 years' experience was $27,946.
Source: 1993–94 Schools and Staffing Surveys

dummy variable for rural location.[15] The variables of interest are at the bottom of the table. Here we see that starting pay in secondary private schools in 1993–1994 was $2,171 higher than in elementary schools, and pay for teachers with a master's was $4,816 higher. These are substantial premiums considering that, in this sample, the average base starting pay was just $17,531, and MA-20 pay just $27,946. Pay at combined primary-secondary schools was below that of high schools, but significantly above that of private elementary schools.

The hundredfold difference in firm sizes between the private and public sectors means that, at least in terms of wage determination, private schools look more like a team and public schools look more like a large factory. Indeed, given the relatively small size of private schools, and the competitive market in which they operate, even if all pay scales are uniform, there will be strong performance incentives simply due to the small size of the team. On the one hand, it will be much easier for supervisors to monitor performance and identify shirking in such a small firm. Economic theory suggests that small firms are more likely to use merit- or performance-based individual pay, while large firms will tend to standardize pay (Brown, 1990).

Once again, a look at the private sector is instructive. Table 6 reports the use of incentive pay in public and private schools. In the first row, we find that 12.1 percent of public schools report that they use merit pay. This compares with just 10.9 percent of private sector schools. There is considerable variation within the private sector, however, with 24.3 percent of nonreligious schools reporting use of merit pay. On closer examination, however, the private sector plans seem to play a much more important role in pay determination. We estimated the effect of these pay plans on earnings in the two sectors (details are in Ballou & Podgursky, 1997, ch. 6). In the public sector, teachers who report that they receive merit pay have earnings just 1.9 percent higher than observationally similar teachers—a very small difference. In the private sector, however, the estimated pay differential is 10.7 percent.

Table 6.   Use of Incentive Pay

			Type of School		
Have a Merit Pay Plan	Public	Catholic	Other Religious	Non-religious	All Private
Percentage of Schools with Plan	12.1%	6.0%	9.3%	24.3%	10.9%
Percentage of Teachers with Plan	13.8%	7.2%	11.8%	33.8%	14.9%
Percentage of Teachers Receiving	10.1%	10.5%	10.2%	28.1%	19.0%
Average Award as percentage of Pay	1.9%	—	—	—	10.7%

Source: Ballou & Podgursky, 1997 (Table 6.4)

The statistics in Table 6 understate pay flexibility in private schools. Many schools that reward more valuable teachers may not report that they have a formal merit pay plan in place. For example, data from the 1993–1994 Schools and Staffing Surveys shows that roughly 99 percent of public schools report that they have a salary schedule to compensate teachers, as compared to just 67 percent of private schools. Even among the two-thirds of private schools reporting that they use salary schedules, we found that academic credentials and experience explained much less of the variation in pay in private as compared to public schools (Ballou & Podgursky, 1997, ch. 6; Ballou, 2000). In our ongoing research on personnel policy in private and charter schools, we have discussed compensation policy with many school administrators. When we ask them if they have a salary schedule that they use to guide teacher compensation, many say that they do. However, when we ask if they are willing to go "off schedule" to retain or recruit a particularly valuable teacher, they invariably reply that they are. This is consistent with our finding that private school pay is much more dispersed about an experience regression line.

I am aware of no national data or academic studies on the use of merit or incentive pay in charter schools. The only data I am aware of come from a Fall 1998 survey of 66 charter schools in Arizona conducted by the Center for Market-Based Education in the Goldwater Institute (Center for Market-Based Education, undated). Thirty percent of respondents reported using a salary structure that tied pay to performance measures. About half of these included student test scores. Others included parent satisfaction surveys, attendance, and classroom observations. Twelve of the charter schools expressed a desire for assistance in developing a performance-based compensation structure.[16]

My own anecdotal evidence, gathered over several years of attending education conferences with charter school administrators and consultants, leads me to believe that many charter schools are moving away from the single-salary schedule and experimenting with alternative and innovative compensation plans. Several examples from "mature" charter schools illustrate this point. The Edison Project now operates 77 schools, serving roughly 36,000 children in 12 states.[17] Edison does not use individual merit pay. Rather, it has created a four-step career ladder associated with the team-teaching model employed in its schools, with the top rung of the ladder the team leader. Promotions up this job ladder, and associated pay increases, are merit-based. There are also schoolwide performance-based bonuses. Edison has also drawn considerable national attention with its policy of providing stock options to its entire staff.

Since Minnesota was the first state to enact a charter school law (1991), it has the some of the most mature charter schools. Designs for Learning operates five schools in the Minneapolis-St. Paul area, the oldest of which is now in its fifth year of operation. All of its schools use a competency-based pay schedule, in which teachers advance through four levels of proficiency in seven competency areas, with fixed additions to the teacher's base salary for each step. These competencies are seen as part of a teacher's ongoing professional development plan. Teachers who do not make regular progress up these competency ladders generally do not have their contracts renewed. Another interesting example is The Edvisions Cooperative in Henderson, Minnesota a teacher cooperative that provides instructional services to the Minnesota New Country School. Formally, there is no principal in this school. Managerial and some administrative functions are instead spread among the co-op members. All members of the cooperative are expected to develop their own 13-point professional development plan, which is reviewed annually by the other co-op members. No pay raises were distributed for several years as the cooperative was in its startup phase. Eventually, pay increases were distributed; however, two members who had failed to meet their professional development goals received no pay raise.[18]

CONCLUSION

Compared to other labor markets, and particularly other professional labor markets, the market for public school teachers is highly regulated. Mandatory licensing imposes costly entry barriers that tend to discourage entry by individuals with good labor market alternatives to teaching. Collective bargaining, teacher tenure, and the single-salary schedule inhibit flexible and performance-driven wage-setting, and make it difficult to reward good teachers and weed out poor ones. The single-salary schedule also exacerbates problems of recruiting teachers in fields with shortages such as special education, math, and science.

I have argued that personnel policies in private schools and, given preliminary data, charter schools are very different from those in traditional public schools and that these differences are explained by two factors. The first is incentives. Competition and, for charter schools, the threat of charter nonrenewal provides strong incentives for employers to adopt efficient and flexible personnel policies. The second is size. The wage-setting unit in private and charter schools is far smaller than in traditional public schools. Among other things, small size means that private and charter employers are better able to monitor teacher quality and performance. I believe that this helps explain why private schools place much less importance on traditional certification as a signal of teacher competence or quality in recruitment and make much greater use of individualized or merit pay in compensation policy. Finally, independent of any differences in intra-school pay structures, the small size of the wage-setting unit in the private sector permits the overall level of wages at the school to be more market sensitive, and to better reflect the skills of the workforce and other characteristics of the school.

Flexibility in recruitment and compensation helps private schools recruit, retain, and motivate a high-quality work force in a cost effective manner. The private school experience, as well as evidence from the unfolding charter school experiment, provide valuable lessons for traditional public schools and, in my opinion, deserve more attention in the current policy debates on teacher quality.

AUTHORS' NOTE

From Margaret C. Wang and Herbert J. Walberg, *Tomorrow's Schools,* Copyright 2001 by McCutchan Publishing Corporation, Richmond, California. Used by permission of the publisher

NOTES

1. The deregulation position was articulated by the Fordham Foundation in its recent policy statement, reprinted in Kanstoroom and Finn (1999).

2. Some states nominally require that private schools hire certified teachers as a condition for voluntary state accreditation. However, our own analysis of certification data in these states suggests that these regulations are not aggressively enforced (Ballou & Podgursky, 1998).

3. An exception is Lieberman (1957).

4. These numbers were provided to the author by officials in the relevant state education agencies. None of these totals include the large number of vocational education certificates, which may add another 40 or more titles to the list. Nor do these include hundreds of "grandfathered" but sill valid codes. In Missouri, there are 600 active certification codes; in New York State there are 800.

5. There also exists an older literature that compares levels of education coursework and student outcomes. For surveys see Druva and Anderson, 1983 and Ashton and Crocker, 1987. In general, these studies do not include controls for other teacher characteristics that might affect student performance such as experience, content knowledge, or general academic ability.

6. There were no controls for student demographics. However, the study design paired each certified teacher with an uncertified teacher in the same school. Since there were no controls on teacher characteristics, it may be the case that the uncertified teachers differed in other respects as well. For example, the uncertified teachers may have had less experience.

7. Sanders' work with the Teacher Value-Added Assessment System (e.g., Sanders & Horn, 1994; Sanders, Saxton, & Horn, 1997) in Tennessee, which

is based on a massive statewide longitudinal student database, holds a great deal of promise as a means for estimating teacher effects and the returns of teacher credentials. An important feature of this database is that it permits repeated observations of teacher effects with successive cohorts of students. Sanders and associates have studies underway to analyze the effect of various teacher-training programs.

8. Students of teachers who are certified, but not math certified, perform significantly worse than students of uncertified teachers.

9. In his survey of this literature Hanushek (1986) writes: "The only reasonably consistent finding seems to be that 'smarter' teachers do better in terms of student achievement." The Greenwald, Hedges, and Laine (1996) study finds that of teacher characteristics, the largest effect on student performance is the academic ability of the teacher. Ferguson (1991) and Ferguson and Ladd (1996) find large effects on student achievement of teacher test scores in basic literacy skills and the ACT, respectively.

10. As the number of applicants grows, the law of large numbers gradually shifts the odds toward the certified applicant. Nonetheless, even with 20 applicants for a single opening (10 certified, 10 uncertified), the probability that an uncertified applicant is the best of the 20 is 6 percent.

11. It should be noted that these studies assess principals' evaluations of the entire teaching workforce, not just new recruits.

12. Obviously, not all private schools set pay independently. One seeming exception is Catholic schools. There are three types of Catholic schools: diocesan, parish, and independent. Many Catholic dioceses establish minimum salary schedules for parish-run elementary schools, but parish schools are free to exceed these minimums. Some dioceses establish salary schedules for high schools, whereas others allow high schools to set their own pay. Independent schools run by Catholic orders set their own pay. Thus, even in large cities, pay determination in Catholic schools is fairly decentralized.

13. Within the public sector, research suggests that district size is inversely related to educational performance (Walberg, 1992; Walberg & Fowler, 1987).

14. Similarly, private schools to date have shown little interest in certification of experienced teachers by the National Board for Professional Teaching Standards. While roughly 13 percent of teachers are in private schools, only 2.4 percent (42) of the 1,781 teachers who are National Board certified are employed in private schools. (These statistics were provided by the National Board.) This suggests that, because of their small size and ability to monitor performance directly, private schools attach little value to an external assessment of their experienced work force (or at least less than $2,000 per teacher the cost of a National Board assessment).

15. The omitted category is indicated by "-." Thus, other things equal, schools in the South have a starting pay level $2,281 below schools in the West.

16. Charter schools in Arizona, as in most other states, are exempt from teacher tenure laws. Most of the charter schools in the Arizona survey had one-year contracts that were not automatically renewed. Most schools noted that a condition for renewal was a satisfactory evaluation. Factors playing a role in renewal were student test scores, parent evaluations, and peer evaluations, among others. Thus, even in schools that do not formally tie pay to performance, if contract renewal is linked to performance, then implicitly pay is

as well. Seniority-based pay increases then reflect satisfactory performance and professional development.

17. Fewer than half of Edison schools are actually charter schools. The remainder are "contract schools," or schools that Edison runs under contract with a local school district. According to Edison officials, the company attempts to implement similar personnel policies in both situations.

18. These charter school cases are based on presentations at a session I organized on compensation policy and on personal interviews conducted at the Edventures conference in Madison, Wisconsin, July 29-31, 1999.

REFERENCES

Armor, D., Conry-Osenguera, P., Cox, M., King, N., McDonnell, L., Pascal, A., Pauly, E., & Zellma, G. (1976). *Analysis of the school preferred reading program in selected Los Angeles minority schools.* Santa Monica, California: RAND.

Ashton, P., & Crocker, L. (1987, May June). Systematic study of planned variations: The essential focus of teacher education reform. *Journal of Teacher Education,* 2–8.

Ballou, D. (2000). Pay for performance in public and private schools. *Economics of Education Review.* forthcoming.

Ballou, D., & Podgursky, M. (1997). *Teacher pay and teacher quality.* Kalamazoo, Michigan: W.E. Upjohn Institute for Employment Research.

Ballou, D., & Podgursky, M. (1998, Summer). Teacher recruitment and retention in public and private schools. *Journal of Policy Analysis and Management, 17*(3), 393–418.

Ballou, D., & Podgursky, M. (2000, February). Reforming teacher preparation and licensing: What is the evidence? *Teachers College Record, 102*(1), 5–27.

Brown, C. (1990). Firm's choice of methods of pay. *Industrial and Labor Relations Review, 43*(Special issue), 1655–182S.

Center for Education Reform. (1999). *National Charter School Directory, 1998–1999.* Washington, DC: Author.

Center for Market-Based Education & Goldhaber Institute. (Undated). *Charter school wage and incentive survey.* Phoenix, Arizona: Author.

Corme, M. A., Hirsch, B. T., & MacPherson, D. A. (1990, October). Union membership and coverage in the US, 1983–1988. *Industrial and Labor Relations Review, 44*(1), 5–33.

Dill, V. S. (1996). Alternative teacher certification. In J. P. Sikula (Ed.), *Handbook of research on teacher education.* New York: Macmillan.

Druva, C. A., & Anderson, R. D. (1983). Science teacher characteristics by teacher behavior and student outcome: A meta-analysis of research. *Journal of Research in Science Teaching,* 20(5), 467–479.

Educational Testing Service. (1999). *The academic quality of prospective teachers: The impact of admissions and licensure testing.* Princeton, NJ: Author.

Ehrenberg, R. C., & Brewer, D. J. (1993). Did teachers' race and verbal ability matter in the 1960s? Coleman Revised. *Economics of Education Review, 14*(1), 1–23.

Ehrenberg, R. C., & Brewer, D. J. (1994). Do school and teacher characteristics matter? Evidence from high school and beyond. *Economics of Education Review*, *13*(1), 1–17.

Evertson, C. M., Hawley, W. D., & Zlotnik, M. (1985, May June). Making a difference in educational quality through teacher education. *Journal of Teacher Education*, 2–12.

Ferguson, R. F. (1991). "Paying for Public Education: New Evidence on How and Why Money Matters." *Harvard Journal on Legislation* Vol. 28, 465–498.

Ferguson, R. F., & Ladd, H. (1996). "How and Why Money Matters: An Analysis of Alabama Schools. In Helen Ladd (Ed.), *Holding Schools Accountable: Performance-Based Reform in Education*. Washington, DC: Brookings Institution.

Feistritzer, C. E., & Chester, D. C. (1998). *Alternative teacher certification: A state-by-state analysis: 1998–99*. Washington, DC: National Center for Education Information.

Friedman, M. (1962). *Capitalism and freedom*. Chicago, Illinois: University of Chicago Press.

Garen, J. (1985, August). Worker heterogeneity, job screening, and firm size. *Journal of Political Economy, 93*(4), 715–739.

Goldhaber, D. D., & Brewer, D. J. (1997, Summer). Why don't schools and teachers seem to matter? *Journal of Human Resources, 32*(3), 505–523.

Goldhaber, D. D., & Brewer, D. J. (1999). Teacher licensing and student achievement. In M. Kanstoroom and C. Finn (Eds.), *Better teachers, better schools* (pp. 83–102). Washington, DC: Thomas B. Fordham Foundation.

Greenwald, R., Hedges, L. V., & Laine, R. D. (1996, Fall). The effect of school resources on student achievement. *Review of Education Research, 66*(3), 361–396.

Hanushek, E. A. (1986, Summer). The economics of schooling: Production and efficiency in public schools. *Journal of Economic Literature, 24*(3), 557–577.

Hanushek, E. A. (1996). School resources and student performance. In G. Burtless (Ed.), *Does money matter?* (pp. 43–73). Washington, DC: Brookings Institution.

Hartocolis, A. (1999, June 24). Crew to shake up worst schools. *New York Times*.

Hawk, P., Coble, C., & Swanson, M. (1985, May June). Certification: It does matter. *Journal of Teacher Education, 36*, 13–15.

Ingersoll, R. (1998, June). The problem of out-of-field teaching. [online]. http://www.pdkinti.org/kappan/king9806.htm.

Kanstoroom, M., & Finn, C. E., Jr. (1999). *Better teachers, better schools*. Washington, DC: Thomas B. Fordham Foundation.

Kershaw, J., & McKean, R. (1962). *Teacher shortages and salary schedules*. New York: McGraw-Hill.

Lieberman, M. (1957). *Education as a profession*. Englewood Cliffs, NJ: PrenticeHall.

Mincer, J. (1974). *Schooling, experience and earnings*. New York: Columbia University Press.

Monk, D. H. (1994). Subject area preparation of secondary mathematics and science teachers and student achievement. *Economics of Education Review, 13*(2).

Murnane, R. (1975). *The impact of school resources on the learning of inner city children*. Cambridge, Massachusetts: Ballinger.

National Commission on Teaching and America's Future. (1996). *What matters most.* New York: Columbia University, Teachers College.

National Commission on Teaching and America's Future. (1997). *Doing what matters most.* New York: Columbia University, Teachers College.

Rottenberg, S. (1962). The economics of occupational licensing. In National Bureau of Economic Research, *Aspects of labor economics.* Princeton, New Jersey: Princeton University Press.

Sanders, W. L., & Horn, S. P. (1994). The Tennessee value-added assessment system (TVAAS): Mixed model methodology in educational assessment. *Journal of Personnel Evaluation in Education, 8,* 299–311.

Sanders, W. B., Saxton, A. M., & Horn, S. P. (1997). The Tennessee value added assessment system: A quantitative, outcomes-based approach to educational assessment. In J. Millman (Ed.), *Grading teachers, grading schools: Is student achievement a valid evaluation measure?* Thousand Oaks, California: Corwin Press.

Summers, A. M., & Wolfe, B. L. (1977, September). Do schools make a difference? *American Economic Review, 67*(4), 639–652.

U.S. Department of Education, National Center for Education Statistics. (1996). *Schools and staffing in the United States: A statistical profile, 1993–94.* (NCES124). Washington, DC: U.S. Government Printing Office.

U.S. Department of Education, National Center for Education Statistics. (1998). *Digest of education statistics, 1997.* Washington, DC: U.S. Government Printing Office.

U.S. Department of Education, National Center for Education Statistics. (1999). *Teacher quality: A report on the preparation and qualifications of public school teachers.* (NOES-1999-080). Washington, DC: U.S. Government Printing Office.

U.S. Department of Education, Office of Educational Research and Improvement. (1999). *The state of charter schools: Third year report* [Online]. Available at http://www.ed.gov/pubs/charter3rdyear/title. html

Walberg, H. J. (1992). On local control: Is bigger better? In *Source book on school size and district size, cost, and quality.* (ERIC Document ED 361 164.)

Walberg, H. J., & Fowler, W. (1987). Expenditure and size efficiencies of public school districts. *Educational Researcher, 16,* 5–15.

Winkler, D. R. (1975, Spring). Educational achievement and school peer group composition. *Journal of Human Resources, 10*(3), 189–204.

Part IV

NO CHILD LEFT BEHIND: A DEBATE

CHAPTER 11

NO CHILD LEFT BEHIND: A DEBATE

Chester E. Finn, Jr.

Signed into law in January 2002, P.L. 107-110, the No Child Left Behind (NCLB) Act, which also reauthorized the LBJ-era Elementary and Secondary Education Act, is a sprawling piece of legislation that touches on hundreds of education issues, big and little. It ranges from bilingual education to "impact aid" to homeless children to magnet schools to (I kid you not) cultural exchanges between Massachusetts and Hawaii that have something vaguely to do with the fact that "whaling" is part of their shared past.

NCLB is best known, however, for its numerous and complex provisions bearing on state academic standards, testing, accountability systems, and teacher qualifications, all in pursuit of an ambitious effort to boost the academic performance of disadvantaged children, to close some long-lasting achievement gaps, and to solve the problem of unsuccessful schools.

George W. Bush came into office committed to vigorous action on this front and, with bipartisan support in Congress, was able to shape NCLB as one of the signature domestic accomplishments of his presidency.

Like it or not, NCLB is a complicated and far-reaching piece of legislation that will have a considerable impact on U.S. K–12 education for the next decade and more.

Is it good or bad or some of both? When I was asked to talk about NCLB at this conference, I asked the organizers whether they expected me to be

Talented Teachers: The Essential Force for Improving Student Achievement, pages 199–211
Copyright © 2004 by Information Age Publishing

for it or against it. In fact, I cannot recall ever being so ambivalent about a major piece of education policy.

Instead of "splitting the difference" in a speech that would necessarily be schizophrenic, replete with innumerable "buts," "howevers," and "on the other hands," I opted to sharpen the differences by debating myself, offering—to the best of my knowledge and abilities—heartfelt and full-throated enthusiasm for *both* sides of ten different issues posed by NCLB. In the text that follows, the opening "argument" represents the supportive or "pro" position. The secondary placement represents the critical or "con" perspective.

THE FEDERAL ROLE IN EDUCATION AS EMBODIED IN NCLB

Pro

The federal government is absolutely right to intrude itself in this major way into U.S. public education so long as the end is worthy and the means are effective. Indeed, there's nothing new about Washington seeking to advance national education objectives by using its money and regulations to alter the practices and priorities of schools, school systems, and educators—not to mention colleges and universities. This practice goes back to the Morrill Land Grant Act in the early 19th century, the G.I. Bill, the National Defense Education Act, a whole raft of "Great Society" programs enacted in the 1960s, the Individuals with Disabilities Education Act, and, more recently, Bill Clinton's Goals 2000 Act. We have plenty of experience, much of it positive, with Uncle Sam trying to call the education shots when a major problem needs fixing and it doesn't look as if state and local actions alone can get it fixed.

In this instance, the problem's diagnosis goes back at least 20 years to the famous *Nation at Risk* report, which, by coincidence, was also a federal product. That national commission, appointed by Education Secretary T.H. Bell, told us that the country had a grave problem posed by the weak academic achievement of its schools and students.

Efforts to solve that problem have been pursued by Washington ever since. There were national education goals set by Bush and his (and Lamar Alexander's) "America 2000" plan. There was even an abortive effort to set national academic standards in core subjects, followed by Clinton's proposal for national testing, enactment of "Goals 2000" legislation, and the 1994 amendments to the Elementary and Secondary Education Act, an obvious precursor to NCLB. Rules, timetables, regulations, funding priorities, the insistence that states set standards and give tests, the threat that federal dollars may be withheld if progress isn't made—none of this is new and none of it is wrong. A serious national problem begs for a national solution and where else could that come from if not Washington?

Con

Nowhere in the federal Constitution does the word "education" even appear. It's one of those areas entrusted to the states by the 10th Amendment. Indeed, every single state has written into its own constitution the self-imposed obligation to educate its citizens. Though most states have delegated the delivery of that education to local school systems, the states still call most of the shots in terms of what must be learned, who can teach it, how long children must attend school, what is required to graduate, and so on. States are the key education policy centers in this country, joined by cities and towns that embody the cherished American belief in local control of education. Moreover, states and communities provide more than 90 cents of every public-education dollar.

It's wrong for Washington to push those states and communities around in the ways we find in No Child Left Behind. Academic standards, tests, and timetables are the states' business and they've gone about it in very different ways. The President and his advisors may think every place should be like Texas but, in fact, Oregon, Vermont, Maryland, and the others have very different notions about education, about what good standards look like, what sorts of assessments to use, what kinds of accountability systems will work best, and who should be accountable for what. They also have very different approaches to training, evaluating, and certifying teachers. For Uncle Sam to crack down on this kind of diversity is wrong in principle and dysfunctional in practice. Besides, it just won't work. On a good day, the U.S. Department of Education can get the checks into the mail with the correct addresses on them. It has no capacity to mastermind what goes on in 50 states, 16,000 school systems, and almost 100,000 schools. And the effort to standardize all this will weaken one of the great strengths of American education, namely its diversity and flexibility. Brandeis wasn't kidding when he called the states our "laboratories of democracy." Why is Uncle Sam trying to lock the doors on those labs?

STATE STANDARDS, NATIONAL TIMETABLE

Pro

The authors of No Child Left Behind were wise to let states set their own standards while giving all of them the same 12-year timeline for getting all children up to "proficiency." While a case can be made for national aca-demic standards, especially in basics like reading and math, America doesn't have the political stomach for that today. Besides, the states have already been setting academic standards for their schools and students. Iowa is the only one that hasn't even tried. It would be disruptive to over-ride these state standards, and it's a fact that some things are more impor-tant in some states than others. Since states will be the main enforcers, they should be the standard-setters.

But if we left it to states to pick their own timetables for getting all chil-dren up to those standards, the timetables would keep getting stretched into the infinite future. Both pragmatically and morally, a deadline is needed for everyone to work back from and Congress was right to set it. Twelve years is a reasonable period that corresponds to the time that most children spend in school. That means school systems have one full student cycle before all children must be proficient, according to state standards. That feels about right. Better still, the tracking of student progress, using states' own test scores and also results from the National Assessment, which all states must now take part in, will enable plenty of sunshine to beam in and comparisons to be made, thus keeping the states' attention and incen-tivizing them, so to speak, to keep at it.

Con

Talk about the worst of both worlds. Talk about perverse incentives. Let-ting standards vary by state, while holding the schedule constant for all, is an invitation to lower standards. And there are signs that some states are doing exactly that. Think how much easier it will be to boost all students to the proficient level in 12 years if proficiency is dumbed down to what might previously have been termed "basic" or "partly proficient." Why encourage states to set easy standards in order to comply with some arbi-trary deadline?

Moreover, the timeline itself seems to allow for some finagling. Though "adequate yearly progress" seems to imply that academic achievement gains are to be made in evenly spaced annual increments, the fine print of No Child Left Behind actually allows states to backload their expected gains into the end of the 12-year sequence, not unlike a "balloon mort-gage." And a number of states are doing just that, proposing, for example, that half the total achievement growth will occur in the final quarter of that period. This is really cynical, violating the spirit if not the letter of the law, and leaving the heavy lifting and potential embarrassment to one's succes-sors. After all, how many governors and chiefs and superintendents who were in office when NCLB was enacted will still be in their present places when the 12-year timetable ends in 2014? We have the appearance of a universal deadline without the reality. That's going to make people even more cynical.

IS IT REALISTIC TO EXPECT THIS OF *EVERY* CHILD?

Pro

Insisting, as NCLB does, that every single girl and boy become academically proficient is true to American values and the only goal worth having. Sure it's ambitious, but imagine Kennedy saying that we would get 90% of the way to the moon or the doctors contending with SARS saying that they'll be satisfied if 85% of their patients get well? Besides, if we start winking when some kids get left behind, or giving waivers to schools, districts, states, guess who will populate the waiver lists? Poor and minority kids, that's who, kids in troubled schools, those with disabilities—in other words, the very children who have forever gotten the short end of the stick. It would confirm school systems and states in their most reprehensible behavior and leave the most troublesome gaps as wide as ever.

No, the only way to be serious about leaving no children behind, and the only formula that is morally defensible and politically palatable in the American democracy, is to insist that we mean every single kid, difficult though that will be to pull off.

Con

It may sound noble and moral, but it's pie in the sky. Only someone who knows nothing about kids OR schools would write a law like that—or someone who doesn't really care whether the law gets obeyed. Everybody who has spent time working with children knows that they're as different as snowflakes. Some are quick, some slow. Some are eager, others apathetic. Some come from supportive homes, others have no homes at all. Some have peers who do homework after school. Others are out on the street playing or making trouble. What's more, the kids are so mobile that half the faces in some classrooms are different in June than in September. Some families return to their home countries. Some move to other states or within the city. Some just disappear, drop out, get sick, whatever. The fact is that few schools retain all of their students even from the beginning to the end of a single year, much less from year to year. How on earth can they be held accountable for all of their results? It's unrealistic about kids and it's unfair to hardworking educators.

The authors of NCLB made a big deal of "disaggregating" the data so that every group of kids in every school is on display in terms of academic achievement and so that failure by one or another group cannot be concealed within a school or district average. Sounds great. But some kids are so far behind their peers when they start that again it's pie in the sky to expect them all to progress at the same rate, especially in relation to fixed standards. A value-added measure would at least take account of how far back some students are when they arrive in a teacher's classroom. But the Education Department doesn't like that approach.

WHY EVERY YEAR?

Pro

Holding schools responsible for "adequate yearly progress"—and making this transparent—is the only way to keep all schools accountable for their students. It's the fairest, surest way of tracking which schools are and are not succeeding and, by disaggregating the results, it'll be clear whether they're succeeding with boys as well as girls, with black and brown as well as white kids, with disabled youngsters, with poor and rich alike, and so forth. Yes, the AYP calculation may be complicated, but we'll get used to it. After all, corporations are audited annually; the auditors poke into everything, all the assets and liabilities, not just the bottom-line profit summary, and they make their findings available to shareholders and government regulators. We should get accustomed to thinking of schools this way. Every child, every group, every school, every year, with a clear set of expectations as to how much progress is acceptable.

Con

Maybe Congress should invite Arthur Andersen to audit schools the way it did Enron. Schools are organic enterprises, full of living, breathing human beings, some of whom aren't the same from one year to the next. Some kids are more fortunate than others. Some teachers are more effective. This endless micro-analyzing of test scores and this effort to fit every group of children in every grade in every one of a state's schools into a fixed set of annual academic gains—well, it's reminiscent of Procrustes demanding that everyone fit precisely into his bed; if you were too tall, he sliced you down; if you were too short, he had you stretched. What's more, we can expect tens of thousands of schools to turn up on the hit list in one year or another for any of a dozen reasons, including simple fluctuations of test scores by school and subgroup. What good will it do a school system or state if two-thirds of its schools wind up on the "needs improvement" list? What an absurd diffusion of resources. And what happens if half of THOSE schools weren't on the list the previous year and a bunch more drop off that list the following year even though nothing really changed except test score fluctuations? This AYP system is going to become the laughing stock of American education even if it's a full employment program for psychometricians and statisticians.

WHAT ABOUT ALL THAT TESTING?

Pro

Annual testing in the core subjects is the only way to know whether progress is being made. When you skip years or grades, you lose track of whether Jamie and Amy are making the gains they should each year. Though some educators are leery of pushing kids into 180-day long "grade levels" instead of letting them move at their own varying speeds through different subjects, parents, taxpayers, and policymakers can only know whether children are making satisfactory progress in relation to their grades in school, and can only know whether the Franklin School's fourth graders are learning what they should, if it's possible to see the difference between how those kids were doing at the start of fourth grade (or the end of third) and the end of fourth grade.

States like Texas that have been doing annual testing in relation to grade-level standards have been making commendable gains in student performance, especially for minority kids. What's more, if there isn't an external check on achievement at the end of each grade, how can we know whether Jamie is qualified to go on to the next grade or whether Amy would benefit from summer school? We then become totally dependent on teacher judgments and run the risk of kids being promoted for dubious reasons, such as a kindly teacher or one who just can't stand having Jamie in her class any longer, instead of on the basis of objective evidence of actual performance.

Yes, people fuss about too much testing and teaching to the test, but if the tests are properly aligned with curricular goals and state standards, then teaching kids what they must know to pass them is an honorable thing to do. The overall burden could be eased if states and districts would get their acts together and simplify their testing systems. The kind of state testing regimen imposed by NCLB is the best possible way to ensure that all of that state's schools are successfully covering the essential skills and knowledge, because the test is how we can audit their results.

Con

We're becoming slaves to standardized tests, which all too often are NOT aligned with curriculum or standards but simply what the low-bidding testing company was willing to provide. There are a million things worth teaching that don't lend themselves to standardized testing, and the surest way to kill a school's distinctiveness or an educator's enthusiasm is to homogenize everything into a test-centered, drill-and-kill system. Why do you think private schools avoid taking part in state tests? It's not just that they're wary of being compared. It's that they know what they want to teach—that's why people choose them—and they know that what they value may or may not be covered on the state test.

As for using annual testing to determine Jamie's and Amy's fate, only someone drinking Potomac River water would think that kids can be standardized like widgets coming out of a factory. They really do learn different things at different speeds and some of them really do test better than others. Some test better on some days, depending on a thousand factors in their lives and their classrooms. To hinge everything on a single annual test score is to defy human nature and cognitive psychology, to cause needless stress for children, teachers, and parents, and to risk a lot of false positives and false negatives depending on what day of the week it is and whether Jamie got a decent night's sleep and whether Amy is distracted by a dog barking outside the room where she's taking that silly test.

WHY JUST THREE SUBJECTS?

Pro

Reading, math, and science are the obvious right subjects to focus on. They're the core of the curriculum in every state and ought to be its core in every school. They're the subjects with the greatest consensus as to what's important for all children to learn. They are the subjects where most states have already done a reasonable job of setting standards. And they lend themselves to fairly reliable testing.

No, they're not the whole curriculum. Many states also have standards for social studies and sometimes for art, music, health, and so on. Where states do not, districts often do. Nobody is saying that the NCLB subjects should be the entire story of what's taught in school. As a matter of fact, it's in other areas that schools may best specialize and distinguish themselves—an art and music magnet, say, or a Spanish-immersion charter school. Every school, though, ought to cover the same essential skills and knowledge in the core subjects—and those subjects ought to be the focus of the state testing and accountability systems.

Con

It's a pipe dream to say that schools are welcome to add history, art, music, and geography to the NCLB subjects. Somebody is drinking that Potomac water again. If there's a single truth in education, it's that what gets tested is what gets taught. What schools are accountable for is what they focus on. All of the pressure in NCLB—the sunlight, the rewards, the sanctions—is concentrated on reading and math and, a few years down the road, science. NCLB doesn't even talk about writing, only reading! In theory, our schools could meet all the federal requirements without ever teaching their pupils to compose a single sentence or know who Abraham Lincoln was or the difference between red and blue or how to find North America on a world map. All of the external attention on a school will focus on how it's doing in just three subjects and nobody will even notice if the rest of the curriculum gets short shrift—or dumped entirely. You can say that we'll turn later to subjects like history and art, after we've got the basics under control, but what about the generations of sixth graders who will pass through school while we're waiting? This could lead to the worst curricular distortion ever.

WHY ALL THOSE DRACONIAN SCHOOL INTERVENTIONS?

Pro

Prescribing a set of interventions in failing schools is the only way to assure that things change. NCLB sets forth a cascade of actions that districts are supposed to take to redirect unsuccessful schools. These come in three big stages, called "improvement," "corrective action," and "restructuring," with a menu of specific actions under each of those headings, some of them options for districts, others prescribed by federal law, depending on how long a school has been in this particular status. Similarly, states are given a menu of interventions that they are responsible for making in unsuccessful districts, five options under the heading of district improvement, and seven more under what NCLB calls "corrective action."

Sure, it's prescriptive and interventionist, but that's what accountability means. Otherwise, what's to keep unsuccessful schools from staying that way? That's been the story of U.S. public education for too long—that's why 20 years after *A Nation at Risk* our results have barely budged. So somebody needs to trigger palpable changes, even unpleasant changes, in faltering schools and districts lest they continue to falter—and to gyp children of a proper education.

Who is that somebody? Public schools in America are creatures of their districts and districts are creatures of their states. So unless you picture a vast army of federal interveners fanning across the countryside, you accept the fact that districts have the primary responsibility for fixing broken schools and states have a similar obligation with respect to faltering districts. NCLB is prescriptive about that part yet it gives districts and states considerable leeway to tailor the cure to the disease.

Con

Get real. Most failing schools are in troubled districts that have allowed them to decay and have no greater capacity to turn around a failing school than to suspend the superintendent's car from a skyhook. We find a huge concentration of dismal schools, especially Title I schools, in dismal districts. Some districts have a majority of their schools on the "needs improvement" list. What are THEY supposed to do? If they knew how to fix these schools, they already would have. They're clueless. Or maybe they have clues but are ineffectual at carrying them out. The same goes for state education agencies. Some employ just a few hundred people, most of whom work on categorical programs and regulations, many of whom are civil servants, not education experts, much less doctors for ailing school systems. I can't picture where a state with dozens of faltering local education agencies (LEAs) is supposed to find the know-how or horsepower to turn them around. That would be an issue even if states weren't facing major budget problems, but it's a bigger issue today, when I'll bet there's not a single state education agency (SEA) in the country that can afford to bring a bunch of education turnaround experts on board. What's more likely is that most failing schools and districts will stay that way because nobody in authority is able to do anything to solve their problems.

THE ROAD TO VOUCHERS?

Pro

Giving kids the right to exit—or take some of their Title I money to private providers—is better than keeping them trapped against their will in failing schools. Especially if schools remain immune to repair efforts, or those responsible for the repair efforts lack the capacity to carry them out successfully, and particularly insofar as the children most directly affected by this institutional failure are poor and minority, we must do something to give them a break. Letting them go to better schools seems pretty obvious—and so does letting them take some of the federal money meant for compensatory services and turn to competent private providers to purchase such services. After all, educating kids is the point, not maintaining the budgets or enrollments of unsuccessful schools. Let the children learn in schools and programs that can do right by them.

In any case, Congress authorized a very limited choice program, a far cry from the Florida-style voucher approach that President Bush first proposed. Under NCLB, the choice of school is limited to other public schools within the same district (including charter schools) unless the district enters into an agreement with other districts. And only a small fraction of a school's Title I money can be redirected into so-called "supplemental services," which may come only from state-approved providers; incidentally, those providers may include other schools and school systems. It's a reasonable, cautious, and limited approach to choice, meant both to create options for kids otherwise stuck in impossible situations AND to build pressure on failing schools to get their acts together.

Con

It's certainly limited and cautious but it's not very reasonable and it's already showing signs of not working. How foolish to confine a child's school choices to other public schools in the same district. We saw last fall that a big fraction of failing Title I schools are in districts crowded with such schools—districts with few if any good schools for students to turn to—and fewer still that have room for more kids. Cities like Chicago had hundreds of schools on the list of schools that, according to NCLB, children should be able to exit for better schools. But they were limited to schools in Chicago. Which meant no realistic options were available to them.

To make matters worse, the LEA is responsible for organizing and publicizing these choice options. Talk about putting the fox in charge of the henhouse. It's not in a district's interest to encourage students to leave some of its schools for other schools, much less to help families make their way to private providers with dollars that would otherwise go to the school system. So with a few happy exceptions, we saw districts dithering, delaying, obscuring, and otherwise minimizing the chances that families would even find out that they had the right to make a move, much less helping them to move. Though the Department of Education is trying to improve this part of NCLB before Fall 2003, it's basically impossible so long as the law leaves the LEA in charge and confines the options to other public schools within the district.

TEACHER QUALITY

Pro

Besides focusing on student achievement, the key ingredient in an effective school is the quality of its teachers. The authors of NCLB were therefore smart to specify "highly qualified teachers" in every classroom and to create a timetable for states in this regard. Otherwise, the neediest kids will continue to get the least qualified teachers and states and districts will continue to fill classroom slots with warm bodies instead of people who really know their subjects, want to teach children, and are good at it.

Yes, it's going to be a challenge for states to comply with the "highly qualified teacher" part of NCLB on the Congressional timetable, especially since these requirements reach beyond traditional certification to include evidence of subject-matter mastery. But here, too, the point is not to keep things the way they've always been but to trigger changes in customary behavior patterns. This is really the one school "input" that NCLB is prescriptive about, but it's hard to dispute. America has a lot of terrific teachers but needs many more of them—and to meet the pupil achievement demands of NCLB it's going to need more than ever.

Con

This is another of those sound impulses that leads to a nightmare of regulation and homogenization and pays no attention to the reality of American public education. School systems aren't hiring unqualified teachers because they want to. They're hiring them because those are the only people applying. Schools can't make people apply who don't want to—and especially in a time of budget stringency, it's hard to picture how they can make abler and better educated people want to apply for these jobs, especially in troubled schools that may be unappealing places in which to work. So the people who end up in those schools—with honorable exceptions, to be sure—are apt to be those with fewest alternatives.

To be sure, if we didn't have uniform salary schedules and bargaining contracts, and if the federal government wanted to pump in billions more for teacher salaries, this marketplace might be altered for the better. But nobody is offering more money. Just laying down more regulations won't change a thing, except maybe aggravating the shortages we already find in certain subjects and schools. Moreover, the Education Department didn't help when it decided a few months back to, in effect, turn alternative certification into a clone of traditional certification—a bad move that was made, apparently, under pressure from the ed schools and their friends on

Capitol Hill. A far better move would be to deregulate entry into teaching, give individual schools much greater authority over personnel decisions (and personnel budgets), and then hold schools accountable for their results. Trying to impose a single definition of highly qualified teachers on American public education is a recipe for failure.

EXCESSIVE BEHAVIORISM OR NEEDED OVERHAUL?

Pro

The whole point of NCLB is to change results by altering behavior—in schools, educators, students, etc.—so it's appropriate that this ambitious law be "behaviorist" in its basic operations, with rewards and punishments, sanctions, and interventions, in pursuit of a much-needed overhaul of American education. If behavior doesn't change, results won't change and we'll still be at risk 20 years from now. Nobody likes to change their accustomed ways of doing things, so we must expect dissent, friction, resistance, and grumbling. But the underlying premise is correct: the status quo isn't working satisfactorily, so we must do whatever is necessary to leverage the reforms that will actually boost the outcomes.

Con

American education didn't become the way it is because of mean spirited people trying to keep kids ignorant. It's a layer cake of differing priorities and local control within the framework of state systems. It's a vast, decentralized enterprise involving thousands of institutions and many millions of people. It doesn't change quickly and won't change just because a few folks in Washington think it should. They seem to believe that the little smidgen of federal dollars going into this system gives them the right to rewrite the ground rules, supersede the decisions of local school boards and professional educators and the wishes of millions of parents, and tell everyone their business. At the very least, you would think, if Washington was going to push for all these changes it would put up the money with which to make them. But funding isn't the key point. What's most troubling is the hubris and naïveté of those folks in Washington about kids and about the forces at work in their lives, not to mention naïveté about curriculum and instruction, about what teachers do, how schools work, and how school systems are run.

Thank you very much for your attention. We both thank you.

Part V

THE GROWTH OF THE TEACHER
ADVANCEMENT PROGRAM

CHAPTER 12

THE GROWTH OF THE TEACHER ADVANCEMENT PROGRAM

Lewis C. Solmon and John Schacter

Lewis C. Solmon

In this presentation we introduce you to the Teacher Advancement Program (TAP), and discuss the growth of TAP. We have a serious problem in this country because not enough of our best and our brightest are pursuing education as a career. Moreover, of those who do, too many leave the classroom after a short time.

My colleague John Schacter and I will talk about the importance of teacher quality and how the Teacher Advancement Program has proven to be an exciting and successful way of attracting, motivating, developing, and retaining high-quality teachers in America's K–12 schools. We have been working on TAP for over four years and, by now national policy has caught up with us. Teacher quality is a major policy issue today, and as you know, by 2005–2006, states have to ensure that all teachers are highly qualified. According to No Child Left Behind, highly qualified means fully licensed or certified, including alternative certification, no waivers, or emergency credentials.

Talented Teachers: The Essential Force for Improving Student Achievement, pages 215–239
Copyright © 2004 by Information Age Publishing

To me, a qualified teacher means a lot of other things, and to some people certified may not necessarily mean qualified. Certification may be neither a necessary nor a sufficient condition. We see in independent schools a lot of Dartmouth history majors teaching history and doing a pretty good job. I have a Ph.D. in economics from the University of Chicago and I have taught at UCLA, Purdue University, and several other colleges. Yet, I am not "qualified" to teach 12th grade economics because I'm not certified. My children were taught by a social science-certified teacher who happened to major in geography. At least they had a chance to be remediated at home.

Research confirms that teacher quality is the most important school-related factor affecting student learning. Bill Sanders's longitudinal work demonstrated that students who performed equally well in math in the second grade showed enormous performance differences three years later, depending on whether they had three consecutive years of effective or ineffective teachers. June Rivers found that average-achieving students assigned to four years of ineffective teachers had only a 40% chance of passing the Tennessee High School Exit Examination. The same type of students assigned to four years of effective teachers had an 80% chance of passing. So teacher quality really is pivotal.

There are many excellent teachers in the profession today, there is no question about that; there are many all around the country, but there are not enough. Some teachers are not as effective, up to date, energetic, as others in the field are. Clearly, most of our best and our brightest do not choose the teaching profession today. To get more of them to do so, we have to understand why those who don't choose teaching do not. We have learned a lot from focus groups and surveys that we have conducted over the years.

Everybody says, if you want more teachers pay them more. We would love to raise all teacher salaries, sort of. Salaries are low, but we have to remember the nine-month contract, and the importance of fringe benefits today. Some surveys say teachers aren't in it for the money. Of course not, that's why they are teachers! We shouldn't ask teachers whether money is important; rather, we should ask those people who didn't go into teaching.

The cost of raising all teacher salaries to levels that are expected by those who are choosing law or medicine or business would be prohibitive. Even the $6,000 that would be required in about 30 states to bring their salaries up to the national average might break the bank, or at least be politically infeasible. This would serve to keep the least effective teachers in the classroom, the ones with the least opportunity costs and fewest other alternatives outside of education, rather than the most effective.

Do we really want to raise the salaries of ineffective teachers by the same amount as effective teachers? Would $6,000 or $10,000 more attract those people who are now thinking about law, medicine, and business? The top people seeking careers don't look at average salaries. In fact, the average salary of lawyers is not as different as the average salary of teachers as you might think when you consider the government lawyers, or the one who puts up a shingle waiting for somebody to get hit by a car. The top people look at how much they could make if they were really the best in their field, if they really succeed. They have always been successful. They have been successful academically, extracurricularly, and they think they're going to be successful in their careers. So they ask how much do the top people make. What really turns off many people to teaching according to our focus groups is that everyone with the same experience and education credits will earn the same regardless of their effort effectiveness.

As we have talked to union leaders over the years, they've said we agree that the best people should get paid more as long as it's fair. I've actually offered to some union leaders that we collaborate on a paper to define fair. Once we get that down, then we can deal with paying people according to their effectiveness. Is it fair, however, to pay two teachers the same amount if one is highly effective, up to date, and gets huge learning gains from their students and another does not? I don't think that's fair. TAP is not only about salaries though. To attract, motivate, and retain people takes more than just money, though money is important. We'll get to the other features of TAP in a moment.

We have to juxtapose the issue of people going into teaching with the demand and supply situations. We've estimated that there will be a shortage of about 870,000 teachers over the next decade. What that says is that there are about two million who will retire and one million in the traditional pipeline. Therefore, we have to come up with another 800,000 to a million teachers. It is not just a shortage of quantity, but it's a shortage of quality as well. Some people say that with the recession and the demise of the tech sector we have enough teachers. Some people have entered teaching because of that, but I fear that many of those who entered teaching for these reasons will leave as soon as the private sector turns around and new jobs appear. Teachers do leave the profession, even in a good economy. Twenty percent of teachers leave within three years, and twice as many do so in urban areas. Unfortunately, it is usually the best teachers that end up leaving.

One other condition of education I'd like to discuss is out-of-field teaching. In high-poverty schools, 65% of physical science teachers are teaching out of field. That means they have neither a major nor a minor and some of them have not had a course since high school.

There are many efforts going on to attract high-quality people into teaching. There are new ideas that you may be familiar with such as increasing salaries, forgiving school debt, housing subsidies, perks like memberships to health clubs have been offered, PR campaigns, and the list goes on. Yet so many of these are small, isolated efforts, not school-centered, poorly designed and poorly implemented, not systemic. They solve one problem only to create another. We want higher quality, we raise standards. We raise standards, we exacerbate the shortage. So there really is a problem.

We at the Milken Family Foundation did not have to be convinced about the importance of teacher quality. Indeed, for well more than a decade we have been working with the Milken Educators who are honored for their achievements. We have studied other reforms for many years and concluded that most of them are pretty ineffective without high-quality teachers. We've looked at early childhood education, standards and assessment, and class-size reduction. The reform effort of decreasing the number of students in a classroom can be explained by a backward analogy. Some people notice I've lost some weight and I did it on Atkins, which is completely counterintuitive. You eat fat, you eat all these crazy things and you lose weight. On the other hand, class-size reduction is completely intuitive, right? Everybody wants their kid in a smaller class, but we don't say *ceteris paribus*, what are you holding constant? Would you rather have your kid in a class of 40 students with a motivated, eloquent, inspiring, up-to-date, knowledgeable teacher, or would you rather have your kid in a class of 20 with an unprepared dullard? Unfortunately, in California when we reduced class size, we got more of the latter than the former to take over those classes.

We studied educational technology for many years at the Foundation and we concluded that you could put in all the hardware, all the software, all the wiring, and do all the training that you wanted, but unless teachers have the ability, motivation, and incentives to actually do things differently, nothing will happen. So we feel that teacher quality is essential to the whole school improvement problem.

We need a bold, new strategy that counters traditional drawbacks of low compensation, lack of career advancement, unsupported accountability, and ineffective professional development that really do plague the teaching profession. Teachers need the ability and motivation to do things differently. We believe that the Teacher Advancement Program (TAP) is that bold, new strategy. It doesn't tinker at the margins. It really changes the essence of the profession while maintaining and supporting the public schools. The goal of TAP is to increase student achievement and the method for getting there is to maximize teacher quality. We do this through a comprehensive reform. The five elements of the reform are multiple career paths, market-driven compensation, performance-based accountability, ongoing applied professional development, and expanding the supply of high-quality teachers.

I want to note that schools could implement TAP along with effective curricula, new management methods, and community involvement, parent involvement, business involvement, and so on. When that's done, TAP conforms to the federal definition of comprehensive school reform and qualifies for the money that's been set aside for that.

Now, the fifth principle, expanding the supply of high-quality educators, is more a state issue than an individual school issue. We talk about speeding up the time to degree, alternative certification, bringing back retired teachers, making private pension plans portable, opportunities for national certification, and multi-state credentialing. Multi-state credentialing… isn't it sad that there are surpluses in some states, but when a teacher moves, let's say to California, they have to go through more hoops in order to be able to go to a classroom, even if they were a Milken Educator, even if they were a Teacher of the Year? At the school level, when we talk about expanding the supply, we really urge schools to look beyond their current staff to find some of the outstanding teachers that are available so that they can get the best teachers possible to serve as master and mentor teachers.

Let's compare the Teacher Advancement Program with the traditional system in terms of career advancement. Today, there's a single career path: you start as a teacher, you end as a teacher with not much difference in the responsibilities. TAP has what we call a multiple career path where you start out as an inductee, then you're a career teacher, mentor, and master. Each of those successive levels has more qualifications, more responsibilities, and more compensation. You can actually grow as a teacher almost like in the university where one starts as an assistant, then moves to associate professor, and so on. Currently, of course, the only way you can grow in the education field is to leave the classroom and become an administrator, whether you're good at that or not. Some of the best baseball players do not become the best managers.

The second principle is market-driven compensation. We are all familiar with the traditional model, the lock-step salary schedule, more money for more time, more money for more credits. In the Teacher Advancement Program, salary is determined by responsibilities and effectiveness of performance. Our model would support higher pay for hard-to-staff fields or schools, as well as for National Board Certification. It pays for the performance of teachers and their students, and for taking on additional responsibilities. Other performance pay plans reject any compensation based on the judgment of others, particularly peers, on student achievement or on subject specialty. They fear bias and they fear competition among teachers, rather than collaboration. But in our program, with the detailed evaluation rubrics, multiple evaluators, and evaluations six or more times during a year, it's pretty difficult to give special treatment to your favorites. In addition, because professional development demands collaboration, and since part of the compensation is based on school-wide performance, collaboration rather than competition, is encouraged. Everybody knows who the best teachers are anyway.

Our system has evolved; because we wanted to gain acceptance by teachers' associations, and by the education community, the performance awards are bonuses each year. They're not cumulative; instead, they're constrained by available funds, but they can, on average, amount to up to $5,000 a year. The performance awards supplement rather than replace the traditional step and column scale in most cases. No one earns less and all teachers can get a bonus. It's not a zero-sum game. It's not that only the top X percent get the awards. Fifty percent of the bonus in our system is awarded for skills and knowledge. Fifty percent is based on student achievement, part of that is school-wide achievement, and part of that is the individual teacher's achievement. Therefore, you can get part of the bonus if you do well on the skills and knowledge, even if your kids don't grow and vice versa. Teachers are paid more for additional contract days as well.

On the issue of accountability, traditionally it has been uneven because there are no rewards or sanctions based on it. You are supported for improvement in skills only if you're deficient. In TAP, hiring, advancing, and compensation depend on evaluation, and support is provided for growth. It's not a pass–fail system. There are five levels of rating on each of the rubrics, and few receive scores of five, which means that everybody has room to improve. Performance is tied to compensation and there's a list of the performance indicators consisting of skills, knowledge, classroom-level gains, and school-wide gains that are necessary to advance.

We want to get away from the teacher going back to their local colleges in the summer to take the course that happens to be offered by the professor who happens to be doing research on something that may or may not be relevant to the problems that the teachers are having in their own classroom. For professional development, we actually alter the schedule of teaching in an elementary or secondary school and provide 90 minutes or more a week where teachers can meet in cluster groups with master and mentor teachers. This way, they are able to actually work on problems that they're facing in their classrooms, whether it's how to teach a unit on gravity or why Johnny is having trouble in mathematics, or what their test scores look like and the topics that kids are getting and the one's they're not. It's ongoing, applied, in school, during the school day, professional development.

You might say this seems like old hat because multiple career paths aren't much different from career ladders. Yet they are different, because with career ladders, if you were the best teacher you got congratulations, you got more work, and you might be honored with a certificate or new title. In TAP, we give you more responsibility and we will pay you for it.

There are many performance pay plans that have not been effective. They've been imposed from the top down. We will not work with a school unless 75% of the teachers agree that it's something worth exploring, so it's bottom up, not top down. Also, in many of the other performance pay plans, if you're really good, you can get a $500 bonus. We're talking $5,000, so the extra work is worth it in our system.

Then there's assessment systems that currently exist like the Sanders system and the National Board. The problem is that many of these systems don't have consequences for assessment good or bad, and in ours, there are consequences for how teachers and their students perform. TAP provides a new kind of professional development, although over the last couple of years, we are seeing more and more schools doing in-school, student-based professional development.

We currently have 31 TAP schools [at time of speech; total is over 70 as of 2004], but that number could more than double next year if all the cards fall into place. It's a very exciting program, not too many double in size in a year. Now, let me just say that it is not an inexpensive program. It costs about $400 per student because we have to have the salary supplements for the master and mentor teachers, which can be up to $15,000 a year for a master teacher. We also have to have a significant bonus pool. The master teachers no longer have their own homeroom. They're teaching model lessons and teaching units in everybody's classroom, so every student gets the benefits of the top teachers, the excellent teachers, but we have to find new teachers to replace them.

The way we get the free time for the teachers to meet in cluster groups during the school day often is to hire specialists so that students will not be deprived of education. For example, sometimes in an elementary school they'll hire a science expert to come in and teach science while the other teachers are meeting. That costs money. Then we have to pay for a lot of training.

But there are sources for funding, for example, No Child Left Behind legislation makes TAP an encouraged use of Title II funds. Most of that goes to districts, but the state has some money as well. Some of it's already allocated, because Title II funds come from the old class-size reduction and Eisenhower Professional Development money. But where there's a will, there's a way. There is also Comprehensive School Reform money and the Fund for Improvement of Education. There is money if schools and districts have the will.

We've seen a new state sales tax increase in Arizona where voters approved Proposition 301, which was sold to the public based on accountability, and there's a performance pay element in that. In Eagle County, Colorado, they increased the property tax levy for performance pay. A couple of years ago, Florida's legislation enacted a law that states that 5% of salaries has to be in the form of performance pay. In South Carolina and Arizona, the state education chiefs found money in their budgets. In Arkansas, there is a $5.4 million grant from the Walton Foundation to support TAP. The Archdiocese of Indianapolis received a $10 million grant from the Lilly Foundation for a number of things, including the Teacher Advancement Program. So there is money if one wants to use it. Of course, there is not a lot of free money floating around. Districts would have to do some other things differently or not at all in order to implement TAP.

It would be well worth the effort though because the outcome is improved student achievement. To discuss this, my colleague John Schacter will present some very exciting early results.

I would just like to add that we've also been doing surveys of teachers in our TAP schools and we find that the acceptance of all the principles is astounding. However, the one principle that people are most cautious about is of course the notion of performance pay. It's interesting to note that in spite of the lower levels of support of performance pay and when I say low, I just mean low compared to the enthusiastic endorsement of the master and mentor teacher concept and of the professional development and so on. In spite of the slightly weaker levels of acceptance of performance pay and accountability, teachers are reporting a stronger degree of collegiality when they're doing TAP than before. That's something that people said would not happen. In addition, there are many other intermediate outcomes including more teachers staying, teachers deciding not to retire, more teachers applying to work at the schools, and so on.

I'll just close with one story. The Madison School District is a long, thin district in central Phoenix, Arizona. There are seven schools; four of them are in the program. At the north of the district are schools serving quite wealthy families. Then at the bottom are the 85% free and reduced-price lunch schools and of course the free and reduced-price lunch schools are the TAP schools. The ones in the north claim not to need TAP because they already have high achievement. They might not be adding a whole lot to their students' achievement, but they already have high achievement. In this district, the pattern usually is that people get jobs at the low-SES schools but as soon as there's an opening at the rich schools, they move up. Yet, in Madison School District, what we are seeing is teachers are applying from the rich schools for jobs at these poorer TAP schools because they are saying we are achieving in our school, I'm achieving as a teacher, I'm getting high value-added, I'm getting improvement from the kids. Why shouldn't I be rewarded for it? So some very excellent teachers are moving from the rich schools to the TAP schools and that's what we want. That will help close the achievement gap.

John Schacter

I'm going to begin with how much in dollars does staying in school matter and then discuss how much teachers matter. Lastly, I'll get into how much does TAP matter. If you notice the logos throughout this conference, the Milkens developed this saying, "The future belongs to the educated." They couldn't be more right.

Here on Chart 12.1 are some statistics that were done by Professor Norton Grubb, an economist at U.C. Berkeley. In the 1960s, we had about

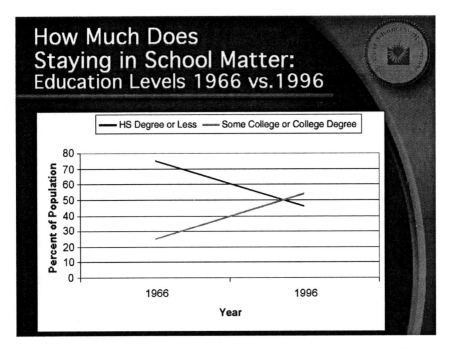

**How Much Does
Staying in School Matter:**
Education Levels 1966 vs.1996

Chart 12.1.   How much does staying in school matter: Education levels 1966 versus 1996.

80% of the people with less than a high school degree and only about 25% who actually graduated from college. Now the lines are intersecting and we have over 50% of folks who are graduating from college, and fewer and fewer folks who are making it without a high school degree. Professor Grubb then ran these analyses where he did pay ratios to determine how much people would earn in each of these categories. So our high school dropouts were earning a decent part of the pie and our people with high school and a little college earning a little bit more, and our college people of course earning the most. This was in 1966.

When we look at 1996, we see that the folks without a high school degree are really having major problems. The people with a little high school, again still doing okay and there is even more money for our college degrees. So what I did was I took Professor Grubb's data from the national economic labor trends and calculated how much people with each one of these degrees would earn 12 years out of school. Chart 12.2 shows that the difference is quite dramatic. A high school dropout earns about $16,000 a year. Those with a high school degree and some college earn $32,000. And college graduates make $51,200 per year. Chart 12.3 shows that over your life, you will earn about a million bucks more if you have a college degree versus a high school degree, about 1.5 million if you have a master's

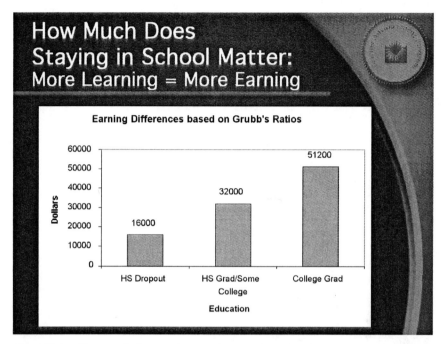

Chart 12.2.   How much does staying in school matter: More learning = more earning.

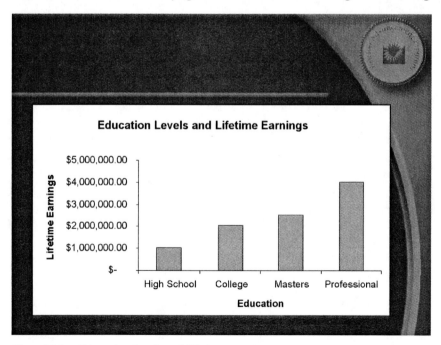

Chart 12.3.   Education levels and lifetime earnings.

degree, and about three million more if you have a professional degree. Therefore, learning equals earning. There's really no question about it, but what most people want to know is, okay if more learning equals more earning, what causes more learning?

Many people are a bit surprised because when we look at what causes more learning, we find that schools and teachers only count for about 20% of the learning in kids. Eighty percent of the variation is due to a student's family and background characteristics (Chart 12.4). However, the interesting thing about this is if we look at teachers compared to schools, we see that individual classroom teachers produce about twice the amount of learning that schools produce. In a book by Bob Marzano published by the Association for Supervision and Curriculum Development (ASCD), he showed that effective schools produce results that overcome student background and effective teachers are about twice as likely to produce those results. So how much do teachers really matter? Let me share with you a couple of studies I have been working on in Arizona.

We studied 300 teachers, second to sixth grade, in Arizona. We linked each one of these teachers to students' reading, language, and math achievement each year over multiple years. We calculated the gain in achievement that each teacher produced from one year to the next. Our results are really quite disappointing: 54% of teachers produce no learning

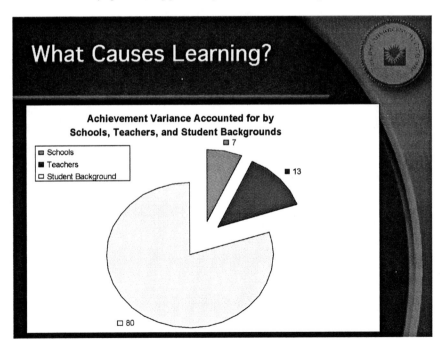

Chart 12.4.   What causes learning.

gains in their classrooms; only 46% produced any type of achievement gains. So we said okay, let's design a study where achievement is not the sole measure of a quality teacher. Let's design studies to look at teaching behaviors. We picked a random subset of 54 teachers and hired six graduate students from ASU, and on 10 random days over the course of the year, we went into their classrooms.

We spent at least one hour during each observation and watched the full lesson, front to back. Eight of our visits were unannounced. Four of our visits were before lunch, and four after lunch. Because I used to be a first-grade teacher, I understand that after lunch there can be problems! Three different graduate students then rated teachers on these teaching behaviors.

The list of teacher behaviors was accrued from the research that found that if these behaviors were enacted, the students would learn more. We wrote rubrics and for each behavior we defined performance at five different levels in really clear language. You could score exemplary, proficient, or unsatisfactory on each of these things. I trained the graduate students to get innerrater reliability so that when they rated the same teacher, they actually had the same scores. We found that about 62% of teachers were ineffective and about 13% were distinguished. Surprisingly, none were classified as exemplary.

When we made the link between these behaviors and student achievement gains in reading, language, and math, we found that for every point increase in teaching behavior ratings, there was a one-standard deviation increase in student achievement on reading, language, and math. What does that mean? Well, let's say that a kid entered a classroom at the 50th percentile. A teacher who scores a five on our scale had kids achieving at the 98th percentile at the end of the year. In contrast, the teachers who scored a one would have students achieving at the 2nd percentile. So, teacher behaviors matter.

Now, let's apply this to your kid. In school, a child has about 48 teachers from K–12. If you applied our results from Arizona, 26 of the 48 teachers your kid has will not produce any achievement gains, so half of the years your child is in school, they're not learning much. Thirteen of the 48 teachers would be rated as incompetent in terms of behaviors. If this were applied to an 800-student elementary school, 430 of the kids would not learn anything from one year to the next, while 496 would be subjected to sub-par instruction. Now, these results seem kind of disappointing, but the TAP results are going to be better, I promise. I don't mean to depress everybody in the audience, but I want to really emphasize how much good teachers matter.

So, how much does the Teacher Advancement Program matter? The backbone of the Teacher Advancement Program is to improve teacher quality by having the most talented, skilled, creative, and exemplary master teachers improve the teaching performance of others in the school. So that's the number-one thing. By providing teachers with a career path to advance by compensating the people who are more expert, by restructuring the school schedule to provide for professional development during the day and by paying teachers based on how well they instruct, and how much their students learn TAP is a comprehensive school reform model.

In TAP, we came up with five research questions to determine how effective TAP is. The first deals with teacher attitudes. What are their attitudes? The second, with how much achievement improves on a yearly basis. Then we wanted to know if TAP schools outperform comparable control schools. Just because the TAP schools are improving in achievement might not mean that they are outperforming schools that are similar to them. We compared TAP teachers' achievement gains to those of teachers at other schools. Then we looked at how well they implemented TAP and its effects on achievement. So what were the results?

1. For teacher attitudes, we have data from all 160 teachers in 2001 and 2002 from our five TAP schools in Arizona. We found results that were pretty much counter to a lot of what we were reading in the literature. There were those that argued that you would never be able to implement multiple career paths because the teachers would reject expert teachers earning more and expert teachers evaluating other teachers. We heard complaints that we'd never be able to do performance pay, especially using a peer review system and especially tying student achievement gains to it.

Many argued that doing multiple career paths and performance pay would deteriorate collegiality between teachers. They would compete more and collaborate less. Chart 12.5 shows you that our results did not find any of this.

Chart 12.6 shows that when we looked at the data over two years, as Lew referenced, yes performance pay was not universally accepted. We attribute this to the fact that the teachers were not paid yet when this survey was conducted and I think they'd be happier when they got the pay. However, we gave the survey in June and the performance payouts were in September, so they went through a year of this rigorous evaluation six times by their peers and then getting no money at the end of the year. I think the support will be higher next year when we have the data.

In terms of student achievement, we matched all of the TAP schools to control schools based on achievement, school size, percent of students receiving free or reduced-price lunch, and configuration. For example, we had a K–2 school, so we matched it with a K–2 school. We had a K–5 school; we matched it with a K–5 school and urban and rural classification. We had

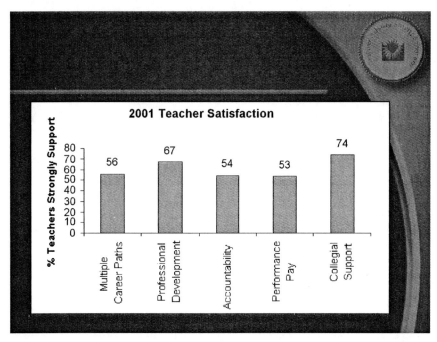

Chart 12.5.   2001 teacher satisfaction.

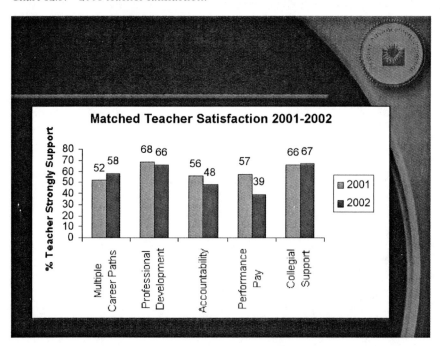

Chart 12.6.   Matched teacher satisfaction 2001–2002.

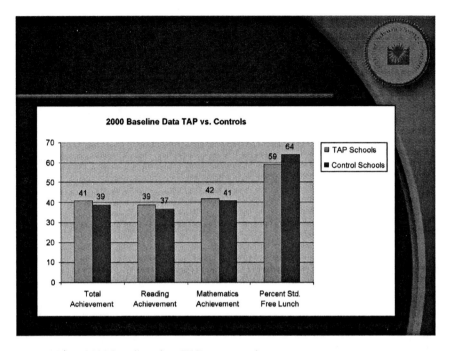

Chart 12.7.   2000 baseline data TAP vs. controls.

five schools in Arizona, but one we had to throw out because they did not test in first grade so we could not calculate a gain for them. From their 2000 baseline data, you can see on Chart 12.7 that they were very well matched. The Arizona State Department of Education helped us out and ran the matches. These control schools were selected from all the schools in Arizona.

What we did when we evaluated the TAP schools is we used something called a value-added assessment model. Bill Sanders travels around the country and gives many talks about what value-added is. Maybe you are familiar or you have read about him, but a value-added model is a model to measure growth in student achievement from one year to the next. Two things are important to understand when you talk about value-added. The first is that where you start can affect the magnitude of your gain. What that means is if you start at the 99th percentile, you are less likely to gain than somebody who starts at the 50th percentile. Therefore, when trying to make comparisons you want to pick schools that start at a similar point, which the Arizona Department of Education did for our control schools. The second thing in value-added is the level of certainty of gain or the probable occurrence of that gain and this is what statistics is all about.

2. Do TAP schools improve student achievement on a yearly basis? Look at Chart 12.8. To read our results, look at the vertical axis, it is going to represent the certainty of the gain. In other words, are we not certain or 100% certain of that gain? The horizontal axis is going to represent the percent of the gain, so how large is the gain? Every TAP school from 2000 to 2001 achieved a gain. Now, the magnitudes of their gains were different. They range from close to 30% to close to 6%.

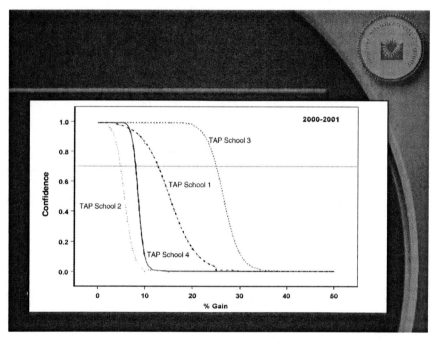

Chart 12.8.

We drew a line at the 70% certainty level and where these curves intersect, the line is how we calculated the gain (see Chart 12.9). You could draw a line, if you wanted to be at the 100% certainty level. You could draw a line at the 50% certain level. In 2002, all schools achieved a gain, with school #3 getting close to a 40% gain. Our lowest-performing school was at a 5% gain. Therefore, the conclusion for whether these schools achieved gains is absolutely yes. The average TAP school gain per year was 11% or 23% over two years. The results are quite promising.

3. Then we said okay, great, TAP schools are gaining. How much are they gaining compared to similar schools? You can see on Chart 12.10 that these results show that TAP schools are significantly outgaining similar schools. Again, the TAP schools got about an 11% gain for 2000–2001 and control school only a 4% gain. When we look at Chart

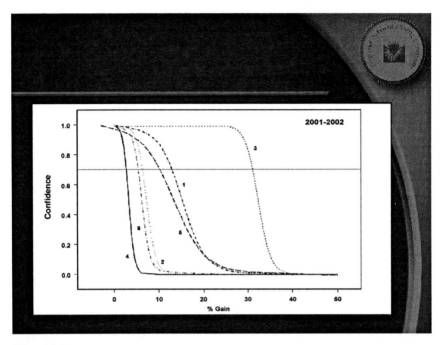

Chart 12.9.

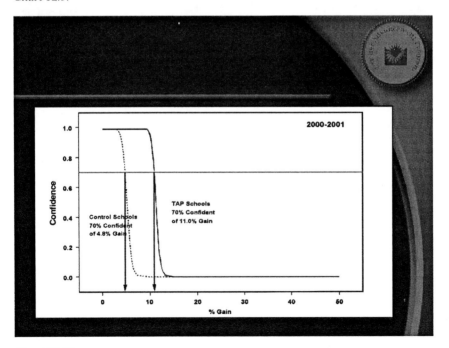

Chart 12.10.

12.11, which shows this in 2002, the gains get better: 12% in TAP schools and about 5% in control schools. Next year, it is going to be bigger because people have learned how to do it. They are internalizing the job and they are improving each year. Are TAP schools outperforming control schools? Yes. TAP schools are significantly outgaining their control schools and over two years, it was 13%.

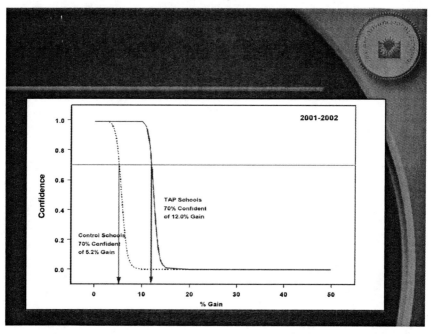

Chart 12.11.

4. Since TAP is about improving the quality of teachers in schools, we want to improve teaching behaviors as well as student achievement. As a result, we wanted to measure what proportion of teachers in TAP schools gain versus the proportion of teachers in control schools. The results from 2001 and 2002 in Chart 12.12 show that the TAP teachers are getting 10% more gains than control school teachers.

5. The final question that we had was, do schools vary in how they implement reforms? What we did was develop a program review in which we visited these schools twice a year and we assessed how well they were implementing each one of the TAP principles: multiple career paths, performance pay, accountability. We interviewed the staff, we watched the cluster groups, and we looked at how master teachers postconferenced with people. We spent a day in the beginning of the year and a day at the end and we rated these schools on compliance. The results are on Chart 12.13.

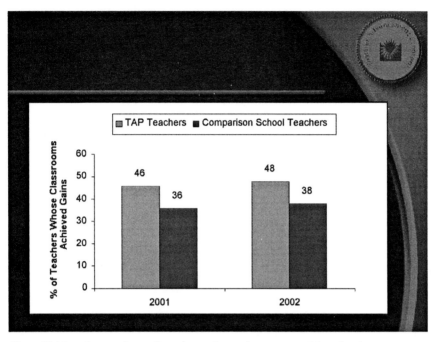

Chart 12.12.   Comparison of teachers whose classrooms achieved gains.

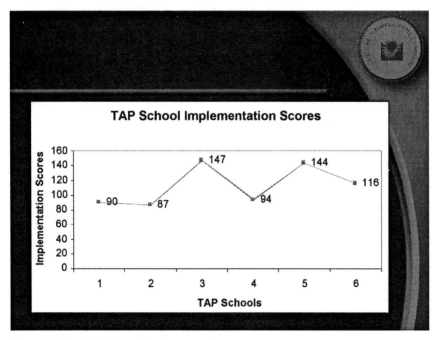

Chart 12.13.   TAP school implementation scores.

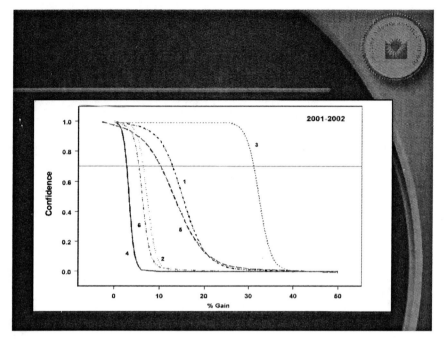

Chart 12.14.

I'd like to point out that TAP school #3 was a very high complier and so was TAP school #5. As you can see on Chart 12.14, compliance and actually implementing the model well matters in terms of getting student achievement gains.

So, our conclusions are that all TAP schools posted achievement gains in both years they implemented the reform. TAP schools significantly out-gain similar comparison schools. TAP teachers were producing larger student achievement gains than non-TAP teachers. Schools that were rigorously implementing the reform were getting much better results than schools that weren't.

Although all TAP schools realized student achievement gains in the first two years, these gains vary dramatically. Our lowest performing school gained 11% over two years. Our highest-performing school gained 51% over two years. Researchers at RAND who studied 160 comprehensive school reform models came up with criteria to determine when a reform is more likely to work than when it isn't. When it's supported by teachers, when there's strong principal leadership, when there's stable and committed district behind the reform, when the school receives ongoing assistance, and when the reform is implemented in smaller rather than bigger schools chances of success are better. Our data confirm the RAND findings.

In our lowest-performing TAP school, there was principal turnover. It was a very large district and a very large elementary school. In our highest-performing school, all of these elements were in place.

On the Milken website (http://www.mff.org/publications/publications .taf?page=304) there is a report on the impact of TAP that has all of our statistical formulas for those of you in the audience that want to look at our model and how we achieved these results. I believe there's also a report in your notebooks on TAP that you can freely distribute. We have a couple of articles coming out, one in an ASCD book and then a couple in journals. Next year, we're really looking forward to the data because we're going to have more schools in South Carolina, Arkansas, Colorado, Indiana, and Florida implement the reform.

Lewis C. Solmon

Before we start out, let me just say that I think it's very courageous of John to give results after only two years and we think that the results are going to get stronger over time. Unfortunately, policy people say they want to see results the day after the program starts. They call and say, have test scores gone up?

Audience Question

I'm Henry Johnson, the chief in Mississippi. The results are impressive and I would like to talk with you more about that. In social science research, isn't a 95% confidence level set? Would you talk a little bit more about why you decided 70 rather than 95?

John Schacter

Yes, and just a note on that, all of our results were significant at the 95% confidence level. We actually developed our metric based on a 70% confidence level for the schools and for the value-added purpose, because we wanted to pay more teachers for getting gains. At 95%, we would have fewer teachers that we were certain achieve a gain. We wanted to be as equitable as possible so we agreed on a 70% confidence level. If you get a gain, if your school gets a gain, we're going to accept it. It was part of the negotiation process, but, in our evaluation, everything is reported at the 95% confidence level and all of our results pertain to that.

We use the Stanford-9 subtests for grades 2–6, testing reading, language and math. We wanted to use the AIMS test; however in Arizona, the AIMS test is given at grades 3, 5, and 8, so we couldn't compute a gain. We had to use the test that the state was administering so that we could compute a gain for it, the Stanford-9. You can compute value-added using any test that has sufficient reliability and validity associated with it.

Audience Question

In implementing this process of change, I'm all for it, but I'm one person and my knowledge base is limited. You have such expertise, so would you be willing to come to a school district?

Lewis C. Solmon

In general, we've worked with the state superintendents who have identified a group of schools. We come and make a presentation to that group of schools and then they decide whether they want to do TAP. Another criterion is that there's got to be some source of funding identified in order to get TAP started. In each state that supports TAP, we supply a state director, we supply a lot of training, and so it's obviously not efficient to have schools scattered all over the state. About five or six schools in a fairly concentrated geographic area of the state is essential in order to make it work, it's just not cost effective beyond that. We generally work with a superintendent who brings together schools that he thinks have got innovative leadership and would be interested.

Audience Question

In regards to the list of teacher quality indicators, in his book, Bob Marzano has 15 or so indicators of teacher qualities. It seems to me that more and more research is showing that teacher quality is of utmost importance. The professional development seems to be essential. Does TAP provide guidance in terms of professional development, what the teachers need in their small learning communities? Or is that left up to the school site?

John Schacter

It's a little bit of both. TAP provides guidelines for what we would like those cluster groups to work on. Schools analyze data then make school goals and cluster group goals. It's the master teachers' responsibility to collect materials, curricular resources, assessments, to do model lessons, to team teach, to evaluate teachers based on the criteria, give feedback, and so on. So there are guidelines that guide the clusters. But in terms of the content that those master teachers bring to it, they're going to bring that content because they are the master teachers.

We provide training for master teachers and mentor teachers, but the master teachers lead those decisions and those activities. Just to give you an example, last night we were talking about clusters. We were asking how do we ensure that this time is used efficiently? When teachers get together, they need to learn how to use time effectively. Cluster groups need to have a clear goal and objective for their meeting. We refer to this as the classroom outcome, meaning whatever you learn in that group gets into your room and then a follow-up by the master and mentor teachers in the classroom to assist and support. That is our framework, more or less, to guide the clusters.

Audience Question

How important is the teacher's union buy-in?

Lewis C. Solmon

It is very important and we find that if we go to schools and explain TAP to teachers and teachers are willing to do it, unions are happy to participate. What we need to do is get strong teacher support and when we have strong teacher support, we get union buy-in.

When developing the performance pay system, we discuss it with schools and unions. That negotiation goes on and the union is involved right from the first day, because of course that's the most controversial proponent at TAP. In one state, the head of the union has worked in developing the evaluation system and other union leaders have said they might like to try to develop TAP schools in conjunction with us.

Audience Question

I can see very clearly how the value-added is measured for classroom teachers. How have you adapted the performance incentives for the specialists such as PE, art, music, special ed, and so on?

Lewis C. Solmon

Their performance pay is based 70% on their skills, knowledge, and responsibilities and 30% on school-wide achievement. What we've found is the specialist teachers are becoming much more involved in helping increase that school-wide achievement by integrating core academic work into their specialty area teaching.

Audience Question

It looks obvious that you couldn't implement TAP in a whole state given the fact that we already have massive programs for teacher evaluation and student evaluation. Do you think that if TAP replaced the money that we're spending on these things already, that it could be cost-effective for a state to adopt it?

Lewis C. Solmon

There are a number of alternative evaluation systems and clearly the trend is to be spending more and more resources on evaluating teachers and on evaluating students. We're hearing that some states are saying that TAP may be the way to go on a statewide basis. That hasn't happened yet, but if your state system is looking at teacher performance, there's no reason why it couldn't happen. I think your question is how to replace and utilize some of the resources that are already there, whether they're from federal funds or state funds and yes, it could happen.

Lowell Milken

I think the answer to the question about allocation of funds is yes, we believe that TAP could benefit greatly if some of the resources that are spent today on professional development were instead allocated to a TAP program. In regards to the union question, it is a difficulty and we're not going to minimize it. I think that's one of the reasons we have not been successful in certain states and gravitated toward other states. Nevertheless, we are looking to work with the unions on this issue.

We're somewhat perplexed why the unions wouldn't embrace something that would offer the kinds of career advancement, compensation, and professional development opportunities that I know everyone of you in the room would want and I know that everyone of us would want for our children, or for any of the students we have if they went into teaching.

We've had many, many discussions with union leaders over the past three years, and we are hopeful that we will make some progress, but the answer to your question is yes it can be a problem.

Audience Question

I'm curious about the additional cost of this program over budget.

Lewis C. Solmon

We generally say the cost of this program is $400 a student, which ends up being about 6% of the per-student allocation. Many assume this implies new money and we don't mean that. For example, in terms of master teachers, some schools have lead teachers, some teachers had science specialists who were already there and so that takes away part of the cost. It also varies according to how much the master, mentor teacher supplements are, and how much is in the bonus pool. Nevertheless, you have to calculate it based on $400 a student. There are schools in Arkansas that have reallocated their Title I and Title II resources and are fully funding TAP out of Title I and Title II. So it's not that this is an impossibility. The superintendent decided they were going to do TAP in all of its schools and he reallocated his Title I and Title II resources to do it. The money is there in Title I and Title II if it's reallocated. But you can't do everything you're doing now and do TAP and say it's not going to cost $400. If you're doing everything you're going to do now, without any changes, you're going to have to come up with another $400. I hope that there would be some reallocation.

Part VI

LEADERSHIP

CHAPTER 13

LEARNING SOME BASIC TRUISMS ABOUT LEADERSHIP

Warren Bennis

If a genuine transformation within any business is to occur, the leadership of that organization must be both willing and able to provide the energy and the power to enable change. Warren Bennis often observes instead men and women suffering under the burden of a high position, still proving themselves, still suffering from battle fatigue, overworked, compulsively intervening, and becoming, ultimately, burned-out victims of the Peter Principle.

In the following article, Bennis discusses how leaders can overcome the obstacles of isolation, cynicism, routine, inertia, and turmoil. He demonstrates how they can instead fuse work and play in a way that makes people feel significant, values learning and competence, and makes work more exciting.

A moment of truth came to me toward the end of my first 10 months as president of the University of Cincinnati. The clock was moving toward 4:00 in the morning, and I was still in my office, still mired in the incredible mass of paper stacked on my desk. I was bone weary and soul weary, and I found myself muttering, "Either I can't manage this place, or it's unmanageable." I reached for my calendar and ran my eyes down each hour, half hour, quarter hour, to see where my time had gone that day, the day before, the month before.

Talented Teachers: The Essential Force for Improving Student Achievement, pages 241–247

Nobel Laureate James Franck has said he always recognized a moment of discovery by "the feeling of terror that seizes me." I felt a trace of it that morning. My discovery was this: *I had become the victim of a vast, amorphous, unwitting, unconscious conspiracy to prevent me from doing anything whatever to change the university's status quo.* Even those of my associates who fully shared my hopes to set new goals, new directions, and to work toward creative change were unconsciously often doing the most to make sure that I would never find the time to begin. I found myself thinking of a friend and former colleague who had taken over one of our top universities with goals and plans that fired up all those around him and who said when he left a few years later, "I never could get around to doing the things I wanted to do."

This discovery, or rediscovery, led me to formulate what might be called Bennis's First Law of Academic Pseudodynamics: Routine work drives out nonroutine work and smothers to death all creative planning, all fundamental change in the university—or any institution.

These were the illustrations facing me: To start, there were 150 letters in the day's mail that required a response. About 50 of them concerned our young dean of the School of Education, Hendrik Gideonse. His job was to bring about change in the teaching of teachers, in our university's relationship to the public schools, and to students in the deprived and deteriorated neighborhood around us. Out of these urban schools would come the bulk of our students of the future—as good or as bad as the schools had shaped them.

But the letters were not about education. They were about a baby, the dean's 10-week-old son. Gideonse felt very strongly about certain basic values. He felt especially so about sex roles, about equality for his wife, about making sure she had the time and freedom to develop her own potentials fully. So he was carrying the baby into his office 2 days a week in a little bassinet, which he kept on his desk while he did his work. The daily *Cincinnati Enquirer* heard about it, took a picture of Hendrik, baby, and bassinet, and played it on page one. TV splashed it across the nation. And my "in" basket began to overflow with letters that urged his arrest for child abuse or at least his immediate dismissal. My only public comment was that we were a tax-supported institution, and if Hendrik could engage in that form of applied humanism and still accomplish the things we both wanted done in education, then like Lincoln with Grant's whiskey, I'd gladly send him several new babies for adoption.

Hedrick was, of course, simply a man a bit ahead of his time. Today, his actions would be applauded—maybe even with a Father of the Year award. Then, however, Hendrik and his baby ate up quite a bit of my time.

Also on my desk was a note from a professor, complaining that his classroom temperature was down to 65 degrees. Perhaps he expected me to grab a wrench and fix it. A student complained that we wouldn't give him course credit for acting as assistant to a city council member. Another was unable to get into the student health center. The teacher at my child's day school, who attended the university, was dissatisfied with her grades. A parent complained about four-letter words in a Philip Roth book being used in an English class. The track coach wanted me to come over to see for myself how bad the track was. An alumnus couldn't get the football seats he wanted. Another wanted a coach fired. A teacher had called to tell me the squash court was closed at 7:00 P.M. when he wanted to use it.

Perhaps 20% of my time that year had been taken up by a problem at the general hospital, which was city-owned but administered by the university medical school. Some terminal cancer patients, with their consent, had been subjected to whole-body radiation as possibly beneficial therapy. Since the Pentagon saw this as a convenient way to gather data that might help protect civilian populations in nuclear warfare, it provided a series of subsidies for the work.

When this story broke and was pursued in such a way as to call up comparisons with the Nazis' experiments on human guinea pigs, it became almost impossible for me or anybody else to separate the essential facts from the fantasized distortions. The problem eventually subsided, after a blue-ribbon task force recommended significant changes in the experiment's design. But I invested endless time in a matter only vaguely related to the prime purposes of the university—and wound up being accused by some of interfering with academic freedom.

The radiation experiment and Hendrik's baby illustrate how the media, particularly TV, make the academic cloister a goldfish bowl. By focusing on the lurid or the superficial, they can disrupt a president's proper activities while contributing nothing to the advancement of knowledge. This leads me to Bennis's Second Law of Academic Pseudodynamics: Make whatever grand plans you will, you may be sure the unexpected or the trivial will disturb and disrupt them.

In my moment of truth, that weary 4:00 A.M. in my trivia-cluttered office, I began trying to straighten out in my own mind that university should be, how they must lead.

Lead, not *manage:* there is an important difference. Many institutions are very well managed and are very poorly led. It may excel in the ability to handle each day all the routine inputs yet may never ask whether the routine should be done at all.

All of us find ourselves acting on routine problems because they are the easiest things to handle. We hesitate to get involved too early in the bigger ones—we collude, as it were, in the unconscious conspiracy to immerse us in routine.

My entrapment in routine made me realize another thing: People were following the old army game. They did not want to take responsibility for or bear the consequences of decisions they properly should make. The motto was, "Let's push up the tough ones." The consequence was that everybody and anybody was dumping his "wet babies" (as the old State Department hands call them) on my desk, when I had neither the diapers nor the information to take care of them. So I decided that the president's first priority—the sine qua non of effective leadership—was to create an "executive constellation" to run the office of the president. It could be a mixed bag, some vice presidents, some presidential assistants. The group would have to be compatible in the sense that its members could work together but neither uniform nor conformist—a group of people who knew more than the president about everything within their areas of competency and could attend to daily matters without dropping their wet babies on the president's desk.

What should the president him- or herself do? The president should be a *conceptualist.* That's something more than being just an "idea man." It means being a leader with entrepreneurial vision and the time to spend thinking about the forces what will affect the destiny of the institution. The president must educate board members so that they not only understand the necessity of distinguishing between leadership and management but also can protect the chief executive from getting enmeshed in routine machinery.

Leaders must create for their institutions clear-cut and measurable goals based on advice from all elements of the community. They must be allowed to proceed toward those goals without being crippled by bureaucratic machinery that saps their strength, energy, and initiative. They must be allowed to take risks, to embrace error, to use their creativity to the hilt, and encourage those who work them to use theirs.

These insights gave me the strength to survive my acid test: whether I, as a "leading theorist" of the principles of creative leadership, actually could prove myself a leader. However, the sum total of my experiences as president of the University of Cincinnati convinced me that most of the academic theory on leadership was useless.

After leaving the university, I spent nearly 5 years researching a book on leadership. I traveled around the country spending time with 90 of the most effective, successful leaders in the nation, 60 from corporations and 30 from the public sector. My goal was to find these leaders' common traits, a task that required more probing than I had expected. For a while, I sensed much more diversity than commonality among them. The group included both left-brain and right-brain thinkers; some who dressed for success and some who didn't; well-spoken, articulate leaders and laconic, inarticulate ones; some John Wayne types and some who were definitely the opposite.

I was finally able to come to some conclusions, of which perhaps the most important is the distinction between leaders and managers. Leaders are people who do the right thing; managers are people who do things right. Both roles are crucial, but they differ profoundly. I often observe people in top positions doing the wrong thing well.

This study also reinforced my earlier insight—that American organizations (and probably those in much of the rest of the industrialized world) are underled and overmanaged. They do not pay enough attention to doing the right thing, while they pay too much attention to doing things right. Part of the fault lies with our schools of management; we teach people how to be good technicians and good staff people, but we don't train people for leadership.

The group of 60 corporate leaders was not especially different from any profile of top leadership in America. The median age was 56. Most were white males, with six black men and six women in the group. The only surprising finding was that all the CEOs not only were still married to their fist spouses but also seemed enthusiastic about the institution of marriage. Among the CEOs were Bill Kiesschnick, then chair and CEO of ARCO, and the late Ray Kroc, of McDonald's.

Public-sector leaders included Harold Williams, who then chaired the Securities and Exchange Commission (SEC); Neil Armstrong, a genuine all-American hero who happened to be at the University of Cincinnati; three elected officials; two orchestra conductors; and two winning athletics coaches. I wanted conductors and coaches because I mistakenly believed that they were the last leaders with complete control over their constituents.

After several years of observation and conversation, I defined four competencies evident to some extent in every member of the group. The first trait apparent in these leaders is their ability to draw others to them, not just because they have a vision but because they communicate an extraordinary focus on commitment. Leaders manage attention through a compelling vision that brings others to a place they have not been before.

One of the people I most wanted to interview was one of the few I could not seem to reach—Leon Fleischer, a well-known child prodigy who grew up to become a prominent pianist, conductor, and musicologist. I happened to be in Aspen, Colorado, one summer while Fleischer was conducting the Aspen Music Festival and I tried again to reach him, even leaving a note on his dressing-room door. Driving back through downtown Aspen, I saw two perspiring young cellists carrying their instruments, and I offered them a ride to the music tent. They hopped in the back of my Jeep, and as we rode I questioned them about Fleischer. "I'll tell you why he's so great," said one. "He doesn't waste our time."

Fleischer finally agreed not only to be interviewed but to let me watch him rehearse and conduct music classes. I linked the way I saw him work with that simple sentence, "He doesn't waste our time." Every moment Fleischer was before the orchestra, he knew exactly what sound he wanted. He didn't waste time because his intentions were always evident. What united him with the other musicians was their concern with intention and outcome.

When I reflected on my own experience, it struck me that when I was most effective, it was because I knew what I wanted. When I was ineffective, it was because I was unclear about it.

So the first leadership competency is the management of attention through a set of intentions of a vision, not in a mystical of religious sense but in the sense of outcome, goal, or direction.

The second leadership competency is management of meaning. To make dreams apparent to others and to align people with them, leaders must communicate their vision. Communication and alignment work together. Consider, for example, the contrasting styles of Presidents Reagan and Carter. Ronald Reagan was called "the Great Communicator"; one of his speech writers said that Reagan could read the phone book and make it interesting. The reason is that Reagan used metaphors with which people can identify. In his first budget message, for example, Reagan described a trillion dollars by comparing it to piling up dollar bills beside the Empire State Building. Reagan, to use one of Alexander Haig's coinages, "tangibilitated" the idea. Leaders make ideas tangible and real to others so they can support them. For no matter how marvelous the vision, the effective leader must use a metaphor, a word, or a model to make that vision clear to others.

In contrast, President Carter was boring. Carter was one of our best-informed presidents; he had more facts at his fingertips than almost any other president. But he never made the meaning come through the facts. I interviewed an assistant secretary of commerce appointed by Carter, who told me that after 4 years in his administration, she still did not know what Jimmy Carter stood for. She said that working for him was like looking through the wrong side of a tapestry; the scene was blurry and indistinct.

The leader's goal is not mere explanation or clarification but the creation of meaning. My favorite baseball joke is exemplary: In the ninth inning of a key playoff game, with a three-and-two count on the batter, the umpire hesitates a split second in calling the pitch. The batter whiles around angrily and says, "Well, what was it?" The umpire snarls back, "It ain't *nothing* until *I* call it!"

The third competency is management of trust. Trust is essential to all organizations. The main determinant of trust is reliability, what I call *constancy*. When I talked to the board members or staffs of these leaders, I heard certain phrases again and again: "She is all of a piece." "Whether you like it or not, you always know where his is coming from, what he stands for."

When John Paul II visited this country, he gave a press conference. One reporter asked how the Pope could account for allocating funds to build a swimming pool at his papal summer palace. He responded quickly, "I like to swim. Next question." He did not rationalize about medical reasons or claim that he got the money from a special source. A recent study showed that people would much rather follow individuals they can count on, even when they disagree with their viewpoint, than people they agree with but who shift positions frequently. I cannot emphasize enough the significance of constancy and focus.

The fourth leadership competency is management of self—knowing one's skills and deploying them effectively. Management of self is critical: without it, leaders and managers can do more harm than good. Like incompetent doctors, incompetent managers can make life worse; make people sicker and less vital. There is a term—*iatrogenic*—for illness caused by doctors and hospitals. There should be one for illnesses caused by leaders, too. Some give themselves heart attacks and nervous breakdowns; still worse, many are "carriers," causing their employees to be ill.

Leaders know themselves; they know their strengths and nurture them. They also have a faculty I think of as the Wallenda Factor. The Flying Wallendas are perhaps the world's greatest family of aerialists and tightrope walkers. I was fascinated when, in the early 1970s, 71-year-old Karl Wallenda said that for him living was walking the tightrope, and everything else was waiting. I was struck with his capacity for concentration on the intention, the task, the decision. I was even more intrigued when, several months later, Wallenda fell to his death while walking a tightrope without a safety net between two high-rise buildings in San Juan, Puerto Rico. Wallenda fell, still clutching the balancing pole he had warned his family never to drop lest it hurt somebody below. Later, Wallenda's wife said that before her husband had fallen, for the first time since she had known him he had been concentrating on falling, instead of on walking the tightrope. He had personally supervised the attachment of the guide wires, which he had never done before.

Like Wallenda before his fall, the leaders in my group seemed unacquainted with the concept of failure. What you or I might call a failure, they referred to as a mistake. I began collecting synonyms for the word *failure* mentioned in the interview, and I found more than 20: *mistake, error, false state, bloop, flop, loss, miss, foul-up, stumble, botch, bungle*...but not *failure*. One CEO told me that if she had a knack for leadership, it was the capacity to make as many mistakes as she could as soon as possible, and thus get them out of the way. Another said that a mistake is simply "another way of doing things." These leaders learn from and use something that doesn't go well; it is not a failure but simply the next step.

2003 NATIONAL EDUCATION CONFERENCE PRESENTERS

Lowell Milken

Widely known as an educational pioneer and reformer, Lowell Milken is chairman of the Milken Family Foundation (MFF), which he co-founded in 1982. Under his leadership, MFF has become one of the most innovative private foundations in the U.S., creating national programs in K–12 education and medical research as well as funding and working with more than 1,000 organizations around the world committed to the interests of young people, K–12 education and medical research. Among his contributions to strengthening education, Mr. Milken conceived both the Milken National Educator Awards and the Teacher Advancement Program (TAP). As a businessman, Mr. Milken is chairman of London-based Heron International, a worldwide leader in property development, and co-founder of Knowledge Universe, a company focused on meeting the lifelong learning requirements of both individuals and businesses. Named by *Worth* magazine as one of the 15 most generous living Americans, Mr. Milken is the recipient of numerous awards from such organizations as the National Association of State Boards of Education, the Horace Mann League, and the National Association of Secondary School Principals. A product of California's public school system, Mr. Milken graduated summa cum laude and Phi Beta Kappa from the University of California at Berkeley in 1970, where he was recognized with the School of Business Administration's Most Outstanding

Talented Teachers: The Essential Force for Improving Student Achievement, pages 249–257

Student Award. He was awarded his law degree from the University of California, Los Angeles, with the distinctions of Order of the Coif and UCLA Law Review. He and his wife of 29 years, Sandy, have four sons.

Jeanne Allen

Jeanne Allen is president of the Center for Education Reform (CER), the national voice for more choices in education and more rigor in education programs. As the nation's leading authority on education reform, CER delivers practical K–12 research and assistance to engage a diverse lay audience to improve all schools for all children. An advocate of bringing the power of ordinary people to bear on policy decisions, Allen is the author of *The School Reform Handbook: How to Improve Your Schools.* She is consulted regularly by lawmakers and national leaders and serves as an advisor to several national and community-based organizations. Allen is also a frequent commentator in print and broadcast media, and her commentaries and thoughts have appeared in more than 200 publications. She received her bachelor's degree in political science from Dickinson College, has worked on Capitol Hill, and has led several organizations in both public and private sectors. She is the mother of four school-aged children.

William J. Bennett

One of America's most influential and respected voices on cultural, political and education issues, William J. Bennett is a distinguished fellow at the Heritage Foundation, co-director of Empower America, and chairman and co-founder of K12, an Internet-based elementary and secondary school. During the 1980s, he served as President Reagan's Secretary of Education and chairman of the National Endowment for the Humanities. Dr. Bennett has written and edited 14 books, including *The Book of Virtues,* which was made into an animated series seen in over 65 countries. His most recent work is *The Children's Book of Home and Family.* He has also written for America's leading news publications and appears on the nation's most influential television shows, including regular appearances on the Fox News Channel's "Hannity and Colmes." Dr. Bennett holds a degree in philosophy from Williams College, a Ph.D. from the University of Texas, and a law degree from Harvard University.

Warren Bennis

Warren Bennis is university professor and distinguished professor of business administration at the University of Southern California, as well as the founding chairman of USC's Leadership Institute. He also serves as chairman of the advisory board of the Center for Public Leadership at Harvard University's Kennedy School and is the Thomas S. Murphy Distinguished Research Fellow at the Harvard Business School. Dubbed the "Dean of Leadership Gurus" by *Forbes* magazine, Mr. Bennis has written or edited 27 books, including the best-selling *Leaders* and *On Becoming A Leader*, and his book of essays, *An Invented Life: Reflections on Leadership and Change*, was nominated for a Pulitzer Prize. Recipient of 11 honorary degrees, Mr. Bennis has served on the faculty at Harvard, MIT, and Boston University, and is a past president of the University of Cincinnati. In 1943-1947, he was one of the youngest infantry commanders in the U.S. Army and was awarded the Purple Heart and Bronze Star.

Philip Bigler

A 1999 Virginia Milken Educator and 1998 National Teacher of the Year, Philip Bigler is director of the James Madison Center at James Madison University in Harrisonburg, Virginia, where he teaches history, American studies and political science. A 25-year veteran of the teaching profession, Mr. Bigler helps his students realize that "civilization rests upon the foundations of the past," and that they are the "inheritors of a rich, intellectual legacy." Under his tutelage, students have debated current issues as members of a Greek polis, argued Constitutional law before a mock Supreme Court and collected oral histories from residents of the Soldiers' and Airmen's Home. For two years, he was historian of the Arlington National Cemetery, after which he returned to the classroom. Mr. Bigler is associate director of the Stratford-Monticello Teacher Seminar and has authored four books including *Hostile Fire: the Life and Death of Lt. Sharon Ann Lane* and *In Honored Glory*.

Jerry Brown

As Mayor of Oakland, California, Jerry Brown has focused on education as a means to lift young people out of poverty. During his two terms as Mayor, he has opened two charter schools in the Oakland Unified School District: The Oakland Military Institute (OMI), where teachers and National Guard personnel run an intensive extended-day academic program, and the conservatory-style Oakland School for the Arts, which opened its doors last year with audition-based admissions. As Governor of California for two terms during the 1970's, Mayor Brown appointed an extraordinary number of women and minorities to prominent government positions and presided over a state that created 25% of the nation's new jobs. In 1992, Mayor Brown entered the Democratic Presidential race, during which he refused to accept contributions larger than $100. He received his B.A. degree in classics from the University of California at Berkeley in 1961, and graduated from Yale Law School in 1964.

David Driscoll

As Commissioner of Education for the Commonwealth of Massachusetts, David Driscoll has a 39-year career in educational leadership. A former secondary school mathematics teacher, he was assistant superintendent, then superintendent of schools, in Melrose, a position he held until 1993 when he was appointed deputy commissioner of education. After appointment as interim commissioner in 1998, Dr. Driscoll was key to obtaining passage of a state law supporting his comprehensive plan for enhancing future educator quality known as the "12 to 62" plan. As commissioner since 1999, Dr. Driscoll has overseen implementation of the Massachusetts Comprehensive Assessment System, the school and district accountability system and the overload of the certification system. These initiatives have led to consistent improvement in student achievement as measured by state standards (MCAS), national measures (NAEP, SAT), and even international tests (TIMMS). Most recently, Massachusetts was named as one of the first five states in the country to have its No Child Left Behind accountability plan approved. Dr. Driscoll holds a doctorate in educational administration from Boston College.

Chester E. Finn, Jr.

Chester E. Finn, Jr., scholar, educator and public servant, has been at the forefront of the national debate on school reform for two decades. He is president of the Thomas B. Fordham Foundation, a senior fellow at Stanford University's Hoover Institution, and chairman of the Koret Task Force on K–12 Education. A former professor of education and public policy at Vanderbilt University, Dr. Finn has been a fellow of the International Academy of Education and the Hudson Institute and was a founding partner and senior scholar with the Edison Project. He serves on the boards of several organizations, including the Center for Education Reform, the Foundation for Teaching Economics and The Philanthropy Roundtable. Author of 13 books and more than 300 articles, Dr. Finn has received numerous honors for his work. He holds degrees in U.S. history and social science teaching and a doctorate in educational policy, all from Harvard University.

Eric A. Hanushek

Eric Hanushek is the Paul and Jean Hanna Senior Fellow at Stanford University's Hoover Institution and a research associate at the National Bureau of Economic Research. A leading expert on educational policy, specializing in the economics and finance of schools, Dr. Hanushek has published numerous articles in professional journals and written several books, including Improving America's Schools and Making Schools Work. He has previously held academic appointments at the University of Rochester, Yale University, and the U.S. Air Force Academy. Dr. Hanushek's government service includes positions as deputy director of the Congressional Budget Office, senior staff economist for the Council of Economic Advisers and senior economist for the Cost of Living Council. Dr. Hanushek is a distinguished graduate of the United States Air Force Academy and served in the U.S. Air Force from 1965-1974. He completed his Ph.D. in economics at the Massachusetts Institute of Technology.

Michael Podgursky

Michael Podgursky is Middlebush Professor of Economics and chairman of the Department of Economics at the University of Missouri–Columbia. He has published numerous articles and reports on education policy and teacher quality and co-authored a book titled Teacher Pay and Teacher Quality. Dr. Podgursky's research has been supported by grants from the U.S. Department of Education, the U.S. Department of Labor, the National Commission on Employment Policy, the U.S. Department of Agriculture, the National Science Foundation and various foundations and state government agencies. Dr. Podgursky is a member of the advisory boards of the National Center for Teacher Quality and the American Board for Certification of Teacher Excellence. From 1980 to 1995, Dr. Podgursky served on the faculty of the University of Massachusetts at Amherst. He earned his bachelor's degree in economics from the University of Missouri–Columbia and a Ph.D. in economics from the University of Wisconsin–Madison.

Nina Rees

As the U.S. Deputy Under Secretary of Education, Nina Rees leads the newly created Office of Innovation and Improvement, overseeing the administration of several competitive grant programs. Ms. Rees also works with the Office of Elementary and Secondary Education, coordinating the implementation of various provisions of President Bush's No Child Left Behind Act. Prior to joining the U.S. Department of Education, Ms. Rees was an aide to Vice President Dick Cheney and helped the Bush campaign draft the blueprint for the No Child Left Behind legislation. Previously, Ms. Rees was chief education analyst for The Heritage Foundation, director of outreach programs at the Institute for Justice and policy analyst at Americans for Tax Reform. A frequent commentator in the media, Ms. Rees has published her articles and views in some of the nation's most prominent national newspapers and magazines and has appeared on several high-profile national television news programs.

John Schacter

John Schacter is president of SPP Enterprises: Educational Consulting. As former vice president for research projects at the Milken Family Foundation, Dr. Schacter designed and developed the teacher performance-based accountability and compensation principle of the Foundation's Teacher Advancement Program. He has conducted a series of longitudinal studies to determine the effect of teachers' instructional behaviors and creativity on student achievement. He has also completed a 21st Century Community Learning centers grant from the United States Department of Education, for which he developed innovative methods to teach reading skills to at-risk first graders while school is not in session. He has published on such topics as early reading, technology, teacher quality and performance-based pay. A former professional educator who taught science at the elementary level, Dr. Schacter came to the Foundation after earning his doctorate in educational psychology at UCLA.

Tamara W. Schiff

As vice president and survey director for the Milken Family Foundation, Tamara Schiff's work on teacher quality in K–12 education is part of the Foundation's Teacher Advancement Program (TAP). As part of the TAP team, Dr. Schiff oversees data collection on teacher attitudes and satisfaction, as well as the development of the multiple career paths principle. Dr.

Schiff has authored numerous monographs and articles on educational issues, including the recently released attitudinal results from the TAP program and the National Association of Secondary Schools' publication, *Priorities and Barriers in High School Leadership: A Survey of Principals*. She is active in the Milken Educator Awards program through her participation in the selection process and National Notifications, and her contributions to the National Education Conference. Dr. Schiff serves on the Board of Trustees for the Milken Community High School where she heads the Education Committee. Prior to coming to the Foundation in 1993, Dr. Schiff received her Ph.D. from UCLA.

Lee S. Shulman

Lee S. Shulman is the eighth president of The Carnegie Foundation for the Advancement of Teaching. As the Charles E. Ducommun Professor of Education and a professor (by courtesy) of psychology at Stanford University, Dr. Shulman's research group laid the conceptual foundations for a reconsideration of the nature of teacher knowledge, emphasizing the role of content understanding in the pedagogical process. Between 1985 and 1990, Dr. Shulman and his colleagues conducted the technical studies and field tests that supported the creation of the National Board for Professional Teaching Standards. He was previously a professor of educational psychology and medical education at Michigan State University and is a past president of both the American Educational Research Association (AERA) and the National Academy of Education. Dr. Shulman has been honored with the American Psychological Association's E.L. Thorndike Award for distinguished psychological contributions to education. In 2002, he was elected a fellow of The American Academy of Arts and Sciences.

Tavis Smiley

Host of "The Tavis Smiley Show" on National Public Radio (NPR) and "The Tavis Smiley Show" on PBS, Tavis Smiley is the first African-American to host his own signature talk show in the history of NPR. Named "one of America's 50 most promising young leaders" by Time, Mr. Smiley was the host of the award-winning "BET Tonight with Tavis Smiley" on Black Entertainment Television, for which he interviewed some of the world's most important figures, including President Clinton, Fidel Castro and Pope John Paul II. Educated at Indiana University, Mr. Smiley was previously a top aide to former Los Angeles Mayor Tom Bradley. He has authored six books, including *Keeping the Faith: Stories of Love, Courage, Healing and Hope from Black America*, and has provided commentary and analysis on national television shows ranging from "The Today Show" to "World News Tonight with Peter Jennings." Mr. Smiley is founder of the Tavis Smiley Foundation, a nonprofit organization whose mission is to encourage, empower and enlighten black youth.

Lewis C. Solmon

Lewis C. Solmon is executive vice president, education, at the Milken Family Foundation, a member of its Board of Trustees, and director of the Teacher Advancement Program (TAP), a major initiative of the Foundation focusing on improving teacher quality. He has recently completed a study on performance-based pay as part of TAP. He has advised several governors and state superintendents in the areas of funding school technology, school finance, teacher quality and charter schools, and served on Florida Governor Jeb Bush's education transition team last December and January. From 1991 to 1997, Dr. Solmon was the founding president of the Milken Institute, which he built into a nationally recognized economics think tank. He served as dean of UCLA's Graduate School of Education from 1985 to 1991. He received his bachelor's degree in economics from the University of Toronto and his Ph.D. from the University of Chicago. He has served on the faculties of UCLA, CUNY and Purdue, and currently is a professor emeritus at UCLA.

Herbert J. Walberg

Herbert J. Walberg is professor emeritus of education and psychology at the University of Illinois at Chicago and a distinguished visiting fellow of Stanford University's Hoover Institution. Recipient of a Ph.D. from the University of Chicago, Dr. Walberg has written and edited more than 55 books and written over 350 articles on such topics as educational effectiveness and exceptional human accomplishments. Among his latest books are the *International Encyclopedia of Educational Evaluation* and *Psychology and Educational Practice*. Dr. Walberg is a founding fellow and vice president of the International Academy of Education, headquartered in Brussels, and has presented lectures to educators and policymakers throughout the world. Dr. Walberg has served on the National Assessment Governing Board and is a fellow of several academic organizations. He currently chairs the board of Chicago's Heartland Institute, a think tank providing policy analysis for the U.S. Congress, state legislators, the media and the public.

Arthur E. Wise

Arthur E. Wise is president of the National Council for Accreditation of Teacher Education (NCATE) in Washington, D.C. Throughout his career, he has advanced education on several fronts, including teacher quality and professionalism, school finance reform and educational research. Dr. Wise first came to national prominence in 1968 with his book, *Rich Schools, Poor Schools: The Promise of Equal Educational Opportunity,* which conceived the idea of the school finance reform lawsuit. Long active in federal education policy, he helped create the U.S. Department of Education in the late 1970s. A former director of the RAND Corporation's Center for the Study of the Teaching Profession, Dr. Wise proposed education policies regarding teacher licensing, teacher evaluation and teacher compensation, many of which have been incorporated into state laws and regulations. At NCATE, he directed the design of performance-based accreditation and led efforts to develop a system of quality assurance for the teaching profession.